The Free-trade Movement

"Were all nations to follow the liberal system of free exportation and free importation, the different states into which a great continent was divided would so far resemble the different provinces of a great empire."

—ADAM SMITH.

The
Free-trade Movement
And its Results

By

GEORGE ARMITAGE-SMITH

SECOND EDITION

Select Bibliographies Reprint Series

BOOKS FOR LIBRARIES PRESS
FREEPORT, NEW YORK

Second Edition First Published 1903
Reprinted 1969

STANDARD BOOK NUMBER:
8369-5063-1

LIBRARY OF CONGRESS CATALOG CARD NUMBER:
77-95061

PRINTED IN THE UNITED STATES OF AMERICA

Preface to the Second Edition

Lord Beaconsfield once remarked that "Protection was not only dead but damned". The remark seems likely to be disproved; we are threatened with a revival of the whole Free-trade controversy. The events which have contributed to this prospect are several. (1) An agitation of many years against the Continental sugar-bounties has culminated in a convention by which bounty-fed sugar will be excluded from Great Britain, to the admitted loss of British consumers. (2) The heavy burden of expenditure entailed by the South African War led in 1902 to the reimposition of the Corn Duty after fifty-six years. Financial exigencies and an attempt to place taxation on a broader basis were the arguments for the measure; it was, however, interpreted by Protectionists as a recantation of Free-trade doctrine and the beginning of a new era of protection, and great was their disappointment when the tax was in the following year repealed as no longer necessary. By its supporters the incidence of this duty, yielding £2,500,000, was variously assigned to foreign exporters, shippers, merchants, &c., but was declared to have no effect on consumers. The Chancellor of the Exchequer, however, in repealing the tax, maintained that it fell upon the poorest classes. (3) An alarm in some quarters respecting the supply of food in case of war has led to the appointment of a Royal Commission to enquire into the subject. (4) But the event of greatest significance, and one which has excited general interest, is the promulgation by the Colonial Secretary (Mr. Chamberlain) of a policy of preferential trading with the Colonies as a means for consolidating the Empire on a commercial basis, and for rendering it a self-supporting unity, independent of other countries. This proposal is the latest development of the Zollverein scheme propounded some years ago; it raises again the whole issue of Free-trade *versus* Protection. It is necessary again to restate the arguments for the policy adopted in 1846 and to consider their applicability to present conditions, since it is maintained in some quarters that circumstances have changed, and that a theory of foreign trading, which was convincing some fifty years ago, is wholly inapplicable to present times; while by others it is held that on the subject of Free-trade the mental attitude may be one of indefinite suspense.

In this edition a special chapter has been added in which the recent proposals are discussed by the light of economic reasoning; for the rest, the book stands as before. The author has only to add that prolonged study and further experience only more deeply convince him that a Free-trade policy is essential to the well-being of this country, and that it is the policy best calculated to strengthen the ties with the Colonies and to secure the consolidation and prosperity of the Empire.

G. A.-S.

July, 1903.

Preface to the First Edition

In a Series dealing with the characteristic features of the Victorian Era it is obvious that the Free-trade Movement demands a place, although the literature of the subject is so extensive that it might be thought the last word had been already said. The old controversies, however, still remain, and have in fact been renewed with fresh vigour, partly owing to the persistence of the United States and other countries in a Protective policy, and also to the movement for federation with our Colonies, most of which are committed to Protection. The subject has a perennial interest, and there is room for a re-statement both of the historical facts and of the arguments. At no time have the arguments of Adam Smith needed to be enforced more than in the present age, when States are vying with one another in attempts to annex markets for their exclusive benefit and to the disadvantage of others. That the welfare of one nation is closely bound up with that of its neighbours is a doctrine that cannot be too strongly emphasized in these days of eager commercial and political rivalries, which seem to threaten a renewal of the old mercantile system.

The aim of the present work is to give in brief compass an historic account of the origin of Protection, and of the prolonged agitation by which it was ultimately overthrown in this country; to state the economic advantages of the Free-trade doctrine, and to estimate the effects of the change upon the well-being of Great

Britain; and to discuss the chief grounds on which Protection is upheld in other countries, and still finds some adherents in our own. To accomplish this end it was necessary to trace the rise of the Protectionist idea, as only by understanding the circumstances of its evolution can we fully estimate its value as a doctrine and explain its relation to existing conditions. The first three chapters, therefore, are devoted to matters antecedent to the Victorian Era.

While I am convinced of the practical wisdom of the policy of the " open door " in commerce, and believe that its adoption by other nations would make for the peace of the world, I have endeavoured to deal with the subject in the scientific spirit of inquiry and explanation, and the conclusions set down are those forced upon me by a careful and long-continued study of the facts.

On such a subject indebtedness to the work of others is necessarily very great, and it is impossible to do more than make a general acknowledgment: special reference, however, should be made to Leone Levi's *History of British Commerce*, the writings of Prentice and Ashworth upon the history of the Corn-law agitation, and Mr. John Morley's *Life of Cobden*. I wish also to express my obligations to Mr. H. J. Tozer, M.A., for suggestions, and to the Editor of the Series for his valuable criticism and advice.

G. A. S.

LONDON, *March*, 1898.

Contents

vii

viii   Contents

The Free-trade Movement.

Chapter I.

Origin of Restrictions on Trading.

The Free-trade Movement, which had for its aim the abolition of artificial restrictions upon commerce, is perhaps one of the most remarkable movements of the nineteenth century, yet one which has been almost confined to the British Isles, although its origin is to be referred to the teaching of French economic writers of the eighteenth century, from whom Adam Smith, the apostle of Free-trade, derived many of his views. This movement reversed in Great Britain the theories and practical maxims which had governed the commerce of nations for centuries. William Pitt had undoubtedly a strong leaning towards a Free-trade policy. He entered upon a course of economic reforms by a commercial treaty with France (1786) and a reorganization of the customs duties, but the unfortunate war which broke out in 1793 converted Pitt, the financial reformer, into a war minister, and brought about events which renewed and intensified the protective policy he would have modified. The reaction against protection began afresh about the year 1820 and was extended over some forty years, culminating in the Anti-Corn-law agitation (1839–1846). With the abolition of the duties on corn and navigation in 1849, the principle of free-trading was fully established, and by various subsequent reforms it was carried out completely, until, in 1860, all duties of an avowedly protective character had been removed from the British fiscal system.

Thus Free-trade came to be adopted as the expression of the correct economic theory of commerce by the greatest manufacturing and commercial nation of fifty years ago. It might with some reason be assumed that a sound theory of international trade would be evolved in an industrial and commercial age when its advantages and necessities became more obvious, rather than during the simpler periods when intercourse was comparatively slight, or in the times when the relations of nations were most frequently of a hostile character.

When means of communication were few and difficult, when people lived mostly by agriculture and population was small and scattered, natural circumstances and limited knowledge presented almost insuperable obstacles to trading. The journey of Jacob's sons into Egypt to fetch corn was an undertaking occasioned only by necessity; the exchanges of Solomon and Hiram for the building of the temple were barter transactions on a scale worthy of being recorded; the visits of the fleets of Venice to Britain in the thirteenth and fourteenth centuries were great commercial enterprises, and the fairs and markets of the Middle Ages were events of importance in the internal trade of the country; yet they appear insignificant when brought into contrast with the wonderfully refined and intricate system of trade by which the familiar daily wants of life are now supplied.

Trading, like other institutions, is an example of evolution. From elementary exchanges it has developed until the links of commerce now encircle the globe. Illustrations of the various stages of evolution are still to be seen in different parts of the world, and some of them are well marked off by a specific character as local, national, or international, exhibiting a progressive organization. Invention and discovery are continually effecting changes in the methods of commerce, and possibly a century hence present modes of trade may seem antiquated.

A theory of trade must be relative to the circumstances under which it is evolved, and to the economic ideas prevalent at the time. Thus we may expect the theory-of an earlier period to reflect conditions differing much from those of the present.   Modern industry is very complex and highly organized; Free-trading claims to be an expression of the recognition of these facts and of their true import.   But it is a curious circumstance that while Great Britain, a few of her colonies, and some of the smaller commercial countries of Northern Europe, have adopted the principle of free exchange and have renounced the protective system, other great industrial nations still retain the artificial restrictions on trade which were once general, and some, like the United States, are extending those imposts against other countries, although they have at the same time generally removed all barriers to free-trading within the areas comprised by their political boundaries.   The practice of creating obstacles to the full enjoyment of free exchange beyond the limits of a country, whilst recognizing the advantages gained by the removal of such impediments to trade within a country, forms a curious paradox, on which some light is cast by a review of the conditions under which trading was developed.

In an inquiry into the origin of restrictions on trade and their economic effects, we are naturally led to compare the civilization and economic conditions of the present and the past.   The first fact that strikes us is the extraordinary complexity of modern life in its interests and its industrial and commercial relations, its interdependence, variety, far-reaching intercourse and cosmopolitan character, when placed in contrast with the simplicity and local independence of more primitive times.   The world has in fact become one vast market or economic area.   Science, by its marvellous command over the subtle forces of nature, has succeeded in reducing the natural obstacles to intercourse, and in so abbreviating operations of trade that the products of each country can now be distributed with wonderful celerity over the whole globe, and all nations may share in the advantages which each can offer.   On the one hand, the telegraph and post have rendered communication quick and constant, and on the other, steam-power has made transport simple and inexpensive.   Intercourse between

London and Japan or Australia is far easier now than
between the extreme north and south of Great Britain a
few centuries ago.   The natural result has been an
enormous interchange of goods, trading on a gigantic
scale has been established, and nations have learned to
appreciate the advantages to be gained by this enlargement of the field of their economic operations.

Free-trading, which appeals to the commercial instincts, and makes for peace and increased comfort,
would seem to be the logical outcome of this close interdependence.   The reduction of *natural* impediments to
simplicity of trading might be expected to be accompanied
by the removal of *artificial* barriers, and yet the latter
are retained.   To remove the one and retain the other is
an apparent contradiction which calls for explanation.
The causes appear to be threefold, and may be summed
up briefly as (1) the prejudices derived from ancient established customs; (2) the existence of national sentiment,
which, on its negative side, is hostile to foreign ideas
and jealous of foreign goods; and (3) the individual and
class interests which grew up and were nourished under
the shelter of the artificial barriers to foreign competition created by those prejudices and jealousies.

For the roots of protection we must look back into
the early history of trading.

Before the Christian era the Phœnicians are said to
have come to Britain for tin.   Under the Roman occupation of Britain agriculture was developed, corn as
well as metals was exported, and London became a
port of some magnitude.   In Saxon times such commerce as existed was conducted mainly by foreign merchants.   English kings endeavoured to stimulate trading,
as is proved by the law of Athelstan, that a merchant
who thrice crossed the sea in his own vessel should
become a thane.   Norman rule led to further intercourse
with the Continent, and the crusades brought Britain into
commercial relations with the city-states of the Mediter-
ranean.   Trade sprang up, and from 1317 to the middle
of the sixteenth century Italian fleets came to England
and the Netherlands with fine cloth, silks, linen and
cotton goods, glass, Greek wines, silver, and other

luxuries, which they exchanged for the grain, leather, wool, skins, and metals of England.

German traders from Hamburg and Lübeck early gained a footing in England, and established here a branch of the Hanseatic League. This was a federation for commercial purposes which became very powerful in the thirteenth and fourteenth centuries, and controlled the trade of the north of Europe. It extended from Bergen to Cologne, and from London and Bruges to Novgorod; by the year 1300 it had factories in about seventy towns. The league gained many privileges, including immunity from taxes; it organized trade, put down piracy, developed industries, and educated the nations in the art of commerce. To England it brought timber, furs, flax, hemp, fish, copper, &c., in exchange for native produce.

Customs or customary duties have a very ancient origin; they seem to have been paid from time immemorial on merchandise entering a district, country, or town. As tolls or transit dues charges were made for the use of roads, safe passage, and permission to trade. The duty was supposed to fall upon the traders, who were generally foreigners, and it became a source of revenue to the lord or sovereign. In the early customary dues in England there appears no trace of any economic or national aim other than revenue and a charge for the privilege of trading.

From the twelfth to the fifteenth century the local trade of towns was regulated by the merchant and craft guilds; these institutions served at the time a most useful purpose; municipal control of trade seems to have been general and beneficial, though at a later period it degenerated into a close monopoly and became the privilege of a few.

Under Henry III. (1216) there was a great influx of foreign merchants, and trade with Flanders increased; wool was exported and manufactured woollens imported. Under this king was established the system of *stapling*, which for several centuries determined the markets for the home and foreign trade in certain staple products, of which wool was the most important.   Such goods were required to be sent to certain towns, called staples, for sale.   It was thought that trade could be thus more easily supervised and regulated, and the customs duties could be more readily collected.   This system flourished through the thirteenth and fourteenth centuries.   A statute of Edward III. (1354) enumerates ten staple towns in England, and gives the customs duties payable on the goods there to be sold.   These towns paid taxes for the monopoly which they enjoyed.   Various foreign staples were appointed for the foreign trade, such as Antwerp, Bruges, and Calais, to which English wool, leather, &c., were sent.   The system declined under the Tudors from the competition of the merchant adventurers, and practically came to an end with the loss of Calais in 1558.

Export duties were first regulated by Act of Parliament in 1275 under Edward I., when the duties on wool, leather, and metals were fixed for revenue.   This tax was known as "the great customs".   In 1303 the tax was imposed upon both imports and exports at an increased rate, on the ground of the protection afforded to traders, and the rate was fixed at 3*d*. in the £ *ad valorem* on all kinds of merchandise.   A further revision followed in 1376 (Edward III.) when tonnage and poundage exacted on wines and merchandise (whether imports or exports) was granted as a subsidy to the king, and the tax became from this time a regular part of the revenue system.

Previous to this reign no particular economic distinction seems to have been drawn between taxes on imports and exports; revenue appears to have been the chief aim.   But under Edward III. Flemish weavers were encouraged to settle in England and follow their industry, direct attempts were made at fostering home industry, and some restraints on the export of wool began to be adopted.   Modifications of the duties made subsequently by Parliament point to the growth of the idea of checking the export of raw materials and limiting the import of manufactured goods.   Thus, in 1463, Edward IV. prohibited the importation of wrought goods in the interests of English artificers; this act was

renewed under Richard III., and, as late as the eighteenth
century, was commended as a most beneficent piece of
legislation.

Later still, under the Tudors, duties on imports were
increased, and exports were prohibited under penalties.
In Elizabeth's reign it was made a capital offence if a
man for the second time exported wool or English rams.
The preservation of the raw material for home industry, and the export of the manufactured article, were
coming to be recognized as a distinct policy; the protective idea was gaining ground.   Under Charles II.
hides and leather were added to the prohibited exports,
and the instruments of industry were also placed under
like restraint in order not to give to foreign manufacturers any advantage which might be reserved for the
home producer.

Under these regulations the number of taxed articles
had increased greatly, and the system of customs administration had become very intricate and troublesome
to merchants.

Import duties were originally levied on the declared
value of the merchandise, but in 1558 a "Book of Rates"
was drawn up, enumerating the articles and specifying
how each should be valued for customs purposes.   This
book, an anticipation of a tariff, was revised on several
occasions with a view to increasing the revenue.   In
1662 the Rate Book enumerated 1139 articles of import
and 212 of export.

The regulation of trading by privilege, charter, staple,
and prohibition was in accordance with the general
ideas of the age, derived from the system of universal
control in feudal times, under which most of the economic
relations of life were determined by custom and authority.   Of the same nature were the interferences with
freedom of labour, of which the Conspiracy Act (1304),
the Statute of Labourers (1349), and the Apprenticeship
Act of Elizabeth (1563), are examples.   In other directions the belief in the right and capacity of regulation
from above was illustrated.   As home-trading increased,
a class of middlemen or dealers had been evolved; and
it was thought desirable in the interests of consumers to

limit their operations and restrain the action of competition, which was then little understood. Thus by acts (1551–1552) forestallers, regrators, and engrossers were forbidden to buy goods or victuals for resale in the same market or locality. These acts aimed at moderating the prices of necessaries, and also the profits of the dealers in corn, fish, wool, &c.

Money came under legislative control at an early period. Acts were passed forbidding the export of gold and silver, lest there should be an insufficiency of currency, and for fear the royal treasure should suffer depletion. An act of 1307, prohibiting the export of gold, is said to have led to the introduction of bills of exchange. A later act of Richard II. imposed severe penalties on the export of gold or silver without a license: "For the great mischief which this realm suffereth and long hath done, that gold and silver are carried out of the realm, so that in effect there is none left thereof, which thing if it should longer be suffered would shortly be the destruction of the same realm, which God prohibit". Under Henry VIII. (1512) an act was passed "that all persons carrying over sea any coins, plate, or jewels, shall, on detection, forfeit double their value".

Trade with Flanders greatly increased in the fourteenth and fifteenth centuries. In 1496 Henry VII. entered into a commercial treaty with the Netherlands (The Intercursus Magnus), which, by mutual concessions, aimed at freeing and extending the trade between the two countries. The prosperity of the fifteenth century stimulated English merchants to enterprise; they organized themselves into trading companies, of which The Merchant Adventurers gained a charter in 1501. The energy of these traders brought them into conflict and rivalry with the Hanse traders, and finally led to the withdrawal of the charter of that corporation in 1597.

This impulse to British enterprise coincides with the rise of a policy which professed to make trading subservient to national welfare, by securing native industry and commerce against foreign competition, by increasing national resources and strengthening national industries. A variety of circumstances in the sixteenth century

favoured the growth of the national spirit and desire for
national greatness. The discovery of the New World
(1492), and of the Cape route to India (1498), opened up
larger ideas of commerce and new fields for enterprise.
The consolidation of states under more settled government and institutions, the Reformation movement, and
the revival of learning, all tended to awaken new sentiments of national life. The accession of treasure to the
first conquerors of the New World suggested to others
fresh sources of wealth. The sack of Antwerp, in 1585,
diverted a portion of her trade to London, and sent over
a number of Flemish skilled artisans, to the advantage
of British manufactures and trade.

Thus there grew up in the reign of Elizabeth a feeling
from which developed a national policy; the aim of this
policy was to make England great, powerful, and wealthy.
This object was to be accomplished by the creation of a
strong navy, the acquisition of new territory by planta-
tions (or colonies), and the development of national resources, and the increase of a treasure in gold and silver
for the purpose of defence and warfare.

A like enthusiasm had seized upon other nations, and
patriotism in the circumstances was displayed in hostility,
in jealousy and menaces, in struggles for maritime
supremacy and commercial monopoly. The regulations
imposing restrictions upon foreign trade were increased,
and progressive nations in the seventeenth century all
adopted the policy of harassing one another's commerce.

Under Elizabeth the spirit of enterprise and monopoly
gave rise to the formation of a large number of trading
companies, which obtained charters for the purpose of
acquiring the sole rights of trading in certain parts.
The Russia Company, 1553; the Baltic Company,
1579; the Levant Company, 1581; the Guinea Company, 1588; the East India Company, 1600, were all
formed on this principle of "authorized trading". Their
charters conferred upon these companies the exclusive
privilege of trading in specified districts, and from such
parts other traders, called "interlopers", were inter-
dicted. The risks incurred in opening up new trade

formed an argument for these monopolies; they were held to be useful in promoting trade in unsettled and dangerous parts, as Adam Smith admits, "by making at their own expense an experiment which the state might not think it prudent to make". The privileges, however, in time became an abuse, they were attacked in the seventeenth century, and were ultimately withdrawn.

The "national policy" which grew up towards the latter part of the sixteenth century developed a *theory of trade* known as "the mercantilist theory"; which dominated foreign trade relations in the seventeenth century, and almost to the end of the eighteenth century. This policy was deemed to be an advance upon earlier principles of trading, inasmuch as it professed to be based upon a regard for the commonwealth, and to seek the public good. Its acceptance as a public policy preceded its formulation as an economic theory, and the popularity of the theory, when put forth by Thomas Mun in 1664, was due in some degree to the fact that it seemed to give a scientific explanation of trading in accordance with the popular sentiment of the times.

The history of the seventeenth and eighteenth centuries is largely a record of struggles for commercial supremacy, for the acquisition of new territory and the control of markets. Wherever colonies were planted exclusive trading was established. During the seventeenth century the Dutch enjoyed the position of the leading commercial nation; they possessed the largest fleet, and had a vast carrying trade. Against them the Navigation Acts of England (1651 and 1660) were directed, with the view of injuring their trade and extending our own maritime power. Notwithstanding the jealousy of Holland, the English copied her methods, and carried on a large trade with her, which amounted in 1703 to £2,250,000 in exports, mostly of wool. During the seventeenth century the English foreign trade increased from £4,628,000 to £11,170,000. Between France and England protection was rife; under the guidance of the minister Colbert, France in 1664 adopted an almost prohibitive tariff, and England in 1678 retaliated by prohibiting the import of French goods, and also the export of wool, raw materials, metals, and implements.

Under the mercantilist system an exaggerated importance was attached to the possession of gold and silver. Money had gained prominence with the increase of trading, but its true functions were not yet clearly understood. It was seen that the precious metals were in universal demand, they were always acceptable in payment for goods, and wealth was commonly estimated in terms of money. The countries which were receiving supplies of the precious metals from the New World had increased their trade, and were enabled to purchase commodities from others. Spain and Portugal for a time appeared to be the proprietors of great wealth. Many circumstances favoured the belief that the precious metals were pre-eminently desirable imports; and measures were adopted to promote their acquisition. Had the influx come about by natural causes, it might have been regarded as an index of prosperity, since the precious metals, like other desirable things, flow to countries in which other forms of wealth are abundant; but an artificial accumulation of money could only take place by surrendering other forms of wealth, as the miser adds to his hoards by denying himself more needful things. Under the delusion that a country profited by increasing its stock of gold and silver, nations struggled to obtain possession of these metals, and their commercial regulations were framed with that object. Exports were encouraged by bounties, imports of useful goods were checked by duties, trading was regarded as injurious to the country if it tended to draw away money, and the advantage of a year's trading to a country was measured, *not* in the increase of useful commodities gained thereby, but in the increase of precious metals which were gained as a "balance of trade". Exporting was thus regarded as more profitable than importing; the mutual advantage of exchange between countries was obscured, and by directing the attention to the mere instrument or mechanism of exchange the one country was supposed to lose in trading what the other gained.

It was also contended that money was a means of employing labour at home, and that the export of bullion was so much money lost as regards that purpose. The business of foreign trade was held to consist in securing markets, and in exporting thither home-produce, the advantage being measured by the amount of the "favourable balance" of treasure. A fundamental economic truth did underlie this argument, namely, that the production of native goods by industry is the real source of wealth, but it was accompanied by a great misconception as to the nature of the advantages gained by trading. These arise from the utility of the goods received in the exchange, and not from the acquisition of money, which may even flow in in such quantities as to be in excess of the requirements of the nation. Mercantilists have sometimes been represented as holding the vulgar error that money was the *only* wealth. This was not so; their error lay in estimating the advantage of foreign trade by the amount of precious metals it introduced, and in neglecting the benefits to be gained by the increase of useful and desirable goods in exchange for their exports. On this point the opinion of John Locke is instructive. He writes: "Gold and silver being little useful to the life of men in proportion to food, raiment, and carriage, has its value only from the consort of men"; and Boisguillebert, even more dogmatically: "It is very certain that money is not a value in itself, and that its quantity adds nothing to the wealth of a country".

In a pamphlet published in 1664 by Thomas Mun, called *England's Treasure by Foreign Trade*, the mercantilist theory of trading is explained "to consist in keeping imports less than exports, thus to secure a favourable balance, and provide an abundance of money which could be drawn upon in time of need". The balance of actual money was advocated in the seventeenth century mainly as a means of providing a treasure for the purpose of national defence. This argument had some weight in an unsettled and warlike period, when bullion was scarce, and the metals were almost the only means of currency. In the eighteenth century, after the loaning system had arisen, and it was no longer deemed necessary to put by stores of money for national purposes, the balance of trade came to be regarded as the measure of the prosperity of industry.   The practical measures urged by Mun to carry out his theory were prohibition of the export of gold and encouragement of its import, encouragement of exports of goods, and discouragement of all imports except the raw materials of industry.   Systems of tariffs and regulations were devised as the machinery to carry into effect this policy, out of which grew up the protective system. Smuggling, as a means of evasion, soon followed, and contraband trade grew into a regular institution.   In course of time the encouragement of manufactures became a more deliberate aim, and the system was pursued with the object of maintaining the prohibition of finished goods, of directing consumption at home, and of stimulating new home industries. The principles which directed the commerce of the eighteenth century embodied in a large degree the chief doctrines of protection as it has been advocated in the present century, and the arguments then advanced in its defence are commonly repeated in the proposals of to-day.

One of the devices of the mercantile system was the promotion of commercial treaties, by means of which it was thought a vent for surplus goods was obtained and some exclusive advantage acquired. England, for example, in 1703 arranged a treaty with Portugal (called the "Methuen Treaty", after its negotiator) in order that she might secure some of the silver which Portugal was importing from Brazil. England undertook to lower her duties on port-wine on condition that Portugal admitted English woollen goods at lower rates.   The treaty was approved in England as much from jealousy of France and the expected increase of bullion by the "balance of trade" as from anticipated advantages to the woollen trade.   England consumed more port and less French burgundy, and the capital of Portugal was directed in a larger degree to the cultivation of the vine. But treaties of this exclusive character always offend some other nation by the diversion of trade, and the Methuen treaty annoyed France by the injury it caused to her wine trade. Less than a century later, with Pitt's treaty of 1786, commercial treaties began to be framed on a better basis, and so as to procure a real reduction of duties between the contracting nations without any attempt at injuriously affecting the trade with others.

When colonization opened up new fields of enterprise to European nations, they applied to the colonies which they acquired the principles of restriction practised in their trade with one another. By the mercantilist statesmen, colonies were treated as the property of the nations which gained them, and their markets and products as the exclusive monopoly of the sovereign nation, and they were allowed no commercial intercourse with foreign nations.[1] This "sole market" policy, known as the colonial system, was adopted by Great Britain in her relations with the American colonies. It impeded their development, though it was argued that the colonies profited by the defence and credit of the mother-country.

Their industries were regulated so as not to compete with the market for goods which they provided for the home industries, their shipping was controlled, and ships built in the colonies were even required to be equipped with sails from England. Even Ireland was included in the system of industrial and commercial restraint. From the year 1660 the importation of meat and dairy produce from Ireland was prohibited in England as adverse to English agriculture, and when this discouragement to cattle-farming had led to the substitution of sheep-farming, Irish wool was excluded from English markets.

This development of the "national policy" brought its natural fruit in smuggling, and discord with the thirteen American colonies, and finally led to the struggle which secured these colonies their independence. The issue of that conflict, together with the growth of the more enlightened ideas of commerce which had been advanced by Adam Smith, led to the abolition of the colonial system by Great Britain, and, at a later period,

[1] See *Wealth of Nations*, book iv. chap. 7, for a full account of the "colonial system".

to the complete commercial independence of her colonies. Other nations (Holland, Spain, and France) did not follow the policy of Great Britain in this respect.

It has often been advanced as a defence of mercantilism that it was a necessary phase in the development of nations; at a critical period in their growth, it is said, statesmen availed themselves of national sentiment by these means to strengthen national life and give it form and character; and only thus could it have been nurtured and sustained. Herr Schmoller, a representative of the historic school of economists in Germany, states this view in his valuable monograph on Mercantilism.[1] He says: "The statesmen who put into form their theories gave the economic life of their people its necessary basis of power, and a corresponding impulse to its economic movement, and they furnished the national striving with great aims. At a time when most advanced nations were carrying on the collective struggle for existence with the harshest national egoism, with all the weapons of finance, of legislation, and of force, with navigation laws and prohibitive laws, with fleets and admiralties, with companies, and with a trade under state guidance and discipline, those who would not be hammer would assuredly be anvil."

The assertion is that mercantilism was in keeping with the spirit of the age. Two questions arise: (1) Was it an unavoidable part of the "national policy" for making nations strong? and (2) Was it economically beneficial? With regard to the former, it must be granted that when the struggle of nations for individual life, and for security and strength, was intense and critical, and while a very jealous and military spirit was the dominating influence, a system of trading framed upon a peace basis was impossible; and it is probable that, as Herr Schmoller suggests, the nations that would not adopt the methods of the stronger powers would have been crushed by them. Historically, the "national policy" of strength was an important phase in the growth of nations; but whether its commercial develop-

---

[1] *The Mercantile System and its Historical Significance,* by Gustav Schmoller.

ments were also necessary is a different question. The
elaborate system of restrictions and regulations, the
struggle for the possession of money, the rejection of
the advantages of exchange, could scarcely have contributed either to national life or to national wealth. The
fact is, that, at a period when economic investigation
had made little progress, the harshness of the struggles
for empire and power was transferred to the domain of
commerce. Trade was made an instrument of warfare,
or was sacrificed to political rivalry. Tariff struggles
grew out of national jealousies, and helped to set up a
system of international barriers, which in time grew
into a protective policy, and came to be regarded as
beneficial to the nation. Mercantilism was a product of
certain conditions of the age; it was in accord with the
general sentiment, and also with the common beliefs, of
those times. That its methods were economically profitable to the nation at any time is, to say the least, very
doubtful.

Free-trading may be regarded as a particular case of
general freedom of action; and this freedom all history
shows to have been of very gradual growth. Sir Henry
Maine holds that "the evolution of society has been
from status to contract". Herbert Spencer states the
same fact in another form when he asserts that "progress has been from communism to individualism".
All early history exhibits society graded, regulated by
custom, and bound down by habit and tradition. The
history of England since the Norman Conquest is a
record of progress from serfdom and feudalism to free
institutions.

> " Freedom slowly broadening down
> From precedent to precedent",

and very slowly did this freedom reach the majority.

Only after centuries of servitude was the right of self-
government attained, but step by step through the
centuries political freedom advanced until finally it has
filtered down and has become the inalienable heritage
of the mass of the people. In religious matters the
country long suffered from the domination of the Church,

and it required years of struggling after the Reformation period before religious freedom and equality were fully admitted and understood.   Freedom of opinion—of speech and of the press—was long denied, and was only attained by slow and painful degrees.   Freedom of discussion and the formation of public opinion by open debate are constitutional safeguards, for men resort to revolutions only when the privileges of free citizens are denied them in order to bring about reforms.   The diffusion of knowledge was a further stage in the advance of freedom.   In the Middle Ages learning was the monopoly of monastics and clergy, at a later period the privilege of the richer classes; in modern times education is the opportunity of all, and it is even forced upon unwilling people.   Knowledge has been truly called the greatest leveller; monopoly and privilege will be doomed when all classes are educated.

Economic freedom came most slowly of all, and is not yet fully attained.   The reason is, that it is dependent upon other forms of freedom, and could not precede them.   The fetters of ignorance must be removed, as well as social and political disabilities, that men may understand and exercise their freedom in pursuit of their own interests.   It was comparatively easy to perceive the injury and injustice of laws fixing wages and restraining men from combining to ask for higher rewards. But it requires a long course of education to make the masses understand that institutions, such as protective tariffs, which they had been accustomed to regard as natural, and which they had been taught to believe beneficial to themselves, are only impediments to liberty and causes of diminished well-being.   To effect this change in public opinion was the special task to which the prime movers in the Anti-Corn-law agitation devoted themselves; and it is one of the most notable features of the Free-trade movement that its chief victories were achieved by a small body of thinkers, who had imbibed large views of constitutional freedom and of personal and economic liberty.   They finally succeeded by their persistence in educating, and in converting to their opinions, not only manufacturers, factory

workers, and agricultural labourers, but even farmers
and land-owners, the prime minister and the House of
Commons itself.

The repeal of the Corn-laws determined the Free-
trade policy of this country, which is commonly dated
from 1846, though it was a policy advocated in the
previous century by Adam Smith, foreshadowed in the
treaty of 1786 by Pitt and by his reforms, actually
commenced by Huskisson in 1823, and practically
adopted by Peel in the budget of 1842.   Since the
abolition of the Corn-laws tariffs have proceeded on
Free-trade lines; the policy of remission of duties was
checked for a time by the Russian war, but it was afterwards resumed, and our fiscal system now contains no
protective element although it raises £21,000,000 from
duties on imported goods, mainly tobacco, wine, spirits,
and tea.

For some years after 1850 there were hopes that a
Free-trade policy would be adopted by other countries;
but a reaction followed the period of the Franco-German
war, and the protective spirit has since been revived
amongst most of the leading commercial nations.   Our
own country has remained firm in its Free-trade principles, though the wisdom of its isolated policy is often
called in question.   Up to the present the great prosperity which has been so marked since the complete
acceptance of the doctrine has been powerfully in its
favour; and, though often assailed, the arguments on
which free-trading is based have not been overthrown.
The following chapters aim at tracing briefly the leading
points in the history of the controversy, the results of
its adoption, and the present position of Free-trade in
Great Britain and the countries with which she is most
intimately connected by commerce.

Chapter II.

Adam Smith and the Decline of Mercantilism.

The overthrow of mercantilism is usually attributed to
Adam Smith's monumental work, *The Wealth of Nations*,
published in 1776; but the revolt against the restraints
and regulations which that system imposed upon industry
and commerce commenced much earlier. The conditions
under which it had been developed had changed materially by the middle of the eighteenth century; the economic problems then arising were of a different order,
and methods of economic inquiry were making some
progress.   In France, writers of the Physiocratic School
of "Economistes"—its founder Quesnay (1768), and
Turgot, minister of Louis XVI. (1774–1776)—had advocated complete liberty both in home and foreign trade;
their demands for freedom of competition were a protest
against impediments to trade on behalf of those who
suffered from the evils of restriction and high prices.
The negative principle of *laissez-faire, laissez-passer*,[1]
which they set up as a scientific maxim, sums up their
views of the functions of the State in commercial and
industrial matters.   Adam Smith owed something to the
teaching of the Physiocrats on "natural liberty", though
he criticised their views respecting the origin of wealth.
Mercantilism was also being questioned by writers on
economic subjects in Great Britain, and the opinion that
greater freedom would be beneficial was not confined to
theorists; the idea that the abolition of duties would be
good for trade was gaining ground, and found expression also among men engaged in commerce.   Sir James
Steuart's dictum, "that it is the combination of every
private interest which forms the public good, and of this

[1] The phrase *laissez-faire* originated in the seventeenth century in the reaction against the attempts of the great French minister Colbert, to foster
industry by a system of state regulation and protection against foreign
countries. As a policy of non-interference with industry and trade, it was
adopted by the Manchester School of economists and politicians a century
later, and became their characteristic doctrine.

the public, that is, statesmen, only can judge" contains
the germ of Adam Smith's reform in political and economic theory, although it relegates to the politician what
is at all events in part the function of the economist.[1]

In the century prior to Adam Smith, statesmen had
given but little attention to the effects of legislation upon
individual welfare; their leading idea was to formulate
a policy for advancing national greatness and obtaining
public revenue; the ultimate end of statecraft was
centred in national strength and defence.   Hence the
importance they attached to a store of treasure and to
an increase of money as supplying the sinews of war.
The legislature busied itself with measures for increasing
the produce of the land as a source of national revenue,
with the regulation of commerce, so as to secure a
favourable balance of trade and a net importation of gold
and silver, and with the encouragement of exports, and
the provision of markets for their disposal.   The economic aspects of this "national policy" were rather over-
shadowed by the political; the importance of individual
enterprise in creating the fund from which revenue is
raised was undervalued.

It is Adam Smith's peculiar merit that he directed
economic legislation towards "the welfare of individuals
and homes".   He gave emphasis to the idea of wealth
"as a means of plentiful subsistence for the people".
To this end he urged that the energies of statesmen
should be mainly directed, subordinating thereto the
supply of revenue for the public service, of which there
would be no lack in a prosperous state.   Adopting the
view of De Gournay, "that private interests are identical
with public interests", he maintained the rights of individuals to dispose of their labour and its fruits in the best
market they can find, and to make, without hindrance, the
best bargains they can for themselves in their exchanges.

---

[1] J. Steuart, *An Inquiry into the Principles of Political Economy* (1767).
Daniel Defoe, also, writing in *The Mercator* at the beginning of the eighteenth
century, had stated very lucidly the real advantages of trading between
nations.   "Trading", he says, "is a matter entirely independent in its
nature, and neither consults other interests nor depends on any interests but
what relate to itself."   And again, "the language of one nation to another
is, I let thee gain by me that I may gain by thee".

The discovery of a great scientific principle usually takes place only when the time and circumstances are ripe for its revelation, but it requires a mind of exceptional genius to grasp the situation, to discern the principle involved, and to enunciate the new truth in a manner at once lucid and forcible, in order that it may gain acceptance from a public biassed by old beliefs.

The doctrine of "natural liberty"—that the national welfare depends upon the exercise of personal freedom in the ordinary business of life by the individuals who compose the state—was of the nature of a discovery in the sphere of political thought, and its application to practice has profoundly affected the course of history. To John Locke (*Civil Government*) the idea of political freedom was mainly due, and Montesquieu (*Esprit des Lois*) had enforced the same doctrine: Adam Smith grasped its force, and gave it application in the domain of economic relations. From his time economics began to be treated as a distinct branch of science, and inquiries into the nature and causes of wealth and of its distribution came to be regarded as more and more important in promoting the welfare of men, both as individuals and as citizens.

Locke had already commented upon the importance of labour in the production of wealth, and Gregory King had emphasized the function of capital in providing a fund for employing labour; Adam Smith demanded that both should be freed from trammels. Capital had already gained some degree of liberty; the trading corporations were declining; new towns were growing up in which the restraints of the old municipal corporations were absent; the usury laws were becoming obsolete; and monopolies granted in connection with certain industries at home, or conferring special privileges in foreign commerce, were tending to lapse. Labour, however, suffered from many disabilities imposed by combination acts, settlement acts, and other impediments to free movement. The whole system of restraints had operated most disastrously for the weaker classes, and the time was ripe for the promulgation of a system of "natural liberty" in matters affecting trade and industry as set forth by Adam Smith.

Whether, as is maintained, this point of view was unattainable at an earlier stage in the growth of nations is a question which scarcely admits of a definite answer; but it is certain that the previous policy had not only impeded industry at home, but had kept up national animosities, and had built up cumbrous systems of commercial legislation, which restricted the development and production of wealth.

By separating the economic problem from the political for purposes of investigation, the conditions favourable to the advance of material welfare were more clearly discerned, and the progress of the masses during the past century has been furthered in no small degree by the practical application of the economic principles thus elucidated.   Legislation also became more humanitarian when the idea had been fully grasped that the well-being of the individuals of which the nation is composed is the true aim of government, that national power and national revenue should subserve this end, and that the removal of legislative hindrances to freedom of action was one of the best means for the attainment of human welfare.

The argument of *The Wealth of Nations* embodied a further idea, which was novel at the time, and which has by no means been universally grasped even yet, namely, that the mutual dependence of nations is a factor in their individual progress, and that exclusiveness is unfavourable to full national development.   This doctrine, a product of the scientific inquiry into the nature and origin of wealth, had a universal application; it tended to remove some of the causes of international jealousy and rivalry, and to promote more cordial relations among nations by the recognition of common interests.   Under the theory of mercantilism, nations were considered necessarily antagonistic to one another; they were always in a state of war or preparing for it,[1] and to attack

1 "Commerce, which ought naturally to be, among nations as among individuals, a bond of union and friendship, has become the most fertile source of discord and animosity.   The capricious ambition of kings and ministers has not, during the present and preceding century, been more fatal to the

or impede the welfare of other peoples was regarded as
a chief means of promoting their own.   The fiscal policy
which these measures entailed injured themselves not less
than their rivals.   The tendency of the new doctrine was
to remove these restraints and burdens, and to foster a
spirit of amity in place of the jealousy which prevailed
between nations.   That the greatest possible liberty of
action would conduce to the comfort and progress of the
people came to be regarded as an economic maxim,
which was progressively adopted by statesmen.   The
analysis of wealth and commerce performed by Adam
Smith made entirely for peace by exposing fallacies
which had been the cause of many conflicts.   His attitude towards trade was cosmopolitan, but not the less
patriotic.   He felt that economic advantages are not
fully secured within political limits.   With scientific insight he saw that commerce benefits all mankind, and is
not merely a device for obtaining gain for one nation at
the expense of others.   He recognized that consumable
goods were what nations required, and what they could
obtain by free exchange, and that gold and silver were
only the instruments of this exchange.   He perceived
also that no special efforts on the part of governments
were necessary to procure the precious metals, since, as
the instruments of commerce, they would necessarily
follow its movements, and that freedom of commerce
would lead to an adequate supply of gold and silver in
countries which did not produce them.[1]

The economic evils of restrictions upon commerce
were very forcibly set forth by Adam Smith; they
checked the growth of wealth, and tended to impoverish
the people by excluding desirable commodities; bounties
upon exports only forced special industries artificially
at the cost of the community, while checks on the

repose of Europe than the impertinent jealousy of merchants and manufacturers " (*Wealth of Nations*, book iv. chap. 3).

[1] Ricardo states this doctrine very clearly in his *Principles of Political
Economy and Taxation*, 3rd edition, p. 143:—" Gold and silver having been
chosen for the general medium of circulation, they are, by the competition
of commerce, distributed in such proportions amongst the different countries
of the world as to accommodate themselves to the natural traffic which
would take place if no such metals existed, and the trade between countries
were purely a trade of barter ".

export of machinery injured the machine-making industries, besides destroying the mutual advantages of exchange. Taxes on food, either home-grown or imported, were, as Adam Smith said, "a curse equal to the barrenness of the earth and the inclemency of the heavens", and an attempt to destroy or reject nature's free gifts. As he suggests in his criticism of the Corn-laws, "were all nations to follow the liberal system of free exportation and free importation, the different states into which a great continent was divided would so far resemble the different provinces of a great empire".[1]   But so numerous were the restrictions upon external trade in his day, so powerful the interests which profited by them, and so deep-rooted the belief in the efficacy and necessity of this State control, that Adam Smith had little expectation that the principles he advocated would ever be realized in practice. In his own words: "To expect, indeed, that the freedom of trade should ever be entirely restored in Great Britain is as absurd as to expect that an Oceana or Utopia should ever be established in it. Not only the prejudices of the public, but, what is much more unconquerable, the private interests of many individuals, irresistibly oppose it."[2]   This quotation substantially expresses the reasons why many other nations still refrain from adopting the Free-trade policy. Adam Smith considered that "freedom of trade should be restored" in such cases "only by slow gradations and with a good deal of reserve and circumspection", since its sudden adoption would destroy the protected industries, and "deprive all at once many thousands of our people of their ordinary employment and means of subsistence".

Although the system of protection prevailing when Adam Smith wrote had originated in a measure of public policy, it had fostered mainly the interests of the trading and mercantile classes, for whom it endeavoured to secure a monopoly of markets. Adam Smith himself attributes its rise to "the clamour and sophistry of the merchants and manufacturers", who had possessed much influence with the Government from the time of

[1] *Wealth of Nations*, book iv. chap. 5.   [2] *Ibid*, book iv. chap. 2.

the Revolution, and had induced a belief among the
ruling classes and land-owners that it was in the public
interest to check the export of wool and to maintain
protective duties.[1] As yet agriculture had not gained
much from protection. For fifty years prior to 1765
Great Britain exported corn; importation then began,
but the duty on wheat was reduced in 1773 to only 6d.
per quarter when the price rose above 48s. The landlords of the eighteenth century had devoted themselves
energetically to developing the resources of the soil;
they had sunk much capital in their estates, and had
shown great enterprise in the introduction of new
methods and new products from Flanders. The century was one of great progress in agriculture. It should
be remembered that the criticism of Adam Smith upon
mercantilism and restrictions generally was not aroused
by dearness of food. That aspect of the system came
into prominence from the end of the century as a result
of bad harvests, the impediments to importation created
by the war, and the efforts of the belligerents to destroy
each other's commerce; as a distinct policy for benefit-
ing agriculture, protection dates from 1815.

In the early periods of interference (from the fourteenth to the end of the eighteenth century) the export
of corn had been checked with the idea of maintaining a
sufficiency at home, and restrictions on its sale were
made with a view of excluding the profit of middlemen
rather than with a protective aim. But under Charles
II. interference began in the interest of land-owners, and
import duties were imposed, which, however, had little
effect on prices. After the Revolution a 5s. bounty was
given on the export of corn when the price fell to 48s. a
quarter. This was expected to raise prices, but in
reality it stimulated production, and led to inclosures
and wider cultivation of corn-land with the object of
gaining the bounty, though, as some maintain, at the

---

[1] " Merchants and manufacturers are the people who derive the greatest
advantage from the monopoly of the home market. . . . Country gentlemen and farmers are, to their great honour, of all people the least subject to
the wretched spirit of monopoly. The undertaker of a great manufactory is
sometimes alarmed if another work of the same kind is established within
twenty miles of him " (*Wealth of Nations*, book iv. chap. 2).

expense of other branches of agriculture. Prices were kept down, and as a fact corn was cheaper by some 30 per cent in the first half of the eighteenth century than in the seventeenth, a circumstance which may in some measure have been owing to the impulse given by the new agriculture, though it was undoubtedly mainly due to the bounty, which lowered prices by calling forth an increased supply.

Though Adam Smith made a general attack upon restrictions on commerce, he admitted two important exceptions which call for special notice:—(1) When the tax which is placed upon an imported article is balanced by an equivalent duty upon the home product, as in the case of our present duties on spirits and beer; such taxes, being levied purely for revenue purposes, are not protective. (2) The second case is that of national defence, which he maintained was "of much more importance than opulence", and his support of the famous Navigation Laws rests upon this ground.[1]

The first Navigation Act was passed as early as 1381, when an attempt was made, not very successfully, to develop a navy by requiring merchants to employ English shipping. The patriotic outburst of the Elizabethan period, coinciding with a spirit of maritime enterprise and great expansion of trade, did much more to stimulate the formation of a navy. The Navigation Acts of 1651 and 1660, however, exercised great influence in developing England's maritime power, in that they crushed the Dutch carrying trade. Their economic aspect was twofold: on the one hand, they benefited ship-owners and merchants by raising prices and rates; on the other, they irritated consumers and shippers (who would either have employed the Dutch carriers or benefited by their competition with the English), and they offended the colonists by setting up monopolies in their

---

[1] "When the Act of Navigation was made, though England and Holland were not actually at war, the most violent animosity subsisted between the two nations. National animosity at that particular time aimed at the very same object which the most deliberate wisdom would have recommended—the diminution of the naval power of Holland, the only naval power which could endanger the security of England" (*Wealth of Nations*, book iv chap. 2).

trade. The justification of the Navigation Acts is political and not economic. Sir Josiah Child's defence of these Acts,[1] made in 1690, rests virtually upon the same kind of argument that has been advanced for strengthening the Navy for Imperial purposes during the past few years. He observes: "This kingdom being an island, the defence whereof has always been our shipping and seamen, it seems to me absolutely necessary that profit and power ought jointly to be considered, and if so, I think none can deny but the Act of Navigation hath, and doth occasion building and employing three times the number of ships and seamen that otherwise we should do; . . . many ships and seamen being justly the reputed strength and safety of England". In the absence of a formidable national fleet and of regular parliamentary votes for the construction and maintenance of ships of war, the Navigation Acts succeeded in providing the stimulus for the creation of a mercantile fleet, which could then supplement the national navy and offer substantial defence for the country in time of war. This is their justification. On purely commercial grounds there is little to be said for them;[2] competition, coupled with the political events which afterwards completed the misfortunes of Holland, would most probably in time have given Great Britain the first place among maritime nations, without the aid of shipping regulations.

It will be seen that the Protection of this century differs in many respects from that of the mercantilists. As has been explained, the latter aimed at "national strength", and the commercial restraints adopted in the light of the economic ideas then prevailing were imposed primarily as conducing to that end. Some of the errors of that system had received their death-blow. The revolt of the American colonies demonstrated the folly of the "colonial system" of trade. Adam Smith had exposed the fallacies respecting money, which led to

---

[1] *Discourse upon Trade*, by Sir Josiah Child (1690).

[2] "The Act of Navigation is not favourable to foreign commerce, or to the growth of that opulence which can arise from it " (*Wealth of Nations*, book iv. chap 2).

regulations for securing a balance of the precious
metals; the growth of a system of credit had introduced
a new method of meeting extraordinary expenditure by
loans, and dispensed with the necessity for accumulating
national treasure.   The adoption of the principle ot
"natural liberty", which aimed at increasing the
national wealth by encouraging individual wealth, destroyed the policy which treated commerce merely as an
instrument for revenue.   Also the original aim of the
Mercantilists had been partly attained; the nation was
becoming consolidated and powerful.   Still, the elements
of a protective policy survived in established practices
and beliefs, and the circumstances of the close of the
eighteenth century were peculiarly favourable for reviv-
ing and strengthening them in the new form which is
the characteristic of nineteenth-century protection.

Some fallacies lingered on—that the gain of one country in trading involves an equivalent loss to the other;
that commerce is a species of warfare, and that to import an article which can be produced at home is an
injury to the country which imports.   These errors,
which are at the root of much Protectionist writing at
the present day, took their rise in less-settled times,
when national animosities and jealousies were easily and
frequently aroused, and mercantilism nourished their
growth.   The struggle with France, that commenced
in 1793, during which France returned to strict prohibition, and which dragged on until 1815, was calculated
to deepen this doctrine; in fact it gained wide currency
at that period.   Patriotism was supposed to demand the
exclusion of the goods of the hostile country, and to
require the nation to encourage its own industries.
National sentiment, aroused by threats of invasion,
supported the rather loose reasoning, that, as hostile
forces must be repelled, so it was equally meritorious to
repel "invasions of goods" from hostile countries.   In
such circumstances it is not difficult to perceive how the
conflict of arms led on to a conflict in the commercial
arena, and how measures which made for national independence and self-sufficiency became the popular policy;
and the spirit of bitter antagonism to foreigners en-

gendered a hatred and fear of dependence upon them
for food, with a strong desire to support those home
industries which provided the national sustenance. A
third cause co-operated with these to favour the exclusion of foreign goods; this was the serious need for
revenue for military purposes, which led to taxes being
levied upon every available object. The result of this
prohibitive policy was that highly-protective duties were
imposed upon foreign goods, and especially corn, during
a period sufficiently long to establish industries on a
protective basis, and to accustom the nation to the protective principle. Out of these various elements the
Protectionist policy of the early part of this century was
evolved.

Adam Smith's advocacy of "natural liberty" has laid
him open to the charge of propounding an uncompro-
mising *laissez-faire* theory. As the philosophical leader
of a great reaction against excessive state regulation in
matters of trade, he has been made responsible by some
of the modern advocates of extended state control for
the views of those of his followers who, at a later period,
pushed the doctrine of non-interference to the extrava-
gant length of opposing factory legislation. The imputation, however, falls to the ground when we consider
the circumstances of the times in which he wrote and
the industrial conditions which then prevailed. He found
economic affairs regulated in every detail; the task which
pressed was that of attacking and overthrowing hurtful
restrictions. To Adam Smith "natural liberty" meant,
economically speaking, the right to dispose of goods or
labour free from unnecessary restraints and taxation.
The period called for destructive criticism, and he supplied it, along with sound economic investigation.
Laissez-faire, as generally understood now, never had
existed in England when he wrote; it was not advocated
by Adam Smith, he simply attacked impediments to
freedom of commerce and labour, common in his day.
It was impossible for him to anticipate the evil of industrial conditions which arose in a new century of
mechanical invention, and the limitations which the
factory-system and methods of large production have

since rendered necessary, in order that labourers may enjoy the liberty of action which he claimed for them, by the removal of disabilities derived from feudal ideas.

Laissez-faire is a doctrine which found favour in England at a much later period, and it is much more a political maxim than an economic doctrine. It was part of the creed of the politicians of the Manchester School (as they have been called), who made the attainment of a peace-policy their leading aim, and advocated Free-trade, the minimum of state intervention with business, and non-interference with the affairs of other nations as the chief means to that end: they represented the most extreme and abnormal development of the non-interference principle. But *laissez-faire*, unadulterated or unalloyed, is not a maxim adopted by economists, least of all by Adam Smith. Ricardo and M'Culloch, who have been regarded as its chief upholders among economists, admitted many exceptions to the principle; their successors, J. S. Mill and Jevons, distinctly repudiated it as an ideal, and indicated many directions in which it is expedient for the state to intervene.

Adam Smith, writing while factory employment and machine-industry were in their infancy, argued for greater liberty in trade and industry, but his opinions must not be identified with views that were propagated some fifty years later. He exposed the errors of his own day, and assailed definite abuses then existing and working great injury and injustice to the majority of the people. His individualism was a reaction against the extreme forms of restriction from which the country had long been suffering, and against the doctrine of state-control, which was the fundamental idea in the moribund mercantilism of his times. It is not surprising if in attacking concrete evils he propounded some principles which need modification when applied to later circumstances, and to later phases of industrial employment; but his doctrine of Free-trade requires no such revision or re-adaptation, —indeed the conditions of modern production make it more than ever applicable—at least to Great Britain. His belief in the beneficent working of enlightened self-interest, and his conviction that the good of society

would be best attained by the removal of impediments
to individual action, are extremely optimistic, and are
not to be taken absolutely, or as true for all circumstances. Experience shows that men are not all enlightened as to their real interests, nor are they equally
capable of pursuing those interests; natural and unavoidable differences in opportunity and ability render
many restraints necessary upon individual action, if the
strong are not to abuse their power and the weak to
suffer wrong. The scope of government action is very
wide in checking injustice and fraud, in limiting abuses
in the employment of power, in aiding and defending
those unable to compete fairly in the struggle for existence, and in helping the ignorant and weak to attain
knowledge and efficiency. But the character of the interferences here indicated is quite in accordance with the
spirit of Adam Smith's teaching, and equally at variance
with the restrictions which he assailed. Both make for
greater freedom of action and opportunity. It was his
task to expose the errors of Protection, and of impediments to free labour and free commerce, and to demonstrate the advantages that would accrue by removing
the fetters which interfered with the natural and beneficial action of men; it was for a later generation, in the
same spirit and with similar enlightened views, to build
up new walls against monopoly, and to impose restraints
upon fresh abuses, which experience has shown will arise
in every age.

Chapter III.

Tariff Reform (1785–1838).

Towards the end of the eighteenth century mercantilism was declining and more liberal ideas were gaining
ground; under the influence of sounder economic doctrine
there was a movement towards moderating restrictions
on trade. This is seen in the numerous treaties of commerce between European nations which were framed

between 1780 and 1790. An attempt had been made in
1713 to arrange a Treaty of Commerce with France, but
it was defeated by the jealousy of the English commercial
and manufacturing classes engaged in the silk, woollen,
and linen trades. After the Peace of Versailles (1783)
a better feeling arose, France showed a more liberal
spirit and a desire to come into closer trade relations;
and overtures for a commercial treaty were begun by
Pitt. Both nations, however, distrusted one another;
their suspicions, together with the attempts to get the
better of one another, created difficulties in arriving at
any agreement on details. After three years of delays,
Mr. Eden, who was sent to Paris to represent Great
Britain, succeeded in negotiating a treaty, which continued in operation from 1786 until the outbreak of the
revolutionary war in 1793 once more roused bitter
animosities and renewed commercial hostilities. By the
terms of this treaty France undertook to reduce the
duties upon British cotton and woollen goods to 12 per
cent *ad valorem*, and those upon hardware, cutlery,
and other goods to 10 per cent *ad valorem* (the duties
had previously been prohibitive); manufactured silks,
and goods composed of wool or cotton mixed with silk,
were still prohibited. Great Britain reduced the duties
on French wines, vinegar, brandy, and oil, on glass and
many other manufactures, to less than one-half. The
result was beneficial to both. Trade between the two
countries doubled in three years, smuggling declined,
and a more friendly feeling prevailed. France entered
into similar treaties with Holland and Russia, and the
liberalizing effect of the policy was seen in a moderate
general tariff drawn up by the Constituent Assembly in
1791.

William Pitt, who was much influenced by the writings of Adam Smith, had set himself to carry out a
policy of peace, retrenchment, and reform. He wished
to remodel the system of taxation, and advanced a stage
towards the adoption of Free-trade principles by reducing the duties on imports. He hoped thus to promote
commerce and to stimulate the national industry and
wealth, to increase the revenue, and put a check upon

the contraband trade which was fostered by the system of high customs duties. As an example of this illicit trading, the duty on tea raised the price 120 per cent, with the result that two-thirds of the tea consumed in the country was smuggled. Pitt lowered the duty to 12½ per cent (1784). He endeavoured to strengthen the finances of the nation by economy in administration and improved methods of taxation. By consolidating the customs (1787) and substituting one rate for the various duties imposed on each article, he gained revenue and reduced the cost of collection, while the public benefited from the simplification and the reduction of vexatious duties. Pitt also devised new taxes, and borrowed some ideas on direct taxation from the Dutch. He imposed a tax upon inhabited houses, and adopted the succession duty; by reducing the taxes upon some necessaries and increasing those upon personal property, he made a very distinct movement from indirect to direct taxation, and shifted part of the burden of taxation from the poorer to the richer classes.

The outbreak of war, in 1793, defeated Pitt's cherished hopes of financial reform, put an end to the commercial treaty with France, and plunged the nations again into commercial hostilities; it also created a demand for fresh revenue to meet the increased expenditure. New taxes had to be levied, old ones reimposed; and it was in the succeeding period of heavy taxation, extending over more than twenty years, that the system of prohibition and restrictions thus adopted developed the modern protective principle of fostering home industries. Each year, from 1793 to 1798, the customs and excise duties were augmented; and in 1798 Pitt imposed an income-tax of 10 per cent upon incomes of £200 and upwards, with a graduated scale for incomes down to £60; this tax was maintained until the close of the war.

The effects of the war were disastrous to British commerce and manufactures, and they were accentuated by several years of bad crops (1793–95), ordinary industries received a check, and an impulse was given to military expenditure. Violent fluctuations in prices ensued, commercial credit collapsed, followed by a crisis which

produced depression and want of employment. The
scarcity of food is curiously illustrated by an agreement
made between members of both Houses of Parliament
in 1796 to reduce their household consumption of wheat
by one-third and to recommend the practice in their
several localities. At this time a bounty of 21s. per
quarter was being offered by the government on wheat
from the south of Europe and other distant parts.

France prohibited the importation of British produce,
Britain retaliated by checking the entrance of food and
merchandise into France. Not content with assailing
one another's shipping, they interfered with the trading
in neutral vessels, and came into collision with other
nations. British commerce suffered; yet with the United
States it doubled between 1793 and 1798, partly owing
to the export of cotton from the States, which commenced in 1794, and stimulated the Lancashire trade.
The Peace of Amiens (1802) gave a short suspension of
hostilities, but the war was resumed in 1803 with greater
vigour and determination, and more strenuous attempts
by both parties to ruin one another's commerce. Great
Britain sought to cut off the trade between France and
the colonies carried on under neutral flags, France
endeavoured to exclude British goods from the Continent.
The decrees of Napoleon (1806–7) and the British Orders
in Council pushed the warfare upon supplies and commerce to a degree hitherto unknown. Each country
sought to cripple the other in resources by the destruction of its commerce. Napoleon ordered British merchandise on the Continent to be seized and burned, and
employed his troops in its destruction. A clandestine
trade meanwhile was carried on by smuggling, and by
a system of evasions, at which both parties connived.
At home trade was in a miserable condition, employment was scarce, wages low, food expensive, and
suffering frequent. The war, though ineffectual in
wholly stopping trade, was successful in producing
great misery.

The vast expenditure of the war in the early period had
called forth the ingenuity of Pitt to provide resources.
From the position of a financial reformer he was driven

to that of a war minister. The outlay was met by two methods: (1) the extension of the system of public borrowing, which built up a huge national debt; and (2) by a large increase of taxation, both direct and indirect. Duties were placed upon almost every article of consumption, both of home production and foreign,—food, raw materials, and manufactured goods alike. At the close of the war (1815) the nation found itself with a debt of £860,000,000, and taxation (which was £17,000,000 before the war) amounting to £72,000,000,[1] for a population numbering less than 20 millions. Military expenditure had averaged £36,000,000 over the 23 years of war, and increased from £4,250,000 in 1791 to £60,250,000 in 1814. Between £50,000,000 and £60,000,000 was paid in subsidies to continental allies. Corn imported in years of scarcity during the war (1796, 1800, 1801, 1802, 1805, 1810) was estimated at more than £25,000,000.[2] Rent of land had risen nearly threefold during the war, and the prices of all consumable goods were high.

It was hoped that with peace would come prosperity, but the country was exhausted by the war, and its cessation even caused some temporary want of employment. There was great distress among both the manufacturing

---

[1] Table comparing Public Revenue for four periods in £s (omitting 0,000). (First 3 cols. from Newmarch, *Statistical Journal.*)

	Year 1815.	Year 1825.	Year 1852.	Year 1896.
	£	£	£	£
Customs, ...	10,53	16,55	20,56	20,76
Excise, ...	26,54	21,00	14,84	26,80
Assessed Taxes and Land and House Duty,	6,34	5,00	3,37	2,50
Income and Property Tax, ...	15,28	—	5,52	16,10
Stamps and Death Duties, ...	6,37	7,45	6,76	18,95
Post Office, ...	1,62	1,60	1,02	11,38
Telegraphs, ...	—	—	—	2,84
Miscellaneous, ...	52	46	1,14	2,64
Ireland (separate for 1815), ...	4,70	—	—	—
	71,90	52,06	53,21	101,97

[2] *The Present State of England*, Joseph Lowe, 1823.

and agricultural classes.   No measures were advanced
to mitigate the burden of taxation upon the poorer
classes, but the House of Commons insisted, in 1816,
upon the abolition of the income-tax (as being a war
tax), though the ministry, under Lord Liverpool, wished
to reduce it only one-half.   The same parliament, composed largely of land-owners, had already passed a bill
(1815) which had for its object to maintain the price of
corn and keep up rents, while it aimed also at keeping
the land under cultivation and providing a sufficient
supply of home-grown corn.   This law practically prohibited the importation of foreign corn.   The Baltic
Provinces and the United States were quite capable of
sending a plentiful supply, and were willing to take our
manufactures in exchange, but they were prohibited
from doing so.   The Navigation Acts also seriously
hampered trade; though some relaxation had been made
in 1796 in the case of the United States, and a further
relaxation was effected by the commercial treaty of
1815, yet no general modification was adopted until
1822.[1]

The period of distress which followed the war per-
plexed the populace, who could not understand its causes;
and it was succeeded by many similar periods during the
next thirty years.   Various causes contributed to the
depression; foremost amongst them, the enormous war
expenditure which had drained the country and produced
a system of taxation pressing upon almost every item
of household expenditure; the restraints upon commerce
checked the manufacturing industries, imposed high
duties on materials, and excluded the corn which would
at the same time have fed the people and stimulated
trade; a demoralizing system of poor-law administration prevailed which was amended only in 1834, and
there were several series of bad harvests and some
periods of speculation, followed by commercial crises in
1825 and 1839, which further disordered trade.   The
poorer classes suffered great hardships from want of
employment, low wages, and dear food.   Riots broke

---

[1] Stephen Dowell (*History of Taxation*, vol. ii. pp. 248–250) gives the
summary of taxation for the year 1815 as follows:—

out in 1816, and bread shops were plundered. In the
Eastern counties the military were required to repress
the disturbances. Incendiarism became frequent, and
corn stacks were often destroyed by famishing men.[1]
There was a revival in the Midlands of the attacks on

GREAT BRITAIN.

	£	£
DIRECT TAXES—		
Land Tax, ...	1,196,000	
House and Assessed Tax, ...	6,500,000	
Property and Income, ...	14,600,000	
Legacy and Succession, ...	1,297,000	
Insurance, Auctions, Licenses, Loco-		
motion and Shipping, ...	1,845,259	
		25,438,259
ON CONSUMPTION—		
Eatables.		
Salt, Sugar, Currants, &c., ...	5,115,663	
Drinks.		
Beer, Malt, Hops, ...	9,596,346	
Wine, Spirits, &c., ...	8,600,772	
Tea, Coffee, ...	3,868,050	
		27,180,831
Tobacco, ...		2,025,663
Raw Materials.		
Timber, Coal, Stone, Cotton, Silk, Hemp, &c.,		6,062,214
Manufactures.		
Leather, Soap, Bricks, Candles, Paper, &c., ...		4,080,721
Stamp Duties.		
Bills, Receipts, &c., ...		2,743,000
Total, Great Britain, ...		67,530,688

IRELAND.

Excise, Customs, Stamps, &c., ...	6,258,723
Total, United Kingdom, ...	73,789,411

[1] "In 1816, at Bideford the mob interfered to prevent the export of a cargo
of potatoes; at Bridport the mob paraded the streets, broke into the bakers'
shops, and proceeded to other acts of violence. Strong able-bodied men in
Essex were often only able to earn but 6d. a day, and wheat was at from £4
to £5 a quarter. Farm buildings, barns, stacks, machinery, business premises were set on fire, and all agricultural property seemed insecure and
liable to destruction by incendiaries. At Swanage six people out of every
seven were paupers, and the poor-rate amounted to 21s. in the £. . . . In
Stafford the manufacturing poor were reduced literally to starvation. Men
were compelled to eat the cabbage stalks in their cottage gardens . . . and
27,500 persons out of a population of 84,000 were in receipt of relief in
Birmingham."—(Spencer Walpole: *History*, vol. i. chap. v.)

machinery. In some places political demonstrations led
to disorder and pillaging of shops. The distress gave
rise in some parts to agitation for parliamentary reform.
The farming classes were not exempt from suffering,
and many farmers who had broken up land for corn
when rents were high, and the price of wheat 100s. a
quarter, found themselves threatened with ruin in the
periods of lower prices and depression which ensued
upon the advent of peace.

The first public movement against the system of
Protection was made in 1820, at a time when not only
corn but nearly every article of manufacture was protected. It came from the merchants of London, who
presented a memorial (drawn up by Thomas Tooke,
author of *The History of Prices*) to the House of Commons, complaining of the "impolicy and injustice of
the restriction system", asking for freedom of trade
except as regards revenue, and adopting definitely the
position and arguments of Adam Smith. The Edinburgh
Chamber of Commerce sent in an equally forcible petition, urging the same enlightened views on trade. Lord
Liverpool's reply was "that the difficulty of the reform
of taxation was in the vested interests which had grown
up and which would be imperilled if any attempt were
made at such a design". The House of Commons re-
ported favourably upon the proposals set forth in the
petitions. The years 1823–1825 were comparatively
prosperous. Huskisson, who was President of the Board
of Trade, then commenced a series of financial reforms
extending over four years, and reducing the tariff-
restrictions upon most foreign manufactures. He also
succeeded in modifying the Navigation Acts,[1] both as

---

[1] The Act of Navigation (1651), which originated in political and commercial jealousy of the Dutch, declared: (1) that no goods or commodities
whatever of the growth, produce, or manufacture of Asia, Africa, or
America should be imported into England or Ireland or any of the planta-
tions, except directly in ships belonging to English subjects, and of which
the master and greater number of the crew were Englishmen. (2) That no
goods of the growth, produce, or manufacture of any country in Europe
should be imported into Great Britain, except in British ships or in such
ships as were the real property of the people of the country or place in
which the goods were produced, or from which they could only be, or
mostly were, exported.

they affected the Colonies and foreign countries, and he paved the way for the ultimate abolition of those restraints on shipping by passing a measure "to place the shipping of any foreign state in the ports of the United Kingdom, on a footing of equality with our shipping, provided such states would afford reciprocal privileges in their ports to the shipping of the United Kingdom".

Huskisson endeavoured to modify the duties on the import of raw materials, and he succeeded in lowering many; he also aimed at a tariff on manufactured imports which should not exceed 30 per cent *ad valorem*.[1] The duty on wool was reduced from 6*d*. to 1*d*. per lb., and its export (hitherto prohibited) was permitted; the import duty on raw silk was reduced from 4*d*. to 1*d*. per lb., that on thrown silk from 14*s*. 8*d*. to 5*s*. per lb., and manufactured silk, previously prohibited, was admitted at a duty of 30 per cent.

The silk trade, carried on in Spitalfields, Coventry, and the eastern counties, had enjoyed a monopoly for sixty years, yet the weavers were in a miserable condition, and often engaged in riots, and French silks were smuggled very plentifully into the country. The industry was declining, there was no improvement in its methods: manufacturers complained that an export trade might be created by the help of a drawback equal to the duty on the imported materials. In proposing the reduction of the duty on silk, Huskisson thus states his opinions on the effects of Protection: "We are far behind other nations in this industry, it (Protection) has a chilling and benumbing effect, men are rendered indifferent to exertion by the indolent security of a prohibitory system".

[1] LEADING MODIFICATIONS OF IMPORT DUTIES BETWEEN 1823 AND 1825.

Silk	manufactures	prohibition,	altered to	30 and 25 per cent.
Cotton	,,	varying from 50 to 75 per cent,	,,	10 ,,
Linen	,,	varying from 50 to 180 per cent,	,,	25 ,,
Paper	,,	prohibition,	,,	same as excise.
Woollen	,,	50 per cent,	,,	15 per cent.
Leather,		75 per cent,	,,	30 ,,
Iron bar,		£6½ per ton,	,,	£1½ per ton.
Earthenware,		75 per cent,	,,	15 per cent.
Olive-oil,		£18, 15s. 7d. per ton,	,,	£4,4s. per ton.
Flax,		5d. per cwt.,	,,	1d. per cwt.
Glass bottles,		8s. per dozen,	,,	4s. per dozen.

Huskisson advanced the cause of free commerce, and removed an injustice to Ireland, by abolishing in 1823 the remaining duties upon her trade with Great Britain, a measure attempted by Pitt in 1785, but then defeated, and not completed at the time of the Union from deference to English interests. He also simplified the administration of the customs and the complicated statutes by which they were regulated.[1] His course of enlightened reform was unfortunately checked in 1827 by the death of Lord Liverpool, and the break-up of the ministry. It was, however, highly satisfactory in its results; consumption increased, trade and revenue improved, and the principle, already proved by Pitt's budget of 1784, was established, that a reduction of duties, by adding to prosperity and commerce, can become a means of yielding greater revenue.

These reforms had been very tentative and cautious, but were a distinct advance on the lines of free-trading. A beginning had been made. They did not, however, touch the stronger interests; the duties on corn and agricultural produce, which were almost prohibitive, remained,[2] while sugar and timber were also heavily burdened by highly differential or prohibitive duties.

When the Whigs again resumed office, in 1830, an attempt to continue the reforms in taxation was made by Lord Althorpe. His object was to give relief to the lower classes, and by removing duties which interfered with manufactures to find them employment. In the budget of 1831 he proposed considerable reductions on manufactured goods, but his scheme was not accepted, and he did not accomplish much. Public interest was now becoming absorbed in the question of political reform. The Reform Bill was passed at length in 1832, and many manufacturing towns, for the first time, received representation in Parliament, and the power of the middle classes was increased. For some years other problems engrossed Parliament. The Poor Law Reform

[1] When Huskisson commenced his reforms, about 1500 Acts of Parliament regulated the administration of the customs regarding entry, export, and custody of goods; he reduced these Acts to 11.
[2] The duty on butter was 21s. per cwt., on bacon 28s., on cheese 11s., lard 8s., on potatoes 2s. per cwt., salt 15s. per bushel.

(1834), Abolition of West Indian Slavery (1833), Municipal Reform (1835), and Tithe Commutation (1836) were among the useful measures passed; the monopoly of the East India Company was extinguished in 1833, and Post Office reforms were carried in 1839 which effected a saving on communication equivalent to a reduction of taxation.

Meanwhile, in 1830, an important contribution was made to the subject of taxation by Sir H. Parnell, who published an analysis of the revenue of 1829, and criticised the system of duties in a work on *Financial Reform*. He showed that taxes on materials were a loss to industry and to the employment of capital and labour, that export duties on machinery were an injury to industry and the export trade, and that excessive duties diminished revenue by checking imports and encouraging contraband trade; this irregular mode of importation had become so general as scarcely to be deemed a serious offence; half the foreign goods consumed were smuggled, and the illicit trading caused a large expenditure to the country on officers for prevention. So bold and open was this contraband trade that smugglers even issued circulars stating the rates they charged for goods by the "indirect channel". Peel read such a circular in the House of Commons (when advocating his reforms in 1842), in which lace, gloves, and other French goods were offered to a London firm at rates "considerably below your custom-house duties".

Sir H. Parnell recommended an income-tax on all property and incomes, and pointed to the results of Huskisson's reforms as demonstrating the gains from reduction of taxes on imports. His arguments, which, like Huskisson's, were derived from Adam Smith, had great weight with Sir Robert Peel, who came into office in 1841, and at once entered upon a course of financial reform. In each year from 1837 to 1842 the national balance-sheet had shown a deficit: in 1842 it amounted to two millions, a result for which bad harvests, the speculation and rash trading fostered by the new joint-stock system of banking which ended in the crisis of

1839, together with the defects of the revenue system, were jointly responsible.

A Parliamentary Committee in 1840, on Import Duties, emphasized the facts set forth by Sir H. Parnell. It exposed the absurdity and wastefulness of the existing customs system in no ambiguous manner. The tariff oppressed every class, but especially the wage-receivers, to whom an extension of commerce meant employment as well as cheap food. Taxes, levied at about 1150 different rates on all articles and on no common principle, realized £23,000,000; of this sum £20,000,000 was raised on 10 articles only, £1,000,000 on 8 other articles, while all the remainder produced less than £1,000,000, some yielding only a few shillings; many duties were entirely prohibitive and imposed a heavy burden on the consumer in high prices while they yielded nothing to revenue. The duties on food alone were estimated to inflict a loss equal in amount to the whole of the revenue derived from other articles; the system of custom-house administration was expensive and irritating.

In 1842 Peel brought in his budget for financial reform, and, in imitation of Pitt, he provided the means for the proposed remission of duties by an income-tax of 7d. in the £, to be levied on incomes of £150 and upwards for five years, during which period he anticipated that the revenue would overtake the deficiency. His principle was, to reduce the cost of living, to remove all prohibitive and reduce all protective duties; to reduce taxes on raw materials to a nominal amount or abolish them altogether; to lower the rates on partly-manufactured goods, which were really materials of manufacture, and to reduce those on manufactures to a moderate and nearly uniform rate of about 20 per cent. He carried his measure, abolishing and reducing duties on 750 articles; but he deliberately left wine and brandy " as instruments of negotiation with a view of effecting a reduction in the duties imposed by other countries on the produce of our country ". Peel had previously introduced his new sliding-scale[1] for corn, and did not on

[1] The sliding-scale system of duties was adopted in France in 1819, and was copied by other countries. It was a scheme by which the duty was

this occasion deal with the corn duties, the Navigation
Act monopolies, or the duties on sugar. As a cautious
reformer, he preferred to remove first the duties which
were obviously wasteful and vexatious, and to establish
the principle and prove its success before proceeding to
those cases in which vested interests would offer strong
opposition. So far, though very sweeping, his measures
were tentative, and calculated to show the advantage
of reduction, and to educate the people to a further
application of the principle.

Peel, however, moved too slowly for the Anti-Corn-
law League, and his long resistance to their urgent
appeals caused him to be generally treated as an opponent
of Free-trade until the final stage of that agitation was
reached. Yet Peel's finance, from 1841, was entirely in
sympathy with Free-trade principles, and his reforms
were steps towards a more complete adoption of that
policy. As a statesman he knew the difficulties of practical politics; though he moved slowly he was progressing surely towards the goal from which, as he explained
later, he knew there was no return.[1] In the domain of
practice many considerations arise, and it is what is
possible, not what the desire for strict application of
principle would dictate, that has to be adopted. Though
leader of the Conservative party, Peel was careful
at no time to pledge himself to the maintenance of a
protective policy. He clearly defined his own position
with regard to the Corn-laws in his speech in the debate
on Mr. Villiers's annual motion in 1839, when he said:
"Unless the existence of the Corn-law can be shown to
be consistent not only with the prosperity of agriculture
and the maintenance of the landlords' interest, but also
with the protection and maintenance of the general interests of the country, and especially with the improvement of the condition of the labouring class, the Corn-

regulated automatically to different circumstances. Peel started with a
duty of 20s. a quarter on wheat when the average price was 50s. a quarter.
As the price rose 1s. a quarter the duty fell 1s. a quarter (with a few exceptions) until at 73s. and upwards it remained at 1s. a quarter.

[1] "But who will re-establish the Corn-laws once abrogated, though from a
casual and temporary pressure."—Letter of Sir R. Peel to Lord Heytesbury.
(*Memoirs of Sir R. Peel*, vol. ii.'

law is practically at an end". And again in 1842: "I should not consider myself a friend to the agriculturist if I asked for a protective duty with a view of propping up rents, or for the purpose of defending his interest or the interest of any particular class". And in his *Memoirs* he writes: "During the discussion in Parliament on the Corn-law of 1842, I was more than once pressed to give a guarantee (so far as a minister could give it) that the amount of protection established by that law should be permanently adhered to; but although I did not then contemplate the necessity for further changes, I uniformly refused to fetter the discretion of the Government by any such assurances as those that were required from me".

Peel's part in the repeal of the Corn-laws is reserved for later discussion; here we continue the brief record of his financial reforms. In 1845 he could point to the success of the measures he had introduced, and he then succeeded in obtaining a continuation of the income-tax for three years in order that he might extend his system of reform. He was thus enabled to further simplify the customs, and to remove 450 duties entirely from the tariff, many of them on raw materials of industries, such as cotton, silk, hemp, flax, hides, &c. Duties on exports were finally abolished; import duties on manufactured articles of cotton, wool, linen, leather, and metals were reduced; the differential duties on sugar (which varied with the country of origin) were cut down. The latter measures encountered opposition from those who wished to retain some duties for the purpose of negotiating commercial treaties. The remaining alterations in the tariff, completing the Free-trade policy, and reducing the British tariff to one for revenue only, were carried out subsequently by Mr. Gladstone, who, as President of the Board of Trade, had shared very fully the labour involved in the details connected with Peel's remissions of duty.

Before entering upon the history of the agitation against the Corn-laws, it may be well to notice the general character of the previous interference by government with the import and export of corn. The great struggle for freedom of trade finally took place upon this interest, and the corn duty is commonly regarded as the central problem of Free-trading, both on account of the severity of that struggle, and because of the extreme importance to this country that attaches to an adequate supply of imported food; but the principle of free importation has almost equal significance for all imported articles which form the materials of British industry. It was mainly to the freeing of these, and to the simplification of our customs system, that Sir Robert Peel devoted his efforts for some years before the climax of the Corn-law repeal was reached; the enormous strides that he made in this direction entitle him to the credit of having accomplished the second considerable stage in the Free-trade movement of this century.

The corn-trade was subjected to legislative interference for many centuries. Regulation may be said to have taken *three* distinct forms: the *first* was prohibition of export, dating from 1360, while free importation was allowed; up to 1793 regulation was mainly directed to export, although importation also came under control. Following the French war, stringent Corn-laws were imposed in 1815, which checked free importation to encourage the growth of home supplies. Neither policy succeeded, for in both cases there were great irregularities in supply, and great and sudden variations in price. Finally, in 1846, the policy of interference was reversed, and freedom of trading was substituted, with no regulation of either importing or exporting beyond a registration duty of 1s. a quarter on wheat, which was removed in 1869.

Legislation during these six centuries was frequent and variable, a fact which demonstrated that each fresh attempt at regulation was a failure, as it had to be superseded by another. The Act of 1360 was relaxed in 1394 to permit exportation to friendly states. In 1436 a limit was placed upon this privilege; in 1463 importation was prohibited until wheat reached 6s. 8d. a quarter. In 1534 exportation of grain was forbidden, except for victualling the English possessions of Calais and Guienne, on the ground that scarcity and high prices ensued at

home. This policy also failed to encourage corn-growing in England, for under Edward VI. it was enacted
that as much land should be tilled in every parish as had
been under the plough since the accession of Henry
VIII., and a penalty was imposed for any failure.

In 1554 exportation was again allowed up to the
6s. 8d. limit, the law against it having proved futile;
after eight years the limit of price was raised to 10s.;
under Elizabeth and the Stuarts various modifications
were made; in 1670 exportation was checked at 53s. 4d.
per quarter, and importation was forbidden until that
price was reached, which was practically prohibitive.
The idea of the necessity for a steady high price in the
interests of agriculture had gained ground, and this idea
prevailed until the abolition of the Corn-laws. In 1689
the landlords secured a bounty of 5s. per quarter on the
export of wheat when it did not exceed 48s., and proportionate bounties on barley and other grain.

From 1697 to 1765 the average export of corn was
500,000 quarters, a large part of which went to Holland.
During this period the imports of grain were small. By
the Act of 1773 the bounty on exported wheat was
altered to begin only when the price fell to 44s. per
quarter, and importation was legal with a duty of only
6d. a quarter when the price of wheat was not less
than 48s.

This was the most liberal scale during the whole history of the corn restriction, and it was obtained largely
by the advocacy of Burke, who pointed out that the
landed interest was not distinct from the trading interest,
and that "he who separates the interest of the consumer
from the interest of the grower starves the country".

The limit of import was raised to 54s. in 1791 on the
plea that the nation might otherwise become dependent
upon foreign countries for food. In 1804 a further change
was made in favour of high prices; the lower limit of
importation, with a duty of 24s. 3d., was raised to 63s.
per quarter; between 63s. and 66s. the duty was 2s. 6d.,
and above 66s. it was 6d. per quarter.

For nearly a century prior to 1773 the exportation
of corn had been stimulated by the aid of bounties;

between 1773 and 1793 little corn was either exported or imported; from 1793 exporting ceased, and succeeding legislation was directed to checking or regulating importation. Towards the end of the century circumstances were altering; new industries had followed on a period of invention; a town population was growing up, and the cotton, iron, and coal trades were developing: Great Britain was becoming a manufacturing country and an exporter of cotton goods. During the first twenty years of the nineteenth century wheat averaged 98s. a quarter. Violent fluctuations in prices occurred during the whole of the war with France. An exceptional number of bad seasons made scarcity at intervals, the war created difficulties in obtaining foreign supplies, taxation was extremely heavy, trade was dislocated and uncertain, the poor-law added to the misery by its mistaken methods, irregularity in employment and violent changes in price created much distress among all classes dependent upon industry. The rise in prices was further increased by the scarcity of labour, as men were withdrawn from agriculture for military service; and during the last five years of the war prices were further raised by the depreciation of the paper currency. The enormous expense of the war and the payment of subsidies (some £60,000,000) to Continental allies created a scarcity of money, which led to the suspension of cash payments by the Bank of England in 1797, and, after a time, to the over-issue and depreciation of the bank-note. This inflation of the paper currency raised gold to a premium of 20 per cent in 1810, and it increased to 29 per cent by 1813. The influence of the inflation upon prices was considerable, though it seems not to have been understood at the time; every variation increased fluctuation; the disturbance was most injurious to commerce, and a source of loss to ordinary consumers.

Owing to the high price of corn which prevailed during the wars, the operation of the Corn-law was slight. Commerce was impeded by the wars, but the deficient harvest of 1809, which raised the price of wheat to £5 and £6 per quarter, led to an importation in 1810 of £7,000,000 worth. During the succeeding

years, when the edicts of Napoleon and the Orders in
Council were in force, importation was checked, and the
price of wheat in 1812 and 1813 averaged £6 per
quarter.

In 1814, with the prospect of peace, the price of corn
fell considerably, and an attempt was made to raise the
duties on importation; the agitation and resistance
aroused in the country prevented the measure from
passing the House of Commons.   But in the following
year, notwithstanding many petitions and much opposition, an Act was passed by which corn was excluded
until the average price was 80s. per quarter for wheat,
40s. for barley, and 26s. for oats.   To the British colonies
(which, however, sent little corn) the limits of price were
67s., 32s., and 22s.   The measure, thus hurried through
Parliament, led to disturbances, and riots took place in
London.

It is interesting to note that a protest against the
Corn-law of 1815 was drawn up in the House of Lords
by Lord Grenville, and signed by ten Peers, on the
ground that it was a restraint on commerce and an
artificial and injurious restriction, adverse to the prosperity of the nation, and more peculiarly so in the case
of that commodity on which depends the existence of a
large portion of the community; that the expectations
from it were delusive, as it would not contribute to produce plenty, cheapness, or steadiness of price; that, in
any case, it would entail a great present evil, giving a
bounty to the grower of corn by a tax levied upon the
consumer; and that Parliament was wholly uninformed
of the causes of public distress.

The seasons of 1816 and 1817 were unfavourable and
the crops deficient; wheat rose to an average of 96s. 11d.
in 1817, and even reached 112s. 8d.   Importation took
place at these times, but great privation had arisen
before the imports were in any degree proportionate to
the demand.[1]   Under a system which was prohibitive in
ordinary years, there could be no regular foreign supply
or organized trade in corn, and it was only after the

---

[1] Corn was imported in 1817, 1818, 1819, at a cost of £2,000,000 (Lowe,
State of England).

scarcity-price had been reached and suffering had become very severe that supplies came in adequately. The imports became most abundant when the period of dearth was coming to an end, so that they coincided with the increased home-supplies of the good years, and forced down prices. The periods of scarcity starved the labourers with high prices, and years of plenty ruined the farmers with low prices.

The fears expressed in the protest of the Peers were amply fulfilled. Rents, which had been lowered after the fall in prices in 1814, again rose, and prices fluctuated; in good years the crops realized less than half that which they produced in bad years. Steady high prices had been expected as the result of legislation, but they were never attained. It might have been foreseen that by restricting the supply to the limited area of the country, prices must fluctuate with every variation in the seasons. From 1820 to 1822 there were no less than 475 petitions to the House of Commons complaining of the distress and of the exhaustion of agricultural capital, of high rents and rates, and of the poverty of the farmers, whose rents had been based on the assumption of the higher prices to be secured under the Corn-laws.

Before a Committee of Inquiry of the Lords and Commons (1821–1822) abundant evidence was produced to show that the act had not realized what its promoters had declared, high rents alone excepted, as these had been based upon anticipated high prices. It was stated that the tenants were paying charges and outgoings from capital and not from profits; and that prices were ruinously low in spite of Protection, which at that time amounted to monopoly, since, with one exception for oats, the ports had been closed against all foreign imports for nearly thirty months. Even some land-owners complained that the act was detrimental, because it led to diminished consumption of food. Statistics were produced from some of the large towns—Birmingham, Leeds, Sheffield,—which showed a greatly decreased consumption of meat; while prices fell, the demand diminished still more, for the paralysis of trade caused by the system of Protection had reduced the employment of those who lived by manufactures for export, and their consumption of food was necessarily cut down in the same degree. Multitudes were thrown upon the poor-rates, which, being augmented in towns, spread the burden more widely. Between 1814 and 1820 poor-rates doubled in many parishes. The vicious poor-law system, which gave relief in kind or money in proportion to the price of bread, aggravated the evil. The Report of the Select Committee of 1821 left no doubt as to the fact of the distress which had overtaken the farmers, and had involved the shopkeeping and other classes. They suggested no remedies, but their faith in Protection was shaken, and they expressed " a doubt whether the only solid foundation of the flourishing state of agriculture is not laid in abstaining as much as possible from interference either by Protection or Prohibition with the application of capital in any branch of industry ".

As a result of the inquiry a small modification of the Corn-law was made in 1823 by Lord Liverpool, and the limit of exclusion was reduced from 80s. to 70s. for the importation of wheat, with similar reductions for other kinds of grain. As prices did not again rise to this level during the six years the law was in force, the Act was a dead letter, it gave no relief. Fluctuations continued as before. In 1829 further legislation took place; the government of the Duke of Wellington, of which Peel and Huskisson were members, introduced a new sliding scale based on 64s. as the standard. At 64s. a quarter, a duty of 23s. 8d. was imposed, and the scale was graduated so that at 73s. the duty was only 1s. per quarter. This was the scale in operation when the agitation for repeal was commenced.

No good results accrued from these manipulations of the tariff. Prices fluctuated as before with the seasons, averaging 61s. 8d. for the five years 1829–1833. The distress among farmers increased to such a degree that a further parliamentary committee was appointed in 1833 to inquire into the state of agriculture. The evidence was most conclusive as to the reality of the farmers' complaints and their inability to meet outgoings from current prices. " Rates had increased, especially poor-

rates, rents had not fallen with prices, and the savings
of many were gone, their credit failing, and their resources generally exhausted." Numbers of farmers had
been ruined, and their capital was so reduced that the
system of farming had retrograded, and land was going
out of cultivation. Labourers were in like distress, and
had resorted to rioting and incendiarism.

The following copy of a petition to the House of
Commons from agriculturists in Somerset (one of many
sent in) describes the condition of that class under the
operation of a law designed to foster agriculture:

"We, the gentry, magistrates, clergy, freeholders, and
occupiers of land in the district of the once opulent Vale
of Taunton most humbly represent to your honourable
House that the cruel distress throughout the district in
which we reside has arrived at an unparalleled height
and is daily increasing to an alarming extent with a
progressive decline in the value of all productions of the
earth, accompanied by an overwhelming burden of taxation such as was never endured by any country, and has
swallowed up the capital of the farmer, and brought the
greater proportion of independent yeomen to the brink
of ruin which without the most speedy relief must ter-
minate in the annihilation of this most excellent and
invaluable body of men".

The chief foreign supplies of corn at this time came
from Russia and Poland, and a small quantity from the
North American colonies. The highest amount of wheat
imported in any year was 1,701,885 quarters (in 1830)
when the price was 64s. 3d., in some years none at all
was admitted; the average from the beginning of the
century to the formation of the League in 1838 was
about 500,000 quarters.

Events demonstrated that tariff legislation could not
determine prices, and that contracts based on any
assumption of a regulation rate were delusive. The
depression in agriculture affected other industries; first
traders, then producers suffered, until the distress became general. The Committee of 1833, after an elaborate examination, conclude their report with the opinion
"that hopes of amelioration in the condition of the

landed interest rest rather on the cautious forbearance than on the active interposition of Parliament". Nothing was done by Parliament upon this report, and three years later (1836) the continued distress led to a further parliamentary inquiry. The evidence is of the same nature —"prices were such that farmers could not recover expenses and rent", they declared the Corn-laws a delusion, since they were expected to keep up prices and had not done it. Further help of some kind they wanted from the state, something which would keep prices up to such a level as to give them an assured profit. Here and there in the evidence we find the opinion that freedom and the prosperity of other trades would create a demand for farming produce, and that in this direction, with reduced rents, would prosperity for farming alone be guaranteed. The Committee of 1836 did not agree upon any report.

A bad harvest in 1836 raised the price of corn; this was followed by a commercial disaster which led to serious failures among the trading firms in the north of England, and produced great distress among the labouring classes, who suffered simultaneously from loss of employment and a rise in the price of food. An attempt was made to obtain some alleviation by a bill to substitute a fixed duty of 10s. per quarter on wheat for the sliding-scale. It was supported by 89 members, including 10 members of the Government, but was defeated by a majority of 134.

The death of William IV. and the accession of Queen Victoria introduced a new era. Lord Melbourne returned to office, and during the year 1838 was mainly engaged with the Canadian rebellion, the settlement of which took place in 1840.

The further history of the movement for the repeal of the Corn-laws is identified with the doings of the Anti-Corn-law Association and League.

Chapter IV.

The Agitation for the Repeal of the Corn-laws (1838–1846).

It was the Reform Act of 1832 which rendered the repeal of the Corn-laws possible. From 1815 to 1832 at every great public meeting for reform the Corn-laws were denounced, and thus the agitation for reform came to be regarded as a step towards cheap bread. At the memorable meeting in Manchester in 1819, which led to the Peterloo Massacre, the banners proclaimed both "No Corn-laws" and "Universal Suffrage".[1] Thus in the minds of the common people the two demands became more or less identified.

A resolution against the Corn-laws was moved in the House of Commons in the year 1826 by Mr. Joseph Hume, a financial reformer and a member of the new school of philosophical radicalism, but the resolution had no success. In 1833 it was suggested by Mr. Archibald Prentice, editor and proprietor of *The Manchester Times*, and afterwards the historian of the Anti-Corn-law agitation, that the press should educate public opinion on the subject of the Corn-laws. The matter was taken up in the Manchester and Glasgow papers, but the good harvests of 1834 and 1835, and the prosperity following thereon, diminished public interest and postponed the movement.

In 1834 Mr. Joseph Hume proposed in Parliament that a fixed duty on corn be substituted for the fluctuating scale then in operation. He was opposed strongly by the landlords, and Sir James Graham contended that "such a law would ruin not only landlords but the state itself"; thus the proposal lapsed. A good harvest in 1835 reduced wheat to 35s. per quarter. Farmers were despondent, and complained that they would be ruined by the plentiful crop, since they could not pay

---

[1] For detailed account see *Rise of Democracy*, by J. H. Rose, M.A., in this series.

their rents.   Labourers, however, profited by the abundant and cheap food, and attempts to prove to them that
scarcity and high prices were a blessing failed, being
met by replies such as that of the old woman who said,
"You'll not persuade me that when there's plenty o'
meal puir folk will get less than when it is scarce".

With the years 1836 and 1837 there began a decline
in prosperity: financial trouble followed on speculation;
trade was checked, employment reduced, and distress
among labourers was wide-spread.   The commercial
crisis was accompanied with a rise in prices.   A proposal was made in Parliament by Mr. Clay to modify
the Corn-laws and to substitute a fixed duty of 10s. per
quarter, but it was defeated.   Early in 1837 an Anti-
Corn-law Association was started in London, which
consisted of seventy-four members.   London, however,
was not the best centre for such an organization at that
time, but it anticipated the later movement in the north.
In February, 1838, Mr. Cobden, whose career will
shortly be noticed, attempted to induce the Manchester
Chamber of Commerce to take up the subject of repeal.
The Chamber had already sent in a protest against the
law, but no further step was taken at this time.

In March (1838) Mr. C. P. Villiers brought forward
in the House of Commons a motion to inquire into the
operation of the Corn-laws, which he repeated annually
until the repeal.   He scarcely gained a hearing.[1]   The
House of Commons was not yet prepared to listen; it
was necessary to bring the pressure of public opinion to
bear upon the Goverment.   When, in the following
July, Earl Fitzwilliam presented a petition from Glasgow
for repeal of the Corn-laws, the prime minister, Lord
Melbourne, replied "that the Government would not
move until they were assured a majority of the people
were in favour of a change", an admission that the
House of Commons would not lead, but would follow
public opinion.   This doctrine, now so fully admitted,

---

[1] Mr. Charles P. Villiers, the last survivor of the repealers, who died on
the 16th January, 1898, at the age of 96, was one of the earliest and
staunchest advocates of the movement.   In Parliament (where Mr. Villiers
represented Wolverhampton for more than sixty-three years) he annually

works well with an educated electorate, but in the circumstances of 1838 it amounted simply to shelving the question.

The agitation for repeal dates from July, 1838, when a lecture on the Corn-laws was given at Bolton by a Dr. Birnie, at which a young medical student, Mr. W. Paulton, who afterwards became a great force in the crusade, made a most effective speech. The following September, Dr. Bowring, who had been abroad endeavouring to promote free commercial intercourse with European states, and was an enthusiastic advocate of Free-trade, lectured in Manchester to a select assembly of some sixty reformers. He advanced many forcible arguments in favour of complete freedom of exchange. Among them he stated that: (1) "In France there are millions willing to clothe themselves in English garments, and you have millions of hungry mouths to take their corn". (2) "In Hungary, not being able to sell their corn to England, the people are turning their capital to manufacturing their own cloth." (3) Holland was dependent upon every country; there were no Corn-laws and no scarcity of food, but high wages and abundant trade. (4) Universal trade was the means of preventing war, for, "who quarrels with his benefactor—with those who confer benefits and blessings?" (5) The victories of commerce and of peace were far more glorious than any gathered in the fields of blood.

From this meeting the Anti-Corn-law League derived

introduced a motion for a Committee to consider and repeal the Corn-laws. The following is a summary of the voting in the House of Commons on Mr. Villiers's motion, and on several other important motions:—

		For.	Against.	Majority.
1838.	Mr. Villiers's motion, ...	97	—	—
1839.	That witnesses should be heard at the bar,	172	361	189
1839.	Mr. Villiers's annual motion, ...	195	342	147
1840.	,, ,, ...	177	300	123
1841.	Sir R. Peel's vote of want of confidence in the government, ...	312	311	1
1842.	Mr. Villiers's motion, ...	90	393	303
1843.	,, ,, ...	125	381	256
1844.	Mr. Cobden's motion for inquiry into agriculture, ...	153	244	91
1844.	Mr. Villiers's motion, ...	124	330	206
1845.	,, ,, ...	122	254	132
1846.	Sir R. Peel's motion for repeal, ...	327	229	98

its origin.[1]   Other earnest addresses were made by
Colonel P. Thompson, author of the *Corn-law Catechism*,
and by Mr. Prentice.   The latter drew attention to the
hard circumstances of the hand-loom weavers, who,
though scarcely able to afford to buy paper, had sent up
a petition with 22,000 signatures in favour of repeal.
As a first step, measures were taken to found an Anti-
Corn-law Association.   Seven enthusiasts for reform
met on the 24th September, 1838, and decided to form
the association upon a popular basis with a five-shilling
subscription.   On October 13th a provisional committee
of thirty-eight members [2] was advertised, including the
names of many who were afterwards prominent speakers
in the agitation, and amongst them that of John Bright.
Richard Cobden's name was added a week later.   The
committee engaged Mr. Paulton of Bolton as lecturer.
The movement was now fairly started, and in December
a request was made to the president of the Manchester
Chamber of Commerce to call a meeting for the purpose
of petitioning Parliament.[3]   Ultimately the chamber
adopted a petition, as drafted by Mr. Cobden, demand-
ing "the repeal of all laws relating to the importation
of foreign corn and other foreign articles of subsistence,
and the removal of all existing obstacles to the un-
restricted employment of industry and capital".

The struggle thus commenced, both as regards the
characters of the agitators, the methods they pursued,

[1] " Manchester would become identified to all ages with the cause; just as
Jerusalem was with the origin of our faith, and just as Mecca was in the
eyes of the Mahometans, so would Manchester be identified in the eyes of
historians as the birthplace and the centre of the greatest moral movement
since the invention of printing; one which would have a greater effect in
the world's history than any struggle that had ever taken place in the annals
of civilization."—(Cobden's speech at Manchester, 23rd December, 1845.)

[2] The following members of the original Manchester Anti-Corn-law
Association were on the Executive Committee when it dissolved in July,
1846: Richard Cobden, Archibald Prentice, George Wilson, W. Rawson,
W. R. Callendar, W. Evans.

[3] Mr. Henry Ashworth, one of the most active members of the League
from its foundation, relates in his *Recollections of Cobden and the League*
how this idea had originated with Cobden a year previously.   "Going
home together one night after a meeting of the British Association, which
they attended at Liverpool, Cobden suddenly stopped and said, 'I'll tell
you what we will do; we'll use the Chamber of Commerce for an agitation
to repeal the Corn-laws' "

and the ultimate issue, was one of the most remarkable in English history, and one which called for unusual energy and determination. It was a deliberate effort to overthrow a system, supposed by its supporters to be not only the bulwark of the agricultural industry, but also necessary to the revenue of the nation, and this system was supported by the richest and most influential classes in the country, who were also directly interested in its maintenance.

From the beginning, Richard Cobden was one of the most active members of the association, and he was soon recognized as the real leader of the movement, which came to engross the best of his life and energies. In order the better to understand and appreciate the motives and actions of Cobden, it may be desirable to give some account of his early life. He was born in 1804 near Midhurst, in Sussex, where his father was a small struggling farmer. He was one of eleven children, and obtained little education at home. His father failed, and he was sent, at the cost of a relative, to a school in Yorkshire for five years, where he received scant instruction and less sympathy. He then entered the office of an uncle in London, who treated him with strictness, but at twenty-one made him his commercial traveller in cotton goods. During this period of hard work and close attention to business the passion for knowledge had developed in Cobden. He educated himself in his leisure hours by assiduous study of the French language, English history and literature; to these at a later time he added mathematics and political economy. His occupation gave him opportunities for gaining knowledge of men and of public affairs, of which he was an acute observer. After a few years' experience as commercial traveller, he started business with two other young men as commission agents in cotton goods. They afterwards became cotton printers, and Cobden travelled now on his own account. Being successful in business, he was enabled to gratify his passion for the acquisition of the knowledge of other countries and peoples by travel. He visited successively France, Switzerland, America, Eastern Europe, Egypt, and Asia Minor. He thus gained larger views of life, and also experience of men, both invaluable for the public duties to which his natural cravings were soon to direct his energies. At the age of thirty-one he published a pamphlet on England, Ireland, and America, and later, one on Russia. These publications displayed a very wide and accurate knowledge of history, commerce, economics, and politics, and his writings, even at this early period, were stamped by an exceptional command of a clear and forcible style. Regarding this, we cannot do better than adopt the words of his biographer, Mr. J. Morley, who speaks of him as possessing "a ringing clearness, a genial vivacity, a free and confident mastery of expression which can hardly be surpassed, . . . what is striking in Cobden is, that after a lost and wasted childhood, a youth of drudgery in a warehouse, and an early manhood passed amid the rather vulgar associations of the commercial traveller, he should, at the age of thirty-one, have stepped forth the master of a style which in boldness, freedom, correctness, and persuasive moderation was not surpassed by any man then living." Of his knowledge of public affairs, Prof. Thorold Rogers writes: "If exact and careful knowledge of history constitutes learning, Cobden was, during the years of his political career, the most learned speaker in the House of Commons; . . . his facts, culled from all sources, were judiciously selected, and were never challenged".

Cobden had in a very high degree the faculty of assimilating knowledge and of giving it practical application; his remarks were always peculiarly apposite; and he displayed remarkable persuasiveness, tact, and self-control, equally in his controversies and in his intercourse with men of all classes.

Sprung from the agricultural class,[1] and educated in business, Cobden's training and sympathies gave him a predilection for commercial and industrial questions.

[1] In his speech in Parliament on the distress of the country, February 1843, Cobden says: "I am the son of a Sussex farmer. My ancestors were all yeomen of the class who have been suffering under this system; my family suffered under it, and I have therefore as good or better right than any of you to stand up as the farmer's friend, and to represent his wrongs in this House."

His mind was eminently practical, regulated by reason
and conviction, and little by sentiment; he grasped with
remarkable clearness and breadth the issues involved in
international commerce; he had no sympathy with war
and struggles for empire; he might be said almost to
have been possessed with the "fixed idea" of an industrial era of peace, such as he believed free commerce
would inaugurate.   His patriotism took the form of
seeking to promote the welfare of the nation by measures
which would increase the efficiency of labour and improve
the general standard of living.   He conceived that a
period of universal peace might be advanced by means
of free international intercourse, and that the mutual
interests of nations in trade would ultimately cause wars
to cease.   He has been called "the international man",
a term which fairly describes the cosmopolitan attitude
he adopted.   Cobden's ideal—a reign of universal peace
based upon industry and friendly commercial relations,
mutually beneficial to nations—was certainly not ignoble,
though it was sneeringly described by the wit of a
brilliant woman of fashion as a "bagman's millennium".
But Cobden greatly over-estimated the effects of commerce upon international relations, and underrated the
jealousies and passions of nations, the ambitions and
other disturbing factors which opposed the attainment
of universal concord; his instincts, however, were right,
his aim was worthy, and his method economically sound.
His views on general politics were mainly determined by
his dominant idea, and naturally included Free-trade.
In his own words: "To prohibit the import of corn,
such as is actually the case at this moment, is to strangle
infant commerce in its cradle".

Cobden fully realized the advantages of free exchange,
and he devoted himself to work for its attainment; his
life and speeches for some years, together with those of
his warm friend and colleague, John Bright, form a
history of the Free-trade movement.   A lucid and close
thinker, no one was better able than Cobden to expound
and illustrate economic principles, or to expose the
fallacies which clung around the Protectionist doctrine.
This he did with vigour and straightforwardness, and

in simple and forcible language, devoid of rhetoric, and
with no attempt at anything but securing conviction by
force of argument.   Some years after his death, his
friend, Bright, described the qualities of his style of
speaking as, "clearness, logic, a conversational eloquence, a persuasiveness, which, when conjoined with
the absolute truth that there was in his eye and in his
countenance, it was almost impossible to resist".
Cobden's method was based upon appeal to reason and
argument; he had enthusiasm and persistence in a high
degree, and often displayed much feeling, but he relied
upon the understanding of his hearers for their conversion to the cause he championed.[1]   To his labours the
success of the Anti-Corn-law agitation was mainly due.

It has been charged against the movement that the
manufacturers were fighting and providing funds for the
League in their own interests.   This was true in a
certain sense, for their trade was languishing; but they
also pleaded the cause of their workmen, who were
starving owing to want of employment, because foreign
markets were practically closed by the tax on the commodity with which foreigners were willing to buy their
goods.   Further, it was a cause in which all purchasers
of food were interested, for the benefits accruing from
activity in trade and an abundant supply of food cannot

---

[1] The following extract will serve as an example of his homely and vigorous
style:—" We have been told by the right hon. gentleman that his object is
to fix a certain price for corn; and hearing that proposition from a prime
minister, and listening to the debates, I have been almost led to believe that
we are gone back to the times of the Edwards, when Parliament was engaged
in fixing the price of a table-cloth, or a napkin, or a pair of shoes.   But is
this House a corn-market?   Is not your present occupation better fitted for
the merchant and the exchange?   We do not act in this way with respect to
cotton, or iron, or copper, or tin.   But how are we to fix the price of corn?
. . . I will ask the right hon. Baronet, Is he prepared to carry out this
principle in respect to cotton or wool?   I pause for a reply."   (Sir R. Peel:
"I have said that it was impossible to fix the price of food by any legislative
enactment".)   "Then upon what are we now legislating?   I thank the
right hon. Baronet for that avowal.   Will he oblige me still further by not
trying to do it?   But supposing he will try, all I ask of him is—and again
I shall pause for a reply—will he try to legislate to keep up the price of
cottons, woollens, silks, and such like goods?   There is no reply.   Then we
have come to this, that we are not legislating for the universal people.   Here
is the simple, open avowal, that we are met here to legislate for a class
against the people."—(Speeeh on Mr. Villiers's Motion, Feb. 1842.)

be restricted to any one class or industry; they concern the nation as a whole. In a speech afterwards made in Manchester,[1] Cobden admitted fully this class-interest in the movement. He said, "I am afraid that most of us entered upon the struggle with the belief that we had some distinct class-interest in the question". As Mr. Morley remarks, however, "The class-interest widened into a consciousness of a commanding national interest. The class-interest of the manufacturers and merchants happened to fall in with the good of the rest of the community."

At a meeting of land-owners in London, a defence of the Corn-laws was drawn up; the following were some of the chief propositions advanced: That a heavy national debt required the tax; that one concession would only lead to another; that the farm labourers profited by wheat being at 80s. to 100s. a quarter, since high prices gave them high wages; and that the agitation was got up by speculators and incendiaries.

In February 1839, the Association sent up delegates to London to offer evidence and present a petition at the bar of the House of Commons. Mr. Villiers moved that the witnesses should be heard, but his motion was rejected. In March Mr. Villiers repeated his annual motion in the House, but with no success. A like resolution, introduced into the House of Lords by Lord Fitzwilliam, was rejected by 224 votes to 24; Lord Melbourne, on that occasion, remarking that to abolish protection of agriculture "was the wildest and maddest scheme that had ever entered into the imagination of man to conceive".

The Association was, in March, 1839, formed into a permanent union to be called the National "Anti-Corn-law League", its objects being to continue the agitation by every constitutional means until the end was secured, to diffuse information through the press, by circulars, pamphlets, and lectures, to raise funds, and generally instruct and organize the country in regard to the Corn-laws.[2] The ensuing agitation, which extended

---

[1] Oct. 19th, 1843.

[2] As Cobden expressed it, "The House had refused to be instructed, but

over seven years, and which ended in the reversal of protective legislation, is perhaps the most remarkable example of a persistent, strenuous, and successful movement
carried out solely by arguments and appeals to facts;
and it should be noted that it was due to, and organized
by, men of business almost entirely, and was quite independent of political parties.   In their pamphlets the
League tried to overthrow the common opinion that the
farmers gained by the duty: they endeavoured to set
forth the solidarity and mutual dependence of society,
and to prove that the real demand for agricultural produce must depend upon the existence of a flourishing
body of labourers of all classes, and that the interests
of the manufacturing and agricultural workers were in-
separable.

The League encountered much opposition in its propa-
ganda.   At some places the lecturers were interrupted,
abused, and threatened, and disorderly persons broke
up the meetings.   The Chartists, who looked to drastic
political reforms as the only means for gaining improved
social conditions, also joined in resisting the Free-traders,
and even defended the Protectionist doctrine.   At a
meeting in Leeds the speakers of the League were vehe-
mently attacked by Feargus O'Connor, who posed as a
leader of the more violent section of the Chartists.   He
had an intolerant contempt for an agitation organized
merely to secure cheap food, which he said " would only
enable manufacturers to lower wages ".   However, the
Anti-Corn-law movement appealed more forcibly to the
hungry people of Leeds than Chartism, and Leeds became a centre of the Association.[1]   That section of the
press which supported the Corn-laws, also indulged in
strong language against the League, and denounced its
members as " unprincipled schemers ", " swindlers ",
" revolutionary emissaries ", " a disloyal faction ", &c.

A paper called *The Anti-Corn-law Circular* was next
started to spread the teachings of the League, and soon

the House must be instructed, and the most unexceptionable and effectual
way will be by instructing the nation ".
[1] For details of Chartist Movement see *Rise of Democracy*, by J. H. Rose,
M.A., in this series.

attained a wide circulation. Finding no hall in Manchester sufficiently large for the meetings, Mr. Cobden
generously gave an open space of land in St. Peter's
Field as a site for a building in which meetings could
be held. A temporary pavilion was erected, which was
subsequently replaced by the Free-trade Hall, opened in
1843. It is an interesting fact that the spot made
notorious in connection with political reform by the
Peterloo massacre of 1819, should thus have been devoted to a reform movement which aimed at obtaining
cheap bread for the people.

Soon after the opening of Parliament in 1840, the
delegates of the League waited in deputation upon Lord
Melbourne; they described the misery of the starving
workmen engaged in the northern industries, explained
the causes of their sufferings, and urged the advantages
of free commerce, but in vain. The prime minister
replied that "repeal was impracticable". His frequently-
repeated objections, which still remain the standing
defences of Protection, though their weakness has been
often exposed, were, that the general opinion of the
world was against Free-trade; that if our ports were
free other nations would not relax their protective duties;
and that to negotiate for reciprocal advantages was the
proper course. Before leaving London the deputation
interviewed the leaders of the Conservative party, but
met with no encouragement from them. The motion of
Mr. Villiers in the House of Commons was opposed
by the ministers. Nothing discouraged, the delegates
promptly met and passed a resolution pledging themselves not to relax their efforts until the grievance was
removed, and, setting aside all political aims, to work
solely for this end until it was achieved.

In May, 1840, Mr. Joseph Hume obtained a Select
Committee to inquire "into the several duties levied
upon imports, and how far those duties were for revenue
only or for protection". This inquiry was most pertinent
to the agitation, as it brought out very clearly the distinction between *taxation for revenue*, and *taxation for
protection* only, thus removing a source of confusion,
and rendering it plain to all reflective men that the

latter species of taxation was a mere burden and a
means of diverting capital and labour to unprofitable
channels.   The report of this Committee was instrumental in modifying the budgets of 1841 and of succeeding years.

During this year the League adopted another plan for
spreading their principles.   The members of the council
themselves went forth as volunteer lecturers.   Their
earnestness, fulness of knowledge, and influence, succeeded in drawing vast crowds, who were favourably
impressed by their arguments.   Party politics were
entirely put aside by members of the League, who devoted
themselves exclusively to the removal of the tax on
bread.   This was made the election test by repealers.
Neither political party gave them any countenance; the
Tories were firm in their support of Protection and the
sliding-scale; the Whigs, who were in office at the time,
professed to advocate a "moderate fixed duty", but no
measure was introduced.

The report of the Import Duties Committee bore fruit.
Lord John Russell, who was unconsciously moving
towards the Free-trade position, proposed in his budget
for 1841 to replace the sliding-scale by a fixed duty of
10 per cent; that is, of 8s. per quarter on wheat, 4s. 6d.
per quarter on barley, and 3s. 6d. on oats, and to
modify the duties upon sugar and timber.   These proposals roused a storm of opposition from the Tory party,
and gained no strong support from his own side.   Sir
Robert Peel therefore proposed a vote of want of confidence, which was carried by one vote, and the Government appealed to the country.

In the succeeding election, August, 1841, Cobden was
returned for Stockport, and henceforth led the cause
in Parliament.   The new Parliament showed a majority
against the Government.   In the Queen's speech, and
in the debate on the address, the Government, by their
attitude towards the Corn-laws, made a bid for the
support of the Free-traders, but their proposals were
regarded by the Free-traders as merely an attempt at
compromise in order to retain office; and from the Protectionists, who were in a majority, they received no

favour. The 8s. duty was not acceptable, and the Melbourne ministry resigned.

In this, his first debate, Cobden at once took rank as
a parliamentary speaker of the first order, and of a new
character. Mr. Morley thus describes him: "He produced that singular and profound effect which is perceived in English deliberative assemblies when a speaker
leaves party recriminations, abstract arguments, and
commonplaces of sentiment, in order to inform his
hearers of telling facts on the condition of the nation.
. . . He insisted that the Corn-law was in reality the
only matter which, at that moment, was worth debating
at all. The family of a nobleman, he showed the House,
paid to the bread tax about one halfpenny on every £100
of income, while the effect of the tax on the family of
the labouring man was not less than 20 per cent."

Cobden made no delay in placing his position clearly
before the House. "I call myself neither Whig nor
Tory, I am a Free-trader", he declared, and under
this banner he consistently fought until the battle was
won.

Peel came into office in September, 1841, as leader of
the Conservative party—a party mainly aristocratic
and agricultural, and consisting of avowed defenders of
the Corn-laws; he remained in office until he had repealed those laws, and he accomplished this with the
same Parliament. Yet Peel, in taking office, was cautious,
while supporting the graduated scale, "not to pledge
himself to plans which, on reconsideration, he might
deem it expedient to modify". He had stated that "he
was for reforming every institution that really required
reform, but he was for doing it gradually, dispassion-
ately, and deliberately, in order that the reform might
be lasting". The term "Conservative" had been in-
vented by Croker as being less objectionable than Tory,
since it more distinctly admitted the idea of progress,
and it had found favourable acceptance with Peel. Peel
was not an economist in the scientific sense, but he was
a statesman and a man of sound judgment; he knew how
to accept the inevitable, and was open to be educated by
the logic of events, and he was capable of leading his

party with him.   His convictions were deep, if slow in
formation, and he was sincere; and, when convinced, he
had the courage of his opinions.   In finance he was
strong and commanded confidence; he had to provide
revenue for a country loaded with debt, with a declining
income, and a revenue system which had no elasticity.
Many of his followers were fanatical believers in Protection; but Peel carried an open mind, and circumstances,
together with the arguments of his opponents, moulded
his ideas on the practical question with which he had to
deal.   His mind was progressive, but he needed to be
convinced not only of the abstract validity of a doctrine,
but of its applicability to the circumstances existing,
before he would give his adhesion to it as a principle of
practical politics.

Peel's accession to office took place at a time when
the country was entering upon a period of acute suffering.   Bad harvests, and a financial crisis which ushered
in a long and severe depression in trade, combined to
produce a winter of exceptional distress.   In the manufacturing districts of England and Scotland many firms
failed, mills were closed, employment almost ceased,
and the destitution which ensued was terrible.   Statistics
give a very inadequate conception of the misery which
was general among the working-classes.   A few facts,
from those gathered by the League and recorded by Mr.
Ashworth, afford some assistance in realizing the extent
of the disaster.   In Manchester, we are told, 116 mills
and many other works were stopped, 2000 families were
reduced to such want as to have pawned even their beds,
12,000 families were receiving poor relief, and thousands
subsisted on charity.   Out of 50 mills in Bolton 30 were
idle, and 6995 persons, whose average earnings were
only 13d. a week, were aided in one month by the Poor
Protection Society.   In Nottingham 10,580 persons were
receiving poor relief.   In Leeds 21,000 persons were
earning on an average 11¾d. a week.   In Stockport so
many firms had failed that work had practically ceased,
and multitudes earned less than 10d. a week.   Bury,
Rochdale, Wigan, Coventry, Paisley, Glasgow, and
many other towns had a similar record of failure and

distress.   While the working-classes were on the verge
of starvation, British corn was 65*s.* a quarter, and the
duty on foreign wheat was 24*s.* 8*d.* per quarter.   The
new Government made no sign of relief, and Parliament
was not summoned during the winter.

The League claimed credit for helping to maintain the
peace and repress disorder among the starving population, by the hope which they inspired of better prospects
when the repeal of the Corn-law should be accomplished.
They increased their efforts and pursued their propa-
ganda in the towns and villages by means of meetings,
lectures, and pamphlets, trusting that, as the public
became enlightened regarding the real operation of restriction on the import of corn, their success would be
assured.   The severity of the suffering in those times is
reflected in the verses to which they gave rise.   Ebenezer
Elliott calls for special mention as the poet of the movement.   In his *Corn-law Rhymes* and subsequent poems
he pours out a fund of indignation mingled with pathos
upon the law which he regarded as the chief cause of
the repeated distress.   A brief specimen must suffice to
illustrate their style:

> " Child, is thy father dead?
>   Father is gone!
> Why did they tax his bread?
>   God's will be done!
> Mother has sold her bed:
> Better to die than wed!
> Where shall she lay her head?
> Home we have none."

Meanwhile the distress continued, and all classes
anxiously awaited the action of the new Parliament.
The Chartists clamoured for political reform as the only
remedy.   The Free-traders continued to draw attention
to the scarcity of home-grown food, the exclusion of
foreign supplies, and the decline in the exports of British
manufactures by means of which an adequate supply of
foreign corn could be obtained.   Others attacked the
new methods of industry as the cause of the distress,
and maintained that machinery was throwing men out

of employment and leading to over-production and general depression in trade.

Cobden replied to this charge by pointing out that the workers in trades like stocking-weaving, in which there had been no change in method for two centuries, were distressed as much as those engaged in cotton spinning and weaving, and that agricultural labourers were almost equal sufferers, although in their trade no machinery had entered. In the cotton trade, again, he showed that the use of machinery had cheapened clothing, increased demand, and gained the trade both at home and abroad, and had for many years supported vast numbers during the time of foreign war and severe taxation. Only after the war was the high protective duty on corn imposed in 1815, and it was able to be tolerated during periods of good harvests. But bad harvests, with a growing population, had raised bread to famine prices; and while the population had been increasing, the existing Corn-laws checked the supply of food, and cut away the foreign demand for British manufactures which would have purchased it. This was the cause which aggravated the distress, though these laws were supposed to be necessary to maintain rents.

It was in the distressing autumn of 1841 that the exceptional powers and energies of John Bright were enlisted actively in the Free-trade campaign. Bright himself told the story many years after the death of Cobden. He had suffered the deep affliction of the loss of his young wife, and was overwhelmed with grief, when Cobden called to condole with him. Before leaving, Cobden said: "There are thousands of houses in England at this moment where wives, mothers, and children are dying of hunger. Now, when the first paroxysm of your grief is past, I would advise you to come with me, and we will never rest till the Corn-law is repealed." Bright accepted, and henceforth his wonderful gifts of eloquence, fervour, and intellectual vigour were devoted to the cause in which he ranks only after Cobden. There was a remarkable contrast in the two men in their temperament and natural endowments, but a common sympathy bound them in the closest friendship throughout the struggle and for the remainder of their life.[1]

Parliament opened in February, 1842, with a sympathetic reference in the Queen's speech to the sufferings in the manufacturing districts, and a recommendation "to consider the laws which affect the imports of corn and other articles". All parties waited with intense excitement for the proposals of the new prime minister. His speech defended the duties on corn as necessary in the interests of agriculture, and to preserve Great Britain from dependence upon other countries. Peel, as he states in his *Memoirs*, was at this time under the belief that special burdens were imposed upon agriculture, and he was also impressed by a fear of dependence upon other countries for food,—both points on which, subsequently, his opinions were completely changed. He desired to keep wheat between 54s. and 58s. a quarter, as a remunerative price for agriculture, and for this purpose he proposed a modified sliding-scale, commencing with a duty of 20s. when wheat was as low as 51s., and falling to 1s. when it reached 73s. The proposal was received in silence, but Lord John Russell's amendment of a fixed duty was rejected. Mr. Villiers's amendment, "that all duties on importations of corn, meal, grain, and flour do now cease and determine", led to an animated debate extending over five days, in which Cobden spoke with great effect. He effectually exposed the common fallacy that high prices made high wages, and urged that it was a well-fed people alone that could either defend the country or produce wealth. He charged the House "with deteriorating the population and thus spoiling both the animal and the intellectual creature". "It is not", said he, "a potato-fed race that will ever lead the way in arts, arms, or commerce." He demanded that, if corn prices were to be fixed by law, prices of other commodities must also be fixed, and if so, a sliding-scale for wages would be equally just and necessary.

During this session 2881 separate petitions, signed by

---

[1] For the account of Bright's work in the campaign, see the volume in this series on *John Bright*, by C. A. Vince, M.A.

1,540,755 persons, were presented against the Government measure, or in support of total repeal.   The bill for a sliding-scale became law on the 29th April.   Peel's new Income-tax Bill followed; it was estimated that this tax would yield £3,750,000, which would be sufficient to cover the deficit and allow of customs reforms affecting 750 articles.   The new tariff now introduced was beneficial, and materially reduced the duties on many articles of consumption.   Peel evidently hoped for a return of prosperity with better harvests and the operation of the new tariff.   He had not yet got rid of the idea that agriculture, as the leading industry, needed special safeguards,[1] and in his concern about dependence upon foreign countries for food, he forgot that starvation was actually existing, and that on every occasion when prices were at famine-level the country did look abroad for assistance, and imported additional food; but, as there was no regular free market in England for foreign corn, and no uniform demand, it was extremely difficult in circumstances of scarcity to purchase corn, except at prices so high as to give no real relief to starving labourers.   A further matter which the ministry had not fully realized was the extent of the large manufacturing industries and the vast population dependent upon them, which found in foreign countries a good market for their produce, while those countries were able to pay for such produce with the food necessary to the support of the labourers in those manufactures.

All the year (1842) the distress in the country increased.   Deputations waited upon the prime minister to explain the suffering and its causes, and to demand the removal of the corn duties on grounds of humanity.   Peel recognized the suffering and expressed his sympathy, but was not yet apparently convinced of the remedy.   He was aware that the duties, once repealed, could not be reimposed, and he hesitated.

The continued depression was, on the whole, borne

---

[1] In his *Memoirs*, part iii. vol. ii. p. 98, Peel writes: "I had adopted at an early period of my public life, without, I fear, much serious reflection, the opinion generally prevalent at the time among men of all parties, as to the justice and necessity of protection to domestic agriculture".

by the suffering classes with remarkable patience.   The
League continued to educate the people, and to teach
them to look for the revival of trade and an increased
supply of food from foreign countries consequent on free
import.   The more advanced Chartist leaders, however,
seized the opportunity to urge their political remedies.
Soon the effect of their more violent agitation made
itself apparent.   The half-starved mill-hands of South
Lancashire were incited to cease working and to make a
demonstration, which threatened a serious disturbance
of the peace.   The turn-out began in Ashton-under-Lyne,
and spread to all the cotton district; crowds of factory-
hands went about compelling the mill-hands in other
towns and villages to cease working, and declaring their
intention not to return to work until they had gained the
Charter and higher wages.

The disturbance in Manchester was soon suppressed
after the reading of the Riot Act, but in other towns of
the cotton district the excitement continued for about a
fortnight, and caused some alarm.   At Rochdale Mr.
Bright helped to restore order and quiet by the publica-
tion of a very temperate and judicious address to the
working-men, in which he calmly discussed the question,
explained the causes of the misery, and showed clearly
that the Charter was no remedy for their condition, and
still less was public disturbance or interference with
work; the problem was economic, and could only be
settled by economic treatment such as the League proposed.   In South Lancashire the agitation ended without violence, but in Staffordshire and other districts
which the Chartists visited serious riots took place, and
the troops had to be called out.

The League now determined to carry the crusade into
the agricultural counties, and to teach the farmers and
rural labourers that they were interested in the success
of manufactures, and had a common cause with the
workers in those industries in their need for cheap food
and enlarged foreign markets.   For this purpose a fund
of £50,000 was asked.   In January, 1843, the spacious
Free-trade Hall, built expressly for meetings of the
League, was opened with a crowded public meeting, at

which the chairman announced subscriptions amounting
to £40,000. In February, 1843, Lord Howick (afterwards Earl Grey) moved in Parliament for a committee
to inquire into the cause of the distress, but the motion
was rejected by 306 votes to 191. The debate acquired
an unfortunate tone from an incident which affected the
relations of the principal opponents, the premier and
Mr. Cobden. Sir R. Peel's private secretary (W. E.
Drummond) had been assassinated in the street by a
lunatic. It was supposed the blow was intended for the
premier, and the rumour was circulated that an attempt
on the premier's life had been sanctioned by the
Leaguers. No proof was offered, and no direct charge
was made, but the movement was discredited by the
rumour, which gained some acceptance.

In the debate in the House Mr. Cobden, with his
usual candour, attacked the Corn-law restriction, and
expressed himself during his speech as holding the
prime minister responsible for the distress and suffering in the country, which could be relieved by the
removal of the duty. Sir R. Peel, in reply, agitated
and overcome by the painful circumstances of the death
of his friend, charged Cobden with making him *individually* and *personally* responsible, and with menacing
him by insinuations. The excitement in the House was
intense. Mr. Cobden denied indignantly the imputation,
or the use of the word *personal*, and repudiated any
possible meaning but that the prime minister, *as such*,
was responsible for the policy of the Government. A
most painful scene followed.

In spite of the disclaimer of Cobden, and its ultimate
acceptance by Peel, the suggestion was promulgated
by the hostile press and by enemies of the League. In
his after life Peel made ample amends for the accusation,
and admitted the honesty of purpose and the purity of
method adopted by the League; but for a time the
charge circulated, and the painful feeling generated
among the members of the League was not readily
removed.

In March, 1843, the League devoted a week to instructing the metropolis in Free-trade views. Drury

customers, and consequently has an injurious effect upon
my profits." The demand for speakers at meetings in
Scotland became so great that Cobden and Bright
separated, each with a group of friends. Cobden went
east, and Bright took the west. On this Scotch tour
Cobden writes: "Our progress has been gratifying in
the extreme. Glasgow, Edinburgh, Kirkcaldy, Dundee,
Perth, and Stirling, have all presented me with the freedom of their burghs, and I have no doubt I could have
become a free citizen of every corporate town in Scotland by paying them a visit. All this is due to the
principles we advocate." Bright was much impressed
by the intelligence of the Scotch, and their keenness in
discerning economic fallacies. He comments humor-
ously on the popularity of himself and his colleagues,
but notes the lack of financial response. Soon after
their return, at Wakefield Lord Morpeth (afterwards
Earl of Carlisle), a new adherent, appeared on the plat-
form, and declared that "the true and permanent
interests of the agricultural, manufacturing, and commercial classes are indissolubly united, and their surest
basis is in the freedom of trade and industry".

At the opening of Parliament in 1844 the prime
minister congratulated the country on the improvement
in trade and prosperity. Lord John Russell, in reply,
attributed whatever improvement had taken place to the
fall in the price of bread, but he still argued in favour of
a fixed duty on corn for revenue purposes only. Sir
R. Peel pointed out that such a duty would have to be
applied equally to home-produced corn; he indicated his
preference and adhesion to the sliding-scale on imported
corn, and stated that "he did not contemplate any
alteration in the existing law".

The belief was, however, growing among the Free-
traders that Peel was rapidly approaching the position
when he would declare for repeal of the Corn-law, and
that he only awaited the suitable opportunity to state
his convictions, when this could be done without com-
promising the Government.

During the month of February, 1844, the League
conducted a special agitation in London; large public

meetings were held in Covent Garden Theatre. In
March, Cobden brought forward in the House of Commons a motion for the appointment of a committee " to
inquire into the effects of the protective duties on the
interests of the tenant-farmers and labourers of this
country". He proved the failure of Protection to maintain farmers' profits or labourers' wages; "many farmers
had taken farms after the act of 1815, calculating on
selling their wheat at 80s.; it had fallen to 50s.; but the
rents remained fixed on the basis of the higher price".
Cobden argued that direct legislation could not regulate
the price of commodities and prevent fluctuations; it
might increase pauperism and destroy trade, banish
capital, and check or expatriate the population; but it
could not keep prices steady and secure the farmer that
price on which he had counted when he undertook his
rent obligations; farmers had been deceived by such
legislation into making contracts which destroyed their
profits. He went on to show that the case of the
labourers was far worse than that of the farmers, and he
produced detailed evidence from many counties to prove
their misery and degradation. Humanity and justice to
them demanded an inquiry into the working of a system
which, while professedly maintained in the interest of
agriculture, allowed those who worked upon the land
to starve. He concluded an address, convincing by its
arguments and descriptions, by moving for a select
committee of inquiry, because " the present system robs
the earth of its fertility and the labourer of his hire,
deprives the people of subsistence and the farmer of
feelings of honest independence".[1] Mr. Bright followed
with a forcible appeal, and urged that " if the majority
thought that the justice of the Corn-laws could be proved,

[1] The following is an extract from this powerful speech :—" The right
hon. Baronet opposite (Sir R. Peel) has confessed that he cannot regulate
the wages of labour or the profits of trade. Now the farmers are dependent
for their prices upon the wages of the labourer and the profits of the trader
and manufacturer; and if the Government cannot regulate these—if it cannot
guarantee a certain amount of wages to the one, or a fixed profit to the
other—how can it regulate the price of agricultural produce? The first
point to which I should wish to make this committee instrumental is to fix
in the minds of the farmers the fact that this House exaggerates its power
to sustain or enhance prices by direct acts of legislation. The farmer's

they would grant the committee at once". The committee was nevertheless refused.

In June Mr. Villiers's motion for repeal again came forward. Mr. Villiers attacked the argument for independence by showing that this country was dependent upon other countries for the materials of its manufactures, and thus for the means by which millions of labourers could earn their bread, while it rejected the bread itself, which could only be obtained in sufficiency by selling the produce of that labour in exchange for foreign corn. He dwelt upon the embarrassed condition of farmers, and the low scale of civilization of the labourers—the consequence of their necessitous condition. Viscount Howick maintained that the question was purely one of rent, in which farmers and labourers received no consideration. Mr. Cobden examined the defence of the Corn-laws, that they enabled the protected classes to pay taxes. He showed that the incidence of the tax on corn was upon the consumer, and argued, moreover, that it caused an absolute loss; he also proved from statistics that revenue rose as corn prices fell, and declined as prices rose.

Mr. Bright attacked the plea of special burdens on land by showing that rents fell when rates were high, that rates fell upon all kinds of industries and property equally with land, and that if it were not so, the proper method was to deal with the particular burden, and not to create another. The motion was lost.

The depression grew and became more severe among the agricultural labourers, whose wages fell to 7s. and 5s. a week in 1844. With wheat at 51s. 3d. a quarter, labourers were existing on potatoes and meal; their standard of living was so degraded as to approach starvation level. More than one-eighth of the population

interest is that of the whole community, and is not a partial interest, and you cannot touch him more sensitively than when you injure the manufacturers, his customers.

"I do not deny that you may regulate prices for a while—for a while you have regulated them by forcing an artificial scarcity; but this is a principle which carries with it the seeds of self-destruction, for you are thereby undermining the prosperity of those consumers upon whom your permanent welfare depends. A war against nature must always end in the discomfiture of those who wage it."

of Suffolk and Essex was upon the poor-rates, and the
wretched peasantry, prompted by their misery and
hunger, once more resorted to incendiarism and set fire
to the ricks of corn,—as some of them admitted—to
raise the price of wheat, since in their ignorance they
had adopted the teaching that "high prices make good
wages", and sought to give it practical effect.

The agricultural distress continued through the winter,
and on March 13th, 1845, Mr. Cobden moved in the
House to appoint a select committee "to inquire into
the causes and extent of the alleged existing agricultural
distress, and into the effect of legislative protection upon
the interests of land-owners, tenant-farmers, and farm-
labourers".   This speech affords perhaps the most perfect example of Cobden's style of debate.   It displays
his masterly and comprehensive grasp of the subject; it
is crowded with pertinent facts narrated in an orderly
and forcible manner, and the conclusions are enforced
by arguments which proved unanswerable.   "How is
it", he asks, "that in a country overflowing with capital,
when there is a plethora in every other business—when
money is going to France for railroads, and to Pennsyl-
vania for bonds—when it is connecting the Atlantic with
the Pacific by canals, and diving to the bottom of Mexi-
can mines for investment,—it yet finds no employment
in the most attractive of all spots, the soil of this country
itself?"   He answers: "Capital shrinks instinctively from
insecurity of tenure, and we have not in England that
security which will warrant men of capital investing their
money in the soil".   He goes on to maintain that "the want
of leases and security deters tenants from laying out their
money in the soil."   "Tenants therefore are prevented
by their landlords from carrying on cultivation properly.
They are made servile and dependent, disinclined to improvement, afraid to let the landlord see that they could
improve their farms, lest he should pounce on them for
an increase of rent."   And he showed from specimens,
that when leases were granted, the "covenants were of
such a preposterous character that I will defy any man
to carry on the business of farming properly under
them".   He quoted the case of one member of the

House who had been publicly rebuking farmers for not
growing flax, while in his own leases there was a clause
which prohibited flax-growing.   But the most powerful
section of this speech is that in which he demonstrates
from agriculture the fundamental fallacy of Protection—
taxing the whole community for the benefit of a section.
Taking clover, beans, oats, hops, cheese, in succession,
he showed that for the sake of giving a monopoly to a
few districts in each of these products, the whole agricultural industry was oppressed and burdened.   He
stated that many farmers had resented this folly, and
had placed their names on the books of the Anti-Corn-law
League, "comprising some of the most intelligent men
that are to be found in the kingdom".   While linseed,
oats, &c., were excluded by duty, fat cattle were imported duty free.   "But to exclude provender for cattle
and to admit fat cattle duty free, was one of the greatest
absurdities in legislation that ever was."   Turning to
the defence that the agricultural classes were large
consumers of manufactures, he asks: "What sort of
consumers of manufactures do you think agricultural
labourers would be with the wages they get?"   "There
are 960,000 agricultural labourers in England and Wales,
and each of them does not spend 30s. a year in manufactures on his whole family, if the article of shoes be
excepted."   "Then", he goes on, "I would ask what
can they pay on 8s. a week to the revenue?"   In a
powerful peroration he appealed to the gentlemen, the
high aristocracy of England, "to play in a mercantile
age that noble part which in feudal times had made their
ancestors the leaders of the people"; but he adds, "if
you are found obstructing that progressive spirit which
is calculated to knit nations more closely together by
commercial intercourse; if you give nothing but opposition to schemes which almost give life and breath to
inanimate nature, and which it has been decreed shall
go on, then you are no longer a national body".

This speech made a marked impression upon Sir
Robert Peel.   Mr. Morley thus describes it:—"The
prime minister had followed every sentence with earnest attention; his face grew more and more solemn as

the argument proceeded.   At length he crumpled up the
notes which he had been taking, and was heard by an
overlooker, who was close by, to say to Mr. Sidney
Herbert, who sat next him on the bench, 'You must
answer this, for I cannot '."

Making use of every legitimate device, the League, in
May, 1845, displayed their enterprise and regard for
orthodox methods of procedure by organizing a great
bazaar in Covent Garden Theatre; by this means they
raised £25,000, gained an immense advertisement of
their aims, and secured many adherents to their cause.

In Parliament Lord John Russell, on May 26th, moved
a series of resolutions, in which, while repeating his
demand for a fixed duty, he practically admitted the
principle of the League, and employed their arguments
The Free-trade doctrine was at length gaining ground,
and it was becoming very evident to the leaders of the
movement that it was only a question of time before the
premier would be completely convinced and would adopt
their views.

In the autumn wet weather caused a bad harvest and
a sudden rise in bread, which created much apprehension
among ministers.   But a more serious evil was at hand.
Ireland had for some time adopted the low diet of potatoes as her standard food, and in some parts potatoes
were almost the only produce of the land, and the sole
means of subsistence.   In the autumn of 1845 the crops
were attacked by blight, and the people were threatened
with famine.   It was necessary to ac romptly if terrible
disaster was to be averted.   The ministry sent a commission to inquire into the state of the food supply in
Ireland, and Mansion House Relief Committees were
formed in Dublin, which demanded free admission of
food to combat the spreading calamity.   In Manchester
the League held a vast meeting and appealed to the
Government to grant relief by opening the ports.   The
Cabinet met frequently, but could not agree to the large
measures for relief proposed by Peel.   Lord John Russell
seized the moment to renounce his belief in a fixed duty,
and in a public letter to the electors of the City he announced his somewhat tardy conversion to complete

Free-trade principles. "Let us then unite", he said,
"to put an end to a system which has been proved to
be the blight of commerce, the bane of agriculture, the
source of bitter divisions among classes, the cause of
penury, fever, mortality, and crime among the people."
Other public men followed, including Lord Macaulay.
The circumstances of the time by their urgency made
many rapid conversions.

The Cabinet meantime hesitated to adopt the prime
minister's plan, until at length the Duke of Wellington
declared that he would give Peel his support, and recommended the rest of the ministers to do the same.
This was at the beginning of December, and on the 4th
The Times startled the country with the announcement
that the Corn-laws were about to be repealed. However, Peel could not overcome the resistance of Lord
Stanley and the Duke of Buccleuch, and he felt it his
duty to resign office, which he did on the 5th December.
He promised Her Majesty to give his personal support
to Lord John Russell in carrying the measure of repeal,
and she accordingly asked Lord John to form a ministry.
He was, however, unable to do so, and Her Majesty
speedily recalled Sir Robert Peel and asked him to resume office. This he did, replacing Lord Stanley by Mr.
Gladstone. His return to office in the altered circumstances left Peel free from past party pledges, except in
the opinion of rabid Protectionists like Lord G. Bentinck.
He came back to save the country from the calamity
with which famine threatened it, and he proceeded at
once to formulate his measure for abolishing the Corn-
laws. The League, meanwhile, was actively urging on
the counties the necessity for action: a great meeting
was held in the Free-trade Hall on the 23rd December,
when it was determined to raise a monster subscription
of £250,000. Towards this sum £60,000 was sub-
scribed on the spot, and in a few days the amount
reached £150,000, so great was the enthusiasm and the
liberality evoked by the critical condition to which the
movement had now been brought.[1]

[1] "The Chairman at once announced his readiness to receive the names
of subscribers; and a scene which defies description immediately followed,

Without delay Peel now brought in his measure for abolishing the Corn-laws. He proposed that they should cease on 1st February, 1849, with the exception of a registration duty of 1s. per quarter, and that in the three years' interval the duty on wheat should be 10s. when the price was under 48s., falling to 4s. when the price reached 53s. The same bill proposed to abolish or reduce duties on 150 other articles of food, raw materials, and manufactures.

After a lengthened debate, in which the opposition to Peel was led by Mr. Disraeli in a virulent personal attack, the bill was carried in the House of Commons on the 16th May. It was passed quickly through the Lords by the Duke of Wellington, and became law on the 25th June, on the very day on which Peel was defeated on the Irish Coercion Bill.

Peel's Corn Bill had passed the third reading by 327 votes to 229. The Irish Coercion Bill, on which he left office, was defeated by 294 votes to 219.

In announcing his resignation of office, Peel made a most eloquent and affecting speech, in which he ascribed to Cobden the chief credit of passing the Corn Bill. He said: " The name that ought to be associated with the success of the measure is the name of a man who, acting, I believe, from pure and disinterested motives, has advocated this cause with untiring energy and by appeals to reason ". He concluded with the dignified and memorable passage: " I shall leave a name execrated, I know, by every monopolist who would maintain Protection for his own individual benefit. But it may be that I shall leave a name sometimes remembered with expressions of good-will in the abodes of those whose lot it is to labour and to earn their daily bread by the sweat of their brow, when they shall recruit their exhausted strength with abundant and untaxed food, the sweeter because it is no longer leavened by a sense of injustice."

Peel has been charged with inconsistency. He took

in which gentlemen were calling out in rapid succession '£1000 for me' and '£1000 for me', until no less than twenty-three names had followed one another for the like sum. There were twenty-two others who put down £500 each, and these, together with other smaller sums then announced, amounted to more than £60,000."—(*Cobden and the League*, Ashworth, p. 200.)

office in 1841 as the minister of a party pledged to maintain the Corn-laws, and he repealed those laws against
the wishes of the majority of that party; yet Peel was
noted for his sincerity and honesty. The solution of the
paradox is in that very sincerity of purpose towards his
country. He became slowly but surely convinced of the
error of Protection: he was not a man of impulse; his
mind was moulded under the influence of facts and strict
logic. The frequent sufferings of the people were the
strongest factor in his conversion; he saw that under
the existing law it had not been possible for them to
obtain sufficient food; finally, the Irish famine made it a
pressing necessity that something should be done. As
Bright expressed it: " Famine itself, against which we
had warred, joined us ". He could have resigned office
and have left the responsibility to his successor, and
thus have escaped the charge of dishonesty to his party;
but he felt the responsibility of a starving people more
than the reproach of a deserted party, and he endeavoured
to induce his Cabinet to relax the prohibitions. Failing
in this aim, he resigned his office and promised his support to his successor in relieving the pressure of the
Corn-laws. When Lord John Russell failed to form a
Government, without hesitation Peel obeyed the request
to resume office, and accepted a task which he knew
would discredit him with his party. He at once candidly
explained his position and his intentions. His views
had undergone a change; the facts of misery and the
menace of famine were the forces that finally convinced
him, and he was courageous and magnanimous enough
to face all the contumely of a charge of dishonesty to
save a nation from starvation and to inaugurate a policy
which he was now assured was the only sound and just
one. His duty was to his country, and he would fulfil
it at any cost. Confident in the consequences of his act,
he left the judgment of his conduct to posterity, in the
assurance that his name would live associated with one
of the most beneficent measures ever passed for the
people of this country. And the judgment of posterity
has not belied his anticipations. Peel ranks as one of
the noblest and truest of British statesmen. The repeal

which he effected is the most permanent of his achieve-
ments. Many financiers regard Peel's bill of 1844 as
the greatest reform in the theory and practice of banking, and as having been the means of placing our currency upon a sound basis; but his fiscal reforms, of
which the repeal of the Corn-law was the climax, became the corner-stone of a new edifice of finance built
up on principles which started this country on a period
of unrivalled prosperity.

The Corn-law of 1815 had been passed in the interests
of land-owners; its avowed object was to enable them to
maintain rents and meet the burdens which they imagined to have been unduly placed upon them by the war.
It was passed in the interests of a class—an aristocracy
of land-owners, and it proved to be inimical to the interests of the majority of the people, who in this struggle
were represented by the manufacturers, a new and
powerful class which had arisen within half-a-century,
and between whom and the landed aristocracy a strong
jealousy then existed. The manufacturers were themselves as much interested in the abolition of Protection
as were the landlords in maintaining it. There is
nothing exceptional in this attempt of "interested
sections" to retain or extend their advantages. Examples are always to be found, and everywhere,—in railways, breweries, trade-unions, manufactures, teachers'
associations, &c.; most questions which are settled by
the votes of groups are determined almost entirely as
they affect the special interests of those groups.

Protection for agriculture exists in France and Germany, where much of the land is held in small portions,
and it would probably have been adopted in England,
in the same circumstances which existed in 1815, had
England been a country of small landholders. In the
United States and most of the colonies it is advocated
and upheld in the interests of the manufacturing classes.
It has been said that the Corn-law question was finally
decided as a class question. This is not strictly correct;
the agitation began partly as a matter of rival interests,
but the larger interest of the community soon outgrew
other considerations. It was argued and discussed on

economic grounds; it was debated and carried by the
convincing reasoning supplied from Adam Smith, who
had written forty years before the duty of 1815 was imposed; and it fell because the principle was shown to be
unsound, and the practice to be economically a loss and
an injury to the community as a whole.

The work of the League was now virtually accomplished. A few days after the passing of the Bill a
meeting was held at the Free-trade Hall, when Cobden
delivered an address, in which he paid a warm tribute
to Sir Robert Peel. "If he has lost office," said Cobden,
"he has gained a country. For my part, I would
rather descend into private life with that last measure of
his, which led to his discomfiture, in my hand, than
mount to the highest pinnacle of human power by any
other means." Mr. Bright followed with a stirring
speech, in which he complimented the House of Lords:
"I must confess that I have a greater respect for the
House of Lords, from watching their passing of this
Bill, and the manner in which they have passed it, than
I ever had at any former period".

Before separating, the League presented their inde-
fatigable chairman, Mr. George Wilson, with a sum of
£10,000 in recognition of the invaluable services which,
during seven years, he had performed gratuitously, and
with remarkable devotion, tact, and sagacity. The
League was then quietly dissolved. It was revived for
a brief period in 1852 when Lord Derby and Mr. Disraeli
came into office, and an alarm was raised by a speech of
Lord Derby's that an attempt would be made to restore
a Protectionist policy.

The removal of the remaining restraints on commerce
are soon chronicled. In 1849 the Navigation Laws
were finally abolished after a brief struggle with the
Protectionists. In 1852 Mr. Gladstone became chancellor
of the exchequer, and immediately proceeded to complete
the policy of his master in finance. He removed the
duties on 123 articles, and reduced those on 133 others,
including most of the remaining duties on food. In
1860, after an interval disturbed by the Russian war, he
resumed the task of simplification, and reduced the

number of taxed imports to 48, removing the last duties on manufactures (wool and silk), and all differential duties.   A few other reforms have since been effected; the timber duty was abolished in 1866, the shilling registration duty on corn in 1869, and sugar was freed in 1875.   The English tariff is now non-protective; it is simple in principle, being levied on only 15 classes of goods and for revenue only; of these, tobacco, tea, spirits, and wine produce about nine-tenths of the whole customs revenue of £21,250,000.

One other matter calls for notice as being part of the direct development of the Free-trade movement.   This was the negotiation of the Treaty of Commerce with France in 1860 by Cobden and Chevalier, with the assistance of the Emperor Napoleon III., who, no doubt, was the more inclined thereto from political motives.   By this treaty Great Britain agreed, on her side, to lower the duties on French brandy and wine, to complete at once the abolition of duties on manufactures, and not to re-impose an export duty on coal to France.   France undertook to abolish prohibition of British goods, to lower the duties on all British staple manufactures of textiles, iron, machinery, tools, leather, glass, &c., to less than 30 per cent *ad valorem*.   The treaty was to be binding for ten years, and to continue afterwards unless denounced.   This last event took place in 1872 after the Franco-German war; but the treaty was temporarily renewed, though finally abandoned in 1882.

The effect of the treaty on the commerce of the two nations was most beneficial.   Between 1858 and 1877 British exports to France increased from £9,000,000 to £25,000,000, and French exports to England from £13,000,000 to £45,000,000.   A further good result followed in the numerous other treaties to which the French treaty gave rise, and in the extension of the principle now adopted of the "most favoured nation", by which negotiations ending in a compact between any two nations may lead to an extension of like advantages to other nations, and thus secure a step towards the removal of obstacles to general free exchange over the whole area of related countries.

Chapter V.

The Economics of Foreign Trade.

In the absence of artificial restrictions, such as tariffs, trade between nations will arise naturally when some advantage is to be derived from it by the nations engaging in it, and will only continue so long as this exists. Sir Dudley North more than two hundred years ago stated this theory of foreign trade: "The whole world as to trade is but as one nation or people, therein nations are as persons. The loss of a trade with one nation is not that only, separately considered, but so much of the trade of the world rescinded or lost, for all is combined together. There can be no trade unprofitable to the public, for if any prove so men leave it off, and whenever the traders thrive, the public, of which they are a part, thrive also."[1]

The advantages gained by home trade are obvious; some parts of a country are fertile and good for agriculture, some yield clay or stone, others iron or coal. To develop these resources and interchange the various products of a country benefits all classes. Certain localities are suitable for the manufacture of tools of iron, and others for that of paper, cloth, or chemicals; proximity to water, coal, the nature of the soil, the humidity or dryness, will determine the character of the local industries. The benefits arising from separation of employments and division of labour need no proof. The principle of specialization of functions is admitted as a sign of higher organization in plants and animals; it is equally true of societies. By localization the special advantages of situation are gained; by specialization those of ability, capacity, aptitude, the gifts of nature and the attributes of man are turned to best account, utility is thereby increased, wealth is augmented, and man rises to a higher civilization. It is only savages who do not co-operate at all; they seek individually to

[1] Sir Dudley North, *Discourses upon Trade*, 1691.

supply their own wants; their condition is very little
above that of the beasts; they are non-progressive. By
contrast, the most advanced and richest nations exhibit
most fully the faculty of combination, and display the
highest differentiation in employments; the greatest
wealth and variety are to be found in the countries where
the application of the principles of subdivision and exchange is adopted; in other words, comfort and wealth
increase as men avail themselves of the circumstances
which promote the exchange of products and services.

The extension of trading to other countries is only an
application of the principle of division and co-operation
to a larger area.   Cobden's saying, " Free-trade widens
the circle of exchange", contains the whole doctrine,
and the possibility of economic advantage increases as
the area is widened.   Nature's bounty has been scattered
lavishly, yet with many limitations; every diversity of
soil and climate is accompanied with diversity of gifts;
metals and minerals are distributed over different lands;
agricultural products exhibit an even greater partiality
in their distribution; the successful cultivation of corn,
the vine, cotton, coffee, tea, oranges, currants, timber,
&c., depends upon conditions of climate and land; they
do not all flourish in the same country. The only way
then in which any one country can enjoy all these products is by foreign trade, *i.e.* by exchange of goods.
Each country may part with something it can produce
easily, and which costs it little, in exchange for other
articles which it could not otherwise obtain at all.   This
merit of foreign trade was the first to commend itself to
early communities.   Self-sustaining as regards their
necessaries, by trading they obtained comforts and
luxuries which their own country did not yield; merchants
came with wares to the nomadic patriarchs in the desert;
the villagers in early England purchased their iron and
salt at the markets and fairs.   The Venetian fleets
brought cotton goods, glass, fine leather, silks, and
many products of the East to be sold at the English
fairs; the strictest Mercantilists and Protectionists bought
gold and silver with English produce. By trading, all
obtained something which their own district did not yield.

But an additional advantage may be obtained by carrying specialization further, and buying abroad things which *can* be produced at home, provided that the foreign article is superior in quality or can be produced under more favourable conditions. Two countries may yield the same kinds of commodities, and yet there may be a great gain by mutual trading, provided one nation has some advantage by nature or skill over the other. The climate or soil of the one may be superior, the ability of the inhabitants may be greater, or some circumstance may favour the development of industry in special directions. In such a case it will benefit both nations if trade is set up, the customer-country paying for the commodity thus imported with some goods of its own production, which the other country is willing to take in exchange; each in fact is customer to the other.

In this manner each country will devote most labour to producing those things for which it is more specially adapted, and the special aptitudes of the countries and their inhabitants being thus utilized, a larger amount of wealth is created, and both may share in the extra produce. The principle here briefly described is called in economic writings the doctrine of "comparative cost"; it is applicable alike to individuals, to localities, and to countries; it is a form of specialization on the simple principle that if each individual or country does by preference what each can do best, the general utility is increased. Increase of utility (serviceableness) is the object of work. Voluntary exchange is a process for increasing utility. Men have many wants, and the desire to satisfy new wants is capable of indefinite expansion. Again, the more we have of anything, the less does an addition to our stock of that article add to its utility. It is therefore a gain in utility to part with a portion of that which we have in abundance, in exchange for things of which we cannot easily produce sufficient to satisfy our wants. By this means our pleasure is augmented, and the serviceableness of the goods is increased. Thus "perfect freedom of exchange tends to the maximizing of utility", to use the expression of Jevons; and since it is its utility which causes a thing to be regarded as wealth, by free exchange wealth is increased. The inability to see that utility is the criterion of wealth, and that it is augmented by exchange, is a radical error of some writers on socialism, which renders much of their reasoning invalid. The same error underlies methods of taxation which have for their object to prevent the free flow of goods to those quarters where their ingress would add to the total enjoyment of the world.[1]

The increase of utility derived by specializing production is regarded by economists as the greatest advantage gained by trading, but protective tariffs prevent this gain by checking the importation of goods which a country can produce for itself though at greater cost. Canada has a sparse population and a soil well suited for the production of corn, fruit, and timber; Great Britain has a dense population, vast capital sunk in machinery, and with her minerals and industrial skill she is specially adapted for manufacturing. If Canada devotes herself by preference to agriculture, and Great Britain to manufactures, by free interchange both countries will be wealthier than if each endeavoured to supply its entire wants in both departments of industry. The gain is obtained by the reduced cost of production arising from the utilization of natural forces. Of course, under perfectly Free-trade some manufactures will flourish in Canada and agriculture in Great Britain; natural conditions alone will determine how far each is profitable. The discovery of better sources of supply is like the invention of a new machine, it is a means of getting an increased amount of wealth from nature with less labour; now the aim of every invention and dis-

[1] No language can state this principle of the efficiency of exchange more simply or forcibly than that of Adam Smith: " It is the maxim of every prudent master of a family, never to attempt to make at home what it will cost him more to make than to buy. The tailor does not attempt to make his own shoes, but buys them of the shoemaker. The shoemaker does not attempt to make his own clothes, but employs a tailor. The farmer attempts to make neither the one nor the other, but employs these different artificers. All of them find it for their interest to employ their whole industry in a way in which they have some advantage over their neighbours, and to purchase with a part of its produce, or, what is the same thing, with the price of a part of it, whatever else they have occasion for. What is prudence in the conduct of every private family can scarce be folly in that of a great kingdom." --(*Wealth of Nations*, book iv. chap. 2).

covery is to cheapen and multiply products and conveniences, thus foreign trade is in its results precisely of the nature of a new discovery or invention.

It by no means follows that the production of the article imported will cease altogether in the country importing, it will only be checked at the point at which it is more profitable to import. For example, corn can be grown in Great Britain at a remunerative price on the land best suited to corn, but it can be imported at such a price as to make it unprofitable to grow corn on inferior land. The trade of Australia with Europe between 1851 and 1870 exactly illustrated the case of a new discovery altering the course of industry, and by the agency of foreign trade conferring benefits on both sides. Prior to the gold discoveries Australia was an agricultural colony, supplying its own food, and sending wool, hides, &c., to Europe in exchange for clothing, tools, and other manufactures. The discovery of gold opened up a much more profitable industry to the shepherds and agriculturalists, who went to the mines in such numbers that Victoria not only ceased for a time to export agricultural produce, but did not produce sufficient food for its wants. Labour expended on gold-digging would yield four or five times as much as it could obtain if applied to agriculture, so Victoria exported gold to Europe and obtained thence butter, flour, timber, and leather in exchange, though all these commodities could have been produced in Australia at much lower prices than they could be imported. To produce gold, however, was more profitable; and the trade, set up naturally, continued until gold-mining became less profitable, when the current was changed and agriculture again resumed its course. This has continued until, at the present day, Australia is one of the largest exporters of wool and meat, and can even send butter to Great Britain at a lower price than British-made butter. Other examples of trade directed to secure the economic gain of exchange are abundant. Some of the West India Isles send fruit to the United States in exchange for meat and flour. Although they could produce those necessaries cheaply themselves, yet they find their greater advantage in the production of fruits, sugar, and coffee. The Channel Isles, in like manner, could obtain corn from their very fertile soil (and in 1844 they exported wheat to Great Britain[1]), but it pays them better now to grow early potatoes and fruit, such as grapes and tomatoes, and with these to purchase their corn in Great Britain.

Sufficient has been said to illustrate the nature of the advantages described under the phrase "comparative cost" in works on economic theory. It amounts to a statement that countries, like individuals, produce most when, in comparing their powers and opportunities in two or more fields of industry, they select for their labour those in which they excel; and with the results of their more efficient labour in those industries they buy the commodities which they themselves are less qualified to produce from countries which, in turn, have some special fitness for the production of those commodities. The total yield is increased by this method of organized production and exchange—there is an addition to the wealth of the world. It is purely a process of adopting the most efficient mode of production in the circumstances.

One great aim of the opportunities for gaining knowledge offered by technical education and the scholarship system is to enable youths to find the sphere in life for which they are best fitted, and thus to increase the national efficiency by employing those gifts and faculties which they possess in any exceptional degree. It is held that the individual advantage will be a national, and, it might be added, an international advantage; for every faculty utilized and developed, every form of latent ability or force rightly directed, becomes a potential increase of power to the world. If this argument be valid, it is difficult to reconcile it with a policy which places artificial limits to the enjoyment of the fruits of such faculty or natural fertility at the boundaries of a nation's territory. Does an *economic* advantage cease at an accidental and even variable line on the earth's surface? Does, for example, the transfer of Alsace and

[1] See Cobden's speech in the House of Commons, March 12, 1844.

Lorraine from France to Germany nullify the economic
gain of free-trading between those territories and
France?

It may be objected that a system of universal free
exchange tends to restrict the number of industries in a
country, and leads to over-specialization, making each
country dependent upon others for the majority of its
wants. To the first complaint it would be sufficient to
point out that in Great Britain, where free exchange
has been in operation for fifty years, there is probably a
larger variety of employments than in any other country,
and that, notwithstanding its manufacturing supremacy,
agriculture is still the largest single industry; it is also
the best-fed country in Europe, and the general standard
of comfort of the inhabitants is higher than that of most
countries which strive to promote many industries by
protective measures.

The great specialization of capital and labour presents
problems of real difficulty; it is, however, a product of
modern civilization, and is equally visible in the United
States, Germany, France, and other progressive countries
which impose high tariffs. Specialization is the outcome of invention, steam-power, the joint-stock system,
the movement towards the organization of production
and distribution on a large scale, and it will continue
independently of all considerations of tariffs. Specialization of industry has recommendations far too valuable to
allow it to be set aside; its danger lies in the readiness
with which trade and industry conducted on a vast scale
can be deranged. A whole district like South Lancashire
may be thrown into idleness by an event such as the
civil war in the United States; a strike of dock-labourers
or coal-miners may almost paralyse the trade of a nation.
These are dangers which arise with the complexity and
interdependence of industries, though they originate in
moral, political, and social causes, and in the imperfect
knowledge of economic laws; the remedies lie, however,
in the direction of removing the causes of wars and
strikes and other interruptions to industry, and along
with these remedies should be classed the reduction or
abolition of tariffs.

The adaptation of demand to supply on so vast and complex a system as trade has now become, presents many difficulties and risks.   Disturbances, crises, and depressions in one part of the world produce effects in remote regions: a famine in India, a convulsion in Australia or Japan, a war between two customer countries, gives a shock to the industries and commerce of England. This is inevitable, but it entails less suffering than did the local failure of crops in times when Great Britain was self-sufficing; and the evil will be much diminished when the economic causes of commercial and industrial depression are more widely understood, and when nations are more disposed to settle their differences by arbitration.   But the extension of the area of trading-relations has many advantages to set against this liability to disturbance: larger and more numerous sources of supply render scarcity less probable, a contraction in one direction is generally met by compensation from some other quarter, there is a levelling and steadying tendency.   In the same manner, a wide and extended area of demand means many markets, and these offer some resistance to disturbing influences, as it is less probable that a large number would fail at one time, and a narrowing in one direction is often balanced by an expansion in another.   Add to these the improved means of communication, diffusion of information and quickness of transit, attained by aid of the same huge forces which have rendered large organization possible, and we find, that on the whole, balancing advantages and disadvantages, the tendency to large markets, complicated trading, and the specialized production which free-trading fosters, is a great benefit to mankind.

The system of complex exchange, free enterprise, and natural trading often leads to the creation of industries in parts of the world where civilization had not previously penetrated; indeed commerce is the greatest civilizing power—it finds out new markets, discovers fresh sources of supply, opens up savage countries, and plants colonies in desolate places to develop products which science has found useful to man; free exchange develops the mechanism which carries to these places the con-

veniences of the most advanced countries.   The nitrate
deposits of Chili and the petroleum wells of Baku, the
gold-mines of Australia and the Transvaal, have drawn
large populations to districts previously almost un-
occupied; by the aid of commerce the various wants of
these populations are able to be satisfied from the
fruits of their specialized industries as easily as those
of the coal-miners of Wales, or the cotton-spinners of
Lancashire.

There are many natural impediments to trading which
are opposed to excessive specialization and the complete
appropriation of industries by any country.   While there
is great disparity in productiveness, yet most countries
can produce many things more conveniently than they
can import them.   Because two countries can produce
the same article it does not follow that trade in that
commodity will arise whenever one of them has a
natural advantage for its production; cost of carriage
will always form a kind of natural protection; distance,
mountains, and seas impose obstacles; differences in
language, in currency, in manners, and in thought
check direct trading; habit and connections tend to keep
trade in local channels; while some causes are expand-
ing trade others interpose barriers, with the effect that a
large number of industries will always of necessity be
local, or have a limited market.

It is sometimes asserted that by permitting complete
freedom in commerce a country may be undersold in *all*
its industries.   This is, however, an impossibility, since
it would imply importing without exporting; but trade
is exchange, the nation that buys must sell, the one
fact is the correlative of the other.   A nation with
nothing to offer cannot buy, and if foreign goods come
into a country some other articles must go out in exchange.   If goods "made in Germany" are plentiful in
Great Britain, goods "made in Great Britain, or purchased with British goods elsewhere", will correspond
to them in Germany; in other words, each nation pays
for its imports *directly* or *indirectly* with its own produce.   Trade depends upon a double demand, each
country's exports are *supply* to others, while to it they

are *demand* for the goods it seeks in exchange. It does not follow that the trade of Great Britain will balance with each country separately. Much trade is circuitous, and the settlement indirect. If Great Britain buys from the United States, the United States from India, and India from Great Britain, their respective debts may be set off against one another; the fact is, that the whole of a nation's imports are purchased by the whole of its exports, and not that its accounts with each country are separately balanced. Here comes in the service of money, and also the function of bills of exchange, which are part of the machinery of trade. Some persons imagine that in foreign trade goods are purchased with money, *i.e.* with gold; in the first place, this is not possible, since the gold does not exist in sufficient quantity to transact all exchanges, and if it were possible to obtain the gold the inconvenience and waste of power would prohibit the attempt. The whole of the gold currency in Great Britain would not provide for one-seventh of its foreign trade alone (£745,000,000 for the year 1897), if we disregard entirely the home trade, which is many times greater and much more directly dependent upon the use of metallic money.

As the United Kingdom does not produce the precious metals, the gold and silver which it employs are imported commodities. The total amount of gold which entered this country in 1895 for all purposes was £36,000,000, and about £21,300,000 was exported; of silver about £12,600,000 was imported, and £10,300,000 was exported during the year. Gold comes plentifully to Great Britain because of its wealth, its free-trading and vast commerce, and its free market for gold.[1] During the fifteen years ending 1895 the import of gold and silver exceeded the export by £77,000,000.[2] Since

---

[1] By the Coinage Act (1870) the British Government undertakes to coin freely and gratuitously *unlimited* gold, at the rate of £3, 17s. 10½d. per oz. of standard gold, which is called the mint price. The gold is purchased by the Bank of England, which acts as agent for the mint, charging 1½d. per oz. for its trouble. This unlimited free coinage constitutes a free market for gold such as does not exist in any other country.

[2] This flow of gold and silver to and from the United Kingdom is sufficiently illustrated by the statistics for five years:—

Great Britain receives much more of the precious metals than she parts with, it is manifest that she is not paying for her imports with money, but with goods, in fact she buys her gold with her merchandise. Trading is done in *terms* of money, that is, in price; gold is the measure and standard, but its transport is avoided as much as possible. And as in the internal trade of the country cheques and bills are estimated to perform some 95 per cent of the exchanges of the nation, so in foreign commerce exchanges are effected by means of bills. The operations are refined and technical; the result is that debts for goods are balanced against one another through the agency of credit documents representing money, and by the aid of the machinery of banking. Thus the foreign trade of the world is carried on with comparatively little metallic currency; goods are bought with goods, imports with exports, balances only being paid in gold.

Since imports are purchased with exports it might be expected that their values would balance one another, and as far as trading alone is concerned this is the case, but international relations are very numerous and complex, and involve many operations besides those of commerce which give rise to indebtedness. Great Britain is a maritime country, with a large mercantile fleet doing a considerable carrying trade for other nations all over the globe. About one-half the ocean commerce of the world is done in British vessels. This carrying trade creates an element of indebtedness, which

	GOLD.			SILVER.	
	Imports.	Exports.	Imports.	Exports.	
1891.	30,275,620	24,167,925	9,215,598	13,060,866	1891.
1892.	21,583,232	14,832,122	10,746,382	14,078,568	1892.
1893.	24,834,727	19,502,273	11,913,395	13,589,745	1893.
1894.	27,572,347	15,647,551	11,005,417	12,165,049	1894.
1895.	36,005,999	21,369,323	12,669,662	10,357,436	1895

TOTAL.

	Imports.	Exports.
1891.	39,591,218	37,228,791.
1892.	32,329,614	28,910,699.
1893.	36,748,122	33,092,018.
1894.	38,577,764	27,812,600.
1895.	46,675,661	31,726,759.

is discharged by the debtor-nations in produce. As an example, suppose a British vessel to carry out £1000 worth of coal to San Francisco and fetch back corn. Let the freight each way be £500. The export of coal from Great Britain will be set down at £1000, on arrival in America the value, enhanced by cost of carriage, will be £1500, and in addition another £500 must be sent to Great Britain to pay the return freight; thus £2000 of corn will be entered as imports, of which £1000 will come in payment for British coal and £1000 will be due for services rendered by British shipping. The additional imports are the earnings of a British industry, the exports do not include the cost of carriage, while the imports, which must include the goods sent to pay for carriage, will necessarily exceed the exports by that amount. The imports received in return for services of British vessels are estimated at about £60,000,000 per annum; this service has been significantly named by Sir Robert Giffen "invisible exports". Not only in foreign trade, but in the ordinary affairs of life, a large part of what is paid for is "service"; but, having none of the attributes of matter to obtrude itself upon the senses, service is apt to be forgotten, and to be overlooked as a factor in exchange, and especially is this the case in comparing values of imports and exports.

Another chief source of the discrepancy between imports and exports arises from the practice of investing capital in foreign enterprises. British subjects have lent to foreign countries vast sums, the interest on which is estimated at about £100,000,000 a year. It is probable that half that amount is reinvested abroad annually; the balance, about £50,000,000, comes in the form of imports, for which no corresponding export is required.

It has been maintained that this mass of imports for interest, while it benefits the investor who receives its value, is a loss to British working-men by competing with their products. The facts are, however, exactly the reverse; at every stage the labourer has shared in the employment and profit afforded by the foreign transaction. The original loans were made in the form of goods, such as railway iron, engines, machinery, clothing, &c.,

all manufactured by British capital and labour, and they were exported in vessels built with British capital and labour. The interest in the form of imports comes home in ships also constructed with British labour; and since these imports consist chiefly of food and material for our industries,[1] they are also beneficial to the working-classes. The imported food provides cheap necessaries, and augments thereby the *real* wages of labour, while the raw materials become the means of future employment in the manufacture of goods either for home consumption or for re-exportation; in the latter case they again employ the labour of those directly or indirectly engaged in the shipping industry. Since there is no scarcity of capital at home, the overflow, sent out as loans in the form of manufactured goods to develop other countries, is wholly an addition to the producing power of the world, and a source of employment, income, and profit to the British nation; it is not a displacement of labour, but an addition to industry and the means of enjoyment which it procures. The right conclusion is that the foreign trade and relations which arise naturally under free competition tend to add to the wealth of a country, and cause industry and capital to flow into the channels which are most lucrative.

Besides the two instances here given, many other relations give rise to indebtedness between countries; such are foreign travel, tribute, remittances of temporary residents, expenses of soldiers and sailors on foreign stations, of colonial government officials, &c. All the debts which arise out of these transactions, though expressed in terms of money, ultimately tell upon imports and exports. Nations do not waste unnecessary power in sending gold and silver to and fro; goods are the real things remitted, exchanged, and consumed in the long run. These various business relations, however, render the balance-sheet more complex, and obscure the simple truth that imported *goods and services* are paid for by exported *goods and services* through the instrumentality of credit documents, and that the pre-

[1] Of British imports about 70 per cent consist of food and materials for manufactures.

cious metals, though the basis and measure of value, play a relatively small part in the actual exchange.

An objection of a different kind may here be considered : it is charged against free-trading that it is in the interests of consumers only, and that producers are left to take care of themselves. The more correct statement, however, would be that it leaves both classes absolutely free to pursue their own interests by buying or selling how and where they choose; it deals out equal measure. Every man is at liberty to produce what he can, and the test of his fitness in the circumstances will be that the community will buy his article in preference to those of other competitors; if its quality and price are such as warrant its success, it will be for the good of the community; if the foreign article is preferred, the principle of comparative cost will show that its production at home would be an economic loss to the community. Again, if any class might claim special consideration, it would be the consumers, who are the more numerous body, seeing they comprise all, and their interests should considerably outnumber those of any group of producers who desire to foster their industry at the expense of the community; but a system which leaves both classes absolutely free cannot be said to favour either.

In a country where Free-trade has already been adopted, and matters are adjusted to its working, to set up Protection would be a method of imposing an unfruitful tax upon consumers; and where equal freedom prevails already no economic ground can be advanced for imposing such a useless burden. The same reasoning applies, only in a less degree, to the proposal to increase a tariff in a country where some degree of Protection exists; this is the case of the United States' tariff (1897), which has considerably increased many duties. But to remove a duty in a protective country is a much more difficult task, as the producers of the article will have acquired the right of a vested interest, and can represent that they committed their labour and capital to their industry with faith in the continuance of a system deliberately adopted and authorized by law. This is a chief difficulty in the way of tariff-reform, and one of the reasons why a country once committed to a protective policy continues to uphold that policy in spite of the great burden which it inflicts upon the consumers. When protection has been adopted for the purpose of starting certain manufactures, a large number of persons in the trades concerned would suffer immediate loss of employment and of capital by the sudden removal of the duties, under the shelter of which the industries were built up. Such persons are naturally vigorous in their efforts to maintain the duties, and they would have some real cause for complaint if, without compensation, they were sacrificed to a change of policy. So impressed with the strength of vested interests was Adam Smith that he doubted whether Free-trade would ever be adopted in Great Britain.

The old theory of trade favoured exporting and aimed at procuring markets; the obstacles to importation led to bounties and other expedients for finding a sale. It is important that a country should be able to dispose of the things which it can most profitably produce; under mercantilism the notion that gold was the most desirable import restricted trading, for there was a limited amount of gold to be procured, and the impediments placed upon other imports did not assist exporting. The fact is, that since importing and exporting are complementary operations, they mutually assist one another, and free imports stimulate exports. Buying implies selling. A country which is open to easy purchasing is more able to dispose of her own produce, for, since she must pay for her purchases, the countries which sell to her will be more disposed to look in her markets for the goods they are willing to import, and if such a country can offer desirable exports they will be more easily accepted. Also, vessels bringing goods to a country which offers a free market will endeavour not to return empty, and will stimulate exporting from such a country by offering low freights. Thus it comes that importing determines exporting, by making it more easy to find markets; it is perfectly true that exporting implies importing, for the exporter will require payment in some form; but it is the importer who takes the initiative, and who makes the market in the first place by his willingness to accept the goods. It would be useless to send goods to a country which would not, or could not, purchase them. Suppose China to determine upon a policy of railway development, and to send a large order to Great Britain for steel rails and steam-engines; the export of iron from Great Britain would lead to an import of produce from China or some country on which she gave us bills; but the prime fact in the whole proceeding would be, not exporting from Great Britain, but importing by China. China, desiring iron goods, would import them from Great Britain, and must be able to pay for them with exports of some kind. The transaction therefore would have its origin in China's desire for imports. It is an elementary economic truth that wants create desires, and these stimulate men to labour for their satisfaction; the fundamental fact is in the wants; and a country which, to satisfy her wants, is willing to import freely, will thus not only increase her imports, but her opportunities for exporting, as a means of paying for them, will be equally augmented. The converse mode of stating the same truth would be that a country which declines imports altogether would sell nothing abroad; every step towards prohibition is a step towards abolishing her export trade. The smoothest method of securing markets abroad for home goods is consistent therefore with a policy which offers the freest market to foreign goods for which they may be exchanged.

Chapter VI.

Arguments for Protection, Reciprocity, Bounties, &c.

Regarded historically and in its origin, Protection is not the outcome of a deliberate policy, adopted after careful weighing of economic arguments. It grew out of the restrictions incidental to early forms of society, and the restraints upon individuals inevitable in the unsettled conditions existing long prior to the modern industrial era; the jealousy of states during the period of their formation and consolidation, the growth of the sentiment of nationality, the need for resources (treasure) to carry on war, and the creation, by means of tariffs, of classes interested in the maintenance of restraints upon commerce, all helped to develop it.   Facts came before theory, and the principle of Protection as a beneficent institution was formulated to explain and support the customs and practices which had grown up.   Until late in the eighteenth century Protection was scarcely questioned as a guiding principle of statesmen; objections were raised to special restraints on commerce, or on freedom of individual action, rather than to the general principle.   The belief that it furthered the material interests of communities sustained the Protective doctrine until Adam Smith changed the stand-point by maintaining that the enlightened pursuit of individual interests harmonized with the national well-being.

In modern times the defence of Protection is undertaken either upon economic, or, more broadly, upon political grounds.   Protection is advocated either as promoting some existing branch of national industry and so securing employment for labourers; or as fostering some new trade which is expected ultimately to be a source of wealth, although it may involve a temporary loss to consumers and tax-payers; or it is demanded upon patriotic grounds as necessary to make the nation independent of foreigners, that it may be self-supporting in the event of war.   Both lines of defence are open to the charge that they are based upon imperfect observation of the whole of the circumstances, and that the conclusions deduced are consequently fallacious.   In examining more at length some of the current arguments for Protection, we shall find that they do not form a harmonious system, that some of them contradict others, and that nobody can consistently uphold them all.   For example, it is urged that a protective tariff will support the home industry by excluding the foreign article and yet raise revenue; that it will keep up prices and yet

benefit the labouring classes, whose real wages it would
by that means reduce; that it will prevent fluctuations
in trade and prices, by excluding foreign competition,
although it thereby creates a monopoly which is a frequent cause of fluctuations and high prices; that while
it is desirable to encourage invention in the interests of
cheapness, it is also beneficial to keep up prices by
tariffs.   These and other paradoxes appear on a survey
of the different arguments in favour of Protection.
They arise by confining the observation to some limited
portion of the industrial field, and identifying its prosperity with the national interest, while other effects are
overlooked.   Thus it comes about that a partial or
temporary effect is mistaken for the whole, and it is not
seen that a benefit in one direction is more than counter-
balanced by a greater loss in another direction, flowing
from the same cause.

Protection is said to encourage home industry by providing work for our own labourers in preference to
foreigners, and it is therefore claimed to be a patriotic
policy.   This statement, however, overlooks the fact
that imports are paid for with exports, and that therefore no goods can be imported unless home industries
are first employed to produce other goods with which to
purchase them.   A country with nothing to sell cannot
buy.   It must employ its labour therefore in producing
the wherewithal to purchase foreign commodities, and if
that labour be diverted to producing those commodities
at home, it will cease to be employed in producing the
other articles which were exported in exchange for them.
Now where there is no artificial direction, and trade is
free, the industries which are most profitable in natural
conditions will be those adopted; but the general effect
of duties imposed for the purpose of regulating trade
will be to direct the labour and capital from more productive to less productive industries.   Labour and
capital being then less efficiently employed, the country
will suffer loss.

To take an extreme case as an example: if Great
Britain were to insist by means of prohibitive tariffs on
making her people grow all their own corn, much labour

would be diverted to agriculture, and vast portions of inferior land would need to be cultivated. Since all imports of corn would now cease, the exports of cloth, machinery, &c., by which they are at present purchased, would cease also, and the industries which supply them would decline; the mercantile marine, which conducts the trade, would be unemployed, shipbuilding and other subsidiary industries, so far as they depend upon this branch of commerce, would collapse, and a vast army of unemployed artisans, now receiving high wages, would be driven to agriculture to provide a bare subsistence from a niggardly soil, or, what is more probable, they would leave the country in search of a better livelihood. The effect upon home industry would thus be disastrous.

The principle, as illustrated in the extreme case of prohibition, is equally valid when the attempt to protect agriculture is less complete; and the results would be proportionally hurtful in whatever degree Protection were applied to any other industry. The effect of a prohibitive duty is to divert industry from a more profitable to a less profitable channel; it creates no new capital, and does not add to production; but it displaces both capital and labour, and it tends therefore, not to increase employment, but rather to diminish employment. The contention that home trade is more profitable than foreign trade, because it employs the capital and labour of both industries at home, is answered by means of the above reasoning. Home trade is more profitable only when it grows up and goes on naturally, without forcing. But where capital and labour are directed to some special home trade by means of Protection, and an industry is fostered on which there would otherwise be loss, that is, where the article could be imported more cheaply, no economic benefit can accrue. If the circumstances of the country are such that it is cheaper to import than to produce a given article, labour and capital should be permitted to find their way to the production of other goods by means of which the desired import may be purchased.

Not infrequently protective duties are advocated as a source of revenue. Protection and revenue are, however,

incompatible aims,[1] since, in so far as Protection is successful foreign articles are excluded and no revenue is
obtained; whereas, if the articles are imported (paying
duty), to that extent Protection is not secured. But if any
revenue is raised the duty is not truly protective, since it
has obviously failed to prevent the goods paying revenue
from entering the country. Protection and revenue
cannot by the same measure both be secured successfully. The fallacy arises in two ways: (a) from confusing
protective duties with other indirect taxes levied on
imports, such as Great Britain places upon tea, wines,
tobacco, &c., but these duties are not protective, they
foster no home industry, their object is revenue; and
(b) because many protective duties are imposed which
fail to give complete protection; some goods are imported under duties not sufficiently high to exclude them
altogether, and then only part of the supply is produced
at home. The cost to the consumer is increased on the
whole of the supply—on the imported portion by the
amount of the duty, on the home-made portion by the
excess of the cost of production over the price at which
the article could have been imported duty free; some
revenue is raised from the imported portion, but none
from the home-made portion; the former is not excluded
by Protection, the latter raises no revenue; such a duty
cannot properly be described as either a protective or a
revenue duty, since it accomplishes neither satisfactorily.

In young countries indirect taxation levied upon imports is generally the most convenient mode of collecting revenue, since the population is spread over wide
and sparsely-settled areas. In such cases duties levied
on many articles, at first for convenience, tend afterwards to become partially protective; that is, industries
are commenced in the colony under the shadow of a
duty which raises the price of the imported article, and
they then supply in part some article which is still also
imported subject to the duty. At length the protected
industry may grow powerful enough to secure an in-

---

[1] "Taxes imposed with a view to prevent or even to diminish importation
are evidently as destructive of the revenue of the customs as of the freedom
of trade."—(Wealth of Nations, iv. 2.)

crease in the tariff sufficient to exclude the article altogether Such a duty is *prohibitive*; but it is obvious that
a duty may be so high as to check importation, and yet
not high enough to prevent it altogether, *i.e.* it may be
partially protective, or protect up to a certain level.   In
all protective countries many duties imposed are only
partially effective, some, but not all the foreign articles
being excluded.   The effect is to raise the price of the
article (whether produced at home or abroad) to the
level of the cost of production of the imported article
plus the duty.   The tax is obtained only from the imported goods; on those produced in the country no
duty accrues to the exchequer, but the consumer suffers
an economic loss as great as if the duty had been levied
on the total product.

Much of the popularity gained by protective proposals
seems to be founded upon the prejudice that foreign
trade on the side of imports is injurious, and an act of a
hostile character initiated by a rival.   If this view were
correct, what should be said of the export of British
goods to other countries?   The fallacy survives in many
current expressions.   "Foreign goods flood our country";
"Great Britain is the dumping-ground for foreign produce"; "An invasion of foreign commodities", are a
few of these question-begging phrases.   Behind these
and similar phrases there lurks the belief that the entrance of foreign products into a country resembles the
descent of a foreign foe upon its shores.   The false
analogy helps to maintain the belief, but the twofold
aspect of trade as exchange is forgotten.   Trade which
arises spontaneously is mutually advantageous; both
parties may be presumed to be studying their interests.
Imports are demanded to satisfy wants, and, as already
shown, they must be paid for by the produce of the importing country.   No nation will continue the process
of exchange unless it is beneficial; foreign goods will
not be sold in Great Britain unless they have something
to recommend them to British consumers, nor unless
British producers can export commodities to pay for
them.   If foreign goods "invade" our shores, British
goods must in return "invade" foreign territory.   Gain

must result to both parties from these peaceful invasions, or the exchange will not be continued.

It has been urged as another argument in favour of protective duties, more particularly in the United States and Australia, that such duties are a means of keeping up wages by excluding the products of what has been called the "pauper labour" of other countries. To this it may be replied, that if money-wages are kept up by this means so also are prices, and the cost of living is proportionally greater; so that real-wages (the commodities and comforts earned by a given amount of labour of the same kind) are not higher. Moreover, experience shows that the standard of living in free-trading Britain is not inferior to that of protective countries, but, on the contrary, distinctly higher than that of most such countries. Comparison of real-wages is very difficult, so many elements enter in, and the conditions of labour and of life are so different as regards hours, severity, cost of food and clothing, rent, means of health and rational enjoyment, &c. In young countries the demand for unskilled labour is plentiful, and such labour gets a high reward; but the skilled artisan living in towns, and paying high rents, does not find the same advantage.[1] Observation has yielded the empirical law, now generally accepted as an economic truth, that the best-paid labour is usually the most efficient, and that low prices may consequently co-exist with high real-wages. The United States tariff is directed principally against British manufactures, and yet it cannot be denied that British labour ranks with the best-paid labour in the world; while the high purchasing power of wages is, in no slight degree, owing to our system of free imports, that cheapens the commodities on which a considerable part of the wages of labour must be expended. Protective duties cannot

---

[1] Mr. Wise writes (*Industrial Freedom*, p. 306): "Personal inquiries from both masters and men have satisfied the writer that the highest grades of the class are less well paid, even in money wages, in Australia than they are in England;" and again (p. 215), "It is no uncommon thing to find among the passengers of homeward-bound steamers skilled English artisans who are returning to England because they cannot make the high wages that they used to earn in any part of Australia—not even in Protectionist Victoria".

therefore be advocated as being levied in the interests of the *real-wages* of skilled labour.

Sometimes it is suggested in support of a proposed tariff, that, if adopted, the foreign exporter will pay the duty. It has been argued, for example, that a duty of 5*s*. a quarter levied upon imported corn would be paid by the exporting country. From the Protectionist point of view this should have nothing to recommend it; for if the duty were paid, and the foreign article admitted, it could afford no protection to the home industry; such a duty becomes a revenue duty and not a protective duty. But the competition of many countries, and of many farmers in corn-producing countries, has long been effective in reducing prices and freights to a very low level, and this far-reaching competition tends to keep prices at a minimum, which leaves the sellers no adequate margin of profit out of which to pay any levy in the form of an import duty. In such circumstances a duty must raise prices, and will ultimately be paid by consumers either in the higher price of the foreign corn, or, if that be excluded entirely, in the increased cost of the home-grown corn which would take its place. It would become in any case a tax upon one of the necessaries of life, which is one of the worst forms of taxation. No one doubts that the import duties upon tea and tobacco are paid by the consumers of those articles; otherwise the demand for a remission of the tea-duty in the interests of the poorer classes is meaningless. Nor will it be maintained that the British manufacturers pay the high duties upon their goods sent to the United States or to Russia, which are in some cases nearly equal to the cost of the product; such duties are ultimately paid by the consumers in those countries. The fact that such goods are imported and are sold, proves that, though thus taxed, they are nevertheless preferred to the home-made articles, owing either to some excellence of quality or style which is wanting in the home products, or to the fact that, with the duty, they are as cheap as the home-made article.

It has been urged as a reason for imposing retaliatory duties, that manufacturers in certain countries are enabled by their protective tariffs to make so much profit on their home business as to permit them to send goods to Great Britain, which can there be offered at prices so low as to undersell British goods. No doubt in many trades there is occasional over-production, and surplus goods, unsaleable at home, are then shipped off to find a market in other countries at any price. But manufacturers making a large profit at home are scarcely to be credited with organizing their industries so as to secure a permanent loss by steady over-production. The passion for underselling will not lead to a regular business of an utterly unprofitable character. Also, an industry protected by a prohibitive tariff, and making profits so much above the average rate as the contention assumes, would soon create competition in its own country, which would lower profits. The export trade, however, would be impossible on other and more convincing grounds; for if a protective duty is required to enable the producers to force the sale of the native product in their own country, it is obvious that the competitor-country, against which the duty is levied, can produce more cheaply. How then can they compete successfully in a country that could undersell them *in their own market* if they were not sheltered by a tariff?

There can be little doubt that, as a general rule, the consumer of taxed goods pays the duty. An import duty may in some instances be shifted to the producing country. If the article be a luxury, such as champagne, which the consumer can discontinue, and he is already paying the highest utility price, a fall in the demand would be occasioned by the imposition of a higher duty. The seller might then be induced to forego part of his profit, and pay the tax by reducing the price rather than lose his market. This happens in the case of any taxed monopoly, where the monopolist has been charging the highest price he can secure. Whether the duty can be shifted from the importer to the exporter depends upon the effect of the duty upon the demand, and also upon the conditions of production in the country of supply. It is also possible that part of an import duty may be borne by a country which is compelled to find its market in the taxing country; but this is not a common case. Further, such a country would soon learn the lesson, and impose retaliatory duties upon the goods sent in payment. The effect of the struggle between the two countries to extract duties from each other would be, that each would be paying higher prices, together with the added cost of the machinery of collection. No real economic advantage would ensue to either. The incidence of taxation is sometimes very difficult to trace with absolute certainty, but it seems clear that duties on ordinary imports fall upon the countries imposing them. If such duties are of a protective nature, and are fixed high enough, they will exclude the foreign article entirely, and if the duties protect in any degree, they *so far* exclude the foreign article, and the consumer pays a higher price to cover the increased cost of producing the article in his own country.

It is very necessary to discriminate between the competition of nations in a neutral market and the mutual commercial intercourse of two nations; for the former is rivalry while the latter is not. In the former case each seeks to secure the advantage of extending its trade to a new area; each endeavours to sell its own goods for the products of the new country. The successful competitor will enlarge its trade at the expense of its rival. The competition of Great Britain and Germany, for example, in a neutral field like South America or China, is of this nature, and the country which gains the trade will expand its own industries thereby, and in exchange will secure fresh products for itself. The mutual trade relations of Great Britain and Germany, however, are not of this nature; it is not a condition of advantage to Great Britain that Germany should lose. They exchange the comparatively superfluous for the relatively desirable, thus satisfying one another's wants and increasing the total of utilities; each is an importer, each an exporter, and both derive advantage. The interchange of produce results in greater concentration upon special industries in the two countries, of much the same kind as that which determines most of the woollen trade to Yorkshire and the cotton trade to Lancashire;

but as there is no hostility in the trade relations of Yorkshire and Lancashire, so neither can trade between two nations, which consists in the mutual supply of conveniences, be properly described as hostile, or as other than beneficial.

A belief that nations trading with one another are engaged in a kind of warfare evidently lies at the root of the desire for "retaliation", which distinctly suggests the notion of paying back " blow for blow".   The belief finds expression in various forms: "They strike us with their tariffs, let us retaliate"; "We have thrown away our weapons, and in this warfare we have no guns with which to fight in the commercial struggle of nations"; and, "We have lost our power to bargain for a reduction of tariffs, we have nothing to offer"; and again, "Others take advantage of our Free-trading policy and give us nothing in return".   Lurking behind all such expressions stands the assumption that trading, so far as the purchaser is concerned, is a mistake; that its object is to get rid of products, not to obtain them.   The fact that the maximum advantage is sought on the easiest terms, which is the prominent feature in individual trading transactions, is ignored when the matter comes to be regarded from a national point of view and in the gross. The object of international, as of individual exchanges, is to obtain the commodities we need, and the goods we part with are merely instruments for gaining as much as possible of those we desire.   Now free importation conduces to this end, and its non-adoption by other nations does not preclude Great Britain from gaining its benefits.   Great Britain gains by allowing foreign goods to enter without impediment, whether other nations copy her example or not.   So long as Great Britain receives in return for her exports a quantity of desirable imports sufficient to cover the cost of production of her exports, she is a gainer by the trade, since she thus gets goods she requires at less cost than she could produce them herself, and, in fact, she gains much more than this, for she makes profit by trading, and carries on a lucrative business as shipper for both parties.   Foreign tariffs may curtail her advantage but cannot destroy it, for if loss occurred trade would cease.

Extreme advocates of reciprocity and so-called Fair-trade ask that we shall only trade with those countries which will accept reciprocal terms, and that we shall punish those who decline by excluding their goods. But while we may regret the methods of other countries, which injure us to some extent by limiting the total trade carried on, we shall not convert them to our views by adopting their methods, and shall only injure ourselves still further by refusing to continue commercial relations which we find profitable even under present conditions. Those who object to the British system of Free-trade as "one-sided Free-trade" fail to recognize the advantages it confers upon both consumers of imports and producers of exports, and are still under the influence of the doctrine which regarded exporting as more profitable than importing, or of that other fallacy which seems to assume that exporting without importing is either possible or desirable.

That we have parted with our means of bargaining for the remission of duties is a matter of little account, when we set against possible petty gains from mutual reduction of duties the enormous advantage of fifty years of free imports, as manifested in the prosperity of the country and in our high standard of living. Commercial treaties and diplomacy are indifferent substitutes for the higher advantages of complete freedom; they are but tentative measures, useful in mitigating the evils of restriction; but which, while securing only partial remissions, are liable to produce mischief or loss in other directions, owing to the jealousy they excite by the diversion of trade. Such treaties may be expedient in dealing with the countries whence we obtain our imports for revenue—wine and spirits, tobacco, tea, &c. The French treaty of 1860, negotiated by Cobden, in which Great Britain lowered the duties on French wines and brandy in return for relaxation of duties on English manufactures, proved that in becoming Free-traders we had not entirely parted with our power of gaining concessions by treaties; the lapse of the treaty and re-

version by France to a more protective *régime* shows
equally the want of permanence in such arrangements;
but the higgling for small concessions which treaties
involve, with all the troublesome details of tariffs, and
the expense attending administration would be superseded by the simpler system of general Free-trade with
its larger economic advantages.

All consumers, as such, prefer Free-trade, because they
know that, to buyers, open competition secures the best
article; but men are apt to become Protectionists when
their view is confined to their own sales. It is then
that they desire to monopolize the market for their own
special profit and not for the good of the nation. The
late Mr. Villiers, in his reply to the address presented
to him in June, 1896, on the completion of fifty years of
Free-trading, summed up the position in a single
sentence: "The land-owner, the ship-owner, the West
Indian merchant, all approve of Free-trade in what they
consume, but in the sources of their income and profit
there are no more staunch supporters of prohibitive law;
they are always reasoning as if the country were made
for them and not they for the country; and in their
ignorance they are ever blind to the fact that while they
seek to profit by the losses of others they are again
injured by a like injustice".

But retaliation in our case is a vain and futile hope.
Great Britain cannot afford to retaliate by taxing food
and the raw materials of her industries, which constitute
quite 70 per cent of what she imports;[1] she would only
starve or ruin herself by such a course, and she would
excite increased commercial hostility on the part of
nations which are already envious of her prosperity. If
it is worth considering, a further objection exists in the
difficulty of making retaliation effective. It is not necessary that trade should be direct. If French silk were
excluded from Great Britain by a high tariff, it might

---

[1] Even most advocates of Protection admit this. Friedrich List, the
author of a *National System of Political Economy*, wrote:—"A nation
which has already attained manufacturing supremacy can only protect its
own manufacturers and merchants against retrogression and indolence by
the free importation of means of subsistence and raw materials, and by the
competition of foreign manufactured goods".

yet enter through Belgium and Holland, while German goods we might wish to exclude could pass through Holland or Sweden. It is almost impossible to determine the country of origin and to make a workable scheme discriminating against the imports of particular countries; the only resource would be thorough-going Protection, which for us is as impossible as it is undesirable.

But, it is objected, a manufacturing nation might, at all events, tax the manufactured articles which enter the country. Now, our imports in 1896 were valued at £441,000,000; of these, food-stuffs amounted to £157,000,000, articles paying duty to £30,000,000, goods which may be classed as raw materials to another £157,000,000, and goods manufactured or in some stage of manufacture to £97,000,000. Some of these last are finished products, such as clocks, watches, French boots, hats, gloves, &c.; others are partly-manufactured goods, such as linen yarn, iron bars, leather, straw-plaiting, &c., all of which are utilized as materials for other British industries. The question has been raised as to what is a manufactured article and what is a raw material. Definition does not solve the practical question, it is entirely a matter of degree; for it might be maintained that every import which has passed through the hands of man, such as fleeces or raw cotton, has already passed through one stage of manufacture. Let us take the example of leather, of which we imported £7,500,000 in 1896. On examination we find that leather imports include hides tanned and curried or dressed, and goat and sheep skins dressed. The whole item might be treated as raw material for the purposes of British industry, since it is here converted into boots and shoes, harness, portmanteaus, and numerous other finished articles, of which, beyond her own consumption, Great Britain exports nearly £2,000,000 worth. The tendency is evidently for the rougher early processes of tanning to be carried out in countries where materials are abundant, and for British industry to be limited to the finer processes which call for greater skill and also afford a higher wage. The same remarks apply to timber, which is now generally imported from Canada

and Scandinavia sawn into given lengths and sizes, or
even advanced a further stage. The complexity of
modern production makes far greater subdivision of
employments, and this is furthered by the advantages
which situation offers for any process. It is thus impossible always to draw a sharp line between the raw
material and the manufactured article, for the latter is
the result of evolution progressing by many stages.
The finished article of one country or locality becomes
the raw material of another, just as bricks are the
materials of house-building; pig-iron, yarn, wire, zinc-
sheeting, and tin plates are the products of certain
industries and the raw materials of others. The country
which in this classification performs the final process,
becomes the finishing-shop; its work is more refined,
less arduous, and better paid; its skill is greater and its
subsistence is gained with less expenditure of toil; and
its finished products, when re-exported, pay for its imports both of raw materials and other consumable
articles. The world-wide organization of industry gives
greater efficiency to the labour of the whole world, and
this kind of efficiency is best promoted by the removal
of all impediments to trading.[1]

Among minor advantages alleged to accrue to a
nation from a protective duty, it is urged that the
protected industries are enabled to employ larger
capitals, and thus call into fuller play the law of increasing returns; also that Protection permits an industry to be started which, without such aid, would at
once be crushed out by the competition of established
organizations operating from foreign shores. As abstract
arguments these hypotheses are valid, and possibly

[1] No doubt it will be here pointed out that highly-finished machinery is
now being imported from the United States and Germany, and that Britain
is being attacked in her most vital part. Circumstances favouring foreign
competition with our staple industries are discussed in a subsequent chapter,
but it may be at once stated that for these Protection affords no antidote.
If the British mechanic allows himself to be surpassed in skill, intelligence,
or industry by others, or if he permits any restraints upon the full efficiency
of his working powers, so that he can no longer compete with foreign
industry, not only in the home markets but in the markets of the world,
neither Protection nor anything else can avail to maintain the supremacy
of British manufactures.

instances might be adduced of very exceptional circumstances in which the conditions would obtain. But in dealing broadly with the subject, while we may be prepared to admit the possibilities, we must recognize that the problems of trade are essentially *practical*, and cannot be kept within the limits of academic discussion. Capital is very plentiful, and highly-organized machinery exists for lending it; capital is easily tempted abroad, and affords opportunities for large production wherever an industry can succeed; but large production by the aid of cheap capital is best illustrated in Free-trading Britain. With regard to the second point, it has not been found that governments have shown either the capacity to discriminate between instances, or the strength to confine their favours to such exceptional cases of interference; they are prone rather to yield to general demands for interference, and indeed when once the principle has been admitted in any country, Protection has been applied all round without any reference to the conditions in which assistance might possibly afford an ultimate economic advantage to the community. The history of tariffs in young countries endorses the opinion aptly expressed by Professor Nicholson, that "Free-trade, like honesty, remains the best policy".

Bounties are a peculiar form of Protection. They were a device of mercantilism to encourage exportation. Under a system of trade which laid stress upon exports and the importance of securing a favourable balance in gold, bounties or premiums were given on certain branches of home industry to enable them to obtain markets abroad by lowering their prices. The bounty system is a natural complement to the system of placing duties on imports; both flourish together. As the latter excludes the cheaper foreign goods in order to protect articles produced at home, so the former subsidizes an industry which could not otherwise succeed in the country, the community being taxed for the amount given to the bounty-fed industry. The French and German sugar bounties are the most notable examples of bounties at the present day. One effect of the bounty-fed sugar industry in France, together with the

French prohibition of foreign sugar, is that sugar is 3*d.*
a pound cheaper in Great Britain than in France, while
the consumption is 86 pounds per head of population in
Great Britain compared with 25 pounds per head in
France. Again, the confectionery, biscuit, jam, marma-
lade, and sweet-drink trades have received an immense
stimulus in Great Britain owing to the advantage
arising out of the cheapening of sugar by foreign
bounties. Fruit gathered in Southern France is sent
to Great Britain in British steamers to be made into jam
with cheap French sugar, and such British-made pre-
serves are re-imported for French consumption. France
also gives a bounty of some 65 francs per ton on iron
and steel ships. These vessels could be bought from
the United Kingdom and the whole bounty saved; but
for the satisfaction of building them in France the
nation is taxed to nearly half their cost, ship-builders
alone being the gainers. Yet, according to *Lloyd's
Register*, in 1895 the United Kingdom launched merchant
shipping to the amount of 950,967 tons, while in the
same period France launched only 22,000 tons, and in
1896 Great Britain completed 1,159,751 tons of merchant
shipping, as against 365,000 tons by all other nations.
Some writers complain of the " disabilities under which
British shipping labours in competition with the vessels
of bounty-paying countries "; but it requires very slight
observation to perceive that the disability lies with
France in this matter; France has a natural disability in
the matter of materials and resources for ship-building,
which renders it more economic for her to purchase
than to build ships. If, in the circumstances, she
persists in building vessels by the aid of bounties, it
must be at the expense of the community which provides
the additional cost from taxation. It is a matter of
common knowledge that M. Thiers gave his support
to the sugar-bounty system with the remark that " he
wished to see the tall chimneys smoke ". To his
imagination these chimneys seemed evidence of manufacturing prosperity and a sign of increasing wealth to
France. The test, however, is not satisfactory when
we learn that such prosperity as it indicates is purchased

at the cost of heavy taxation to the remainder of the community. Of 3,000,000 tons of sugar produced on the Continent two-thirds are exported by the aid of bounties, the population pays this bounty, and for the remaining one-third which it consumes it pays more than it receives for all it exports. To find a market for the produce of sugar-refining by selling it to another country at less than cost of production cannot enrich a nation, though the loss may be obscured by the indirect methods of bounties, and the erection of refineries with smoky chimneys may give the appearance of additional employment.[1]

Meanwhile European sugar is practically excluded from the United States by a bounty on home-produced sugar and a 40-per-cent duty on imported sugar. The result is that a syndicate has been formed which controls about 80 per cent of the supply of sugar consumed in the States. It is strong enough to fix its own price, and

[1] The report of the West India Commission (issued October, 1897) gives the latest information about the sugar-bounty system and its effects.

Germany pays an export bounty of 25s. a ton, and has a protective customs duty of £10 a ton. France gives a bounty of 90s. a ton, and has a protective duty of £24 a ton. In both countries there is an excise duty equal to the amount of the customs duty, which, under the monopoly, the producers recover in the price. The effect is that on the Continent sugar is 3d. or 3½d. a lb. dearer than in England.

It is calculated that the cost to consumers from the continental system in Germany, France, and Austria amounts to £47,000,000 a year, and that those countries pay in bounties £5,000,000 a year. Deducting from the total cost the excise of £20,000,000, this leaves a loss of £32,000,000 for the three countries.

Between 1882 and 1896, the period during which the continental bounty system has been in full operation, the world's production of sugar has increased from 3,799,284 to 7,474,000 tons, and prices have fallen quite one-half. The fall is explained as mainly due to reduced cost of production, and in British Guiana, where the latest improvements have been adopted, the price of cane-sugar has fallen from £16 a ton to £8 and £9 a ton. But these improved methods are not generally adopted throughout the West Indies. Of the total exports (£6,106,000) of the West Indies, one-half (£3,250,000) consists of cane-sugar, and this is threatened by the continental competition of beet-sugar. The commissioners reject the proposal to give a bounty on West Indian sugar, and two out of three reject also the proposal of countervailing duties, while the third recommends a duty of one halfpenny per lb. This, on the average consumption of 80 lbs. per person in the United Kingdom, would mean 3s. 4d. per head of population, or £6,500,000 a year. Other suggestions point to more direct aid in encouraging other industries in the West Indies and to developing the other resources of these colonies.

has made a profit of about £5,000,000 a year.   In such
stupendous monopolies we have a natural fruit of Protection.   In Great Britain, however, owing to her Free-
trade system, these syndicates have had little success in
raising prices.   They have to encounter, sooner or later,
the consequence of the large area of supply which open
competition creates, and which responds to the certainty
of a free market.   The area is too vast to be readily
brought under the control of a single combination in the
case of a necessary of life.   Trusts exist in Great Britain,
but their tendency is to steady production and effect
economy and cheapness by the organization of the industry and the distribution of the product on a larger
scale.   The safeguard is in free competition.   A similar
economy, accompanied by a fall in price, is claimed for
the American Standard Oil Trust, which has, however,
to compete with all other illuminants, and finds a large
market in Europe only by its cheapness.

The working of the bounty and protective system has
recently been illustrated in Argentina.   Following the
lead of other countries, Argentina imposed a heavy duty
on imported sugar, amounting to some £18 a ton.
Consequently sugar-planting received a great impulse,
so that the production soon began to exceed the home
consumption.   It was necessary then to find a fresh
market, and the experiences of France were repeated
almost exactly.   The Government placed an internal
duty upon sugar, and gave a drawback on its exportation which amounted to a bounty.   This was a further
influence favourable to planting, and production again
went on rapidly until it was found to have greatly exceeded the consumption.   The sugar manufacturers are
now (1897) attempting to form a trust to deal with the
surplus, to force sales abroad (of course at a loss) and
to check production at home.   Such are the difficulties
which arise when the natural progress of industry is
interfered with to foster a special trade.

It is often maintained that Great Britain ought to
"countervail" the bounties of other countries by imposing duties equal to the bounties, and frequent efforts
have been made to secure this kind of legislative inter-

ference on the grounds that our industries are unfairly opposed by assisted competition. The attempt of this mode of retaliation, if made, would most probably not be successful, for the bounties might easily be augmented, and it is exceedingly difficult to ascertain their exact amount and actual effect on trade.

But a fatal objection to countervailing duties is, that we cannot draw a clear distinction between them and protective duties; all aim at raising prices by state intervention. Countervailing duties are a form of retaliation upon bounties in favour of some other source of supply.

Bounties, tariffs, differential duties, and countervailing duties are all alike interferences with production or consumption. If England adopted countervailing duties against continental sugar bounties, she would enter once more into the conflict of adjusting tariffs—an expensive and disturbing process, and there would be no limit to the attempts to exclude foreign goods on some pretext or other. In fact, the principle of non-intervention being surrendered, the path would be opened for the re-introduction of all kinds of interference. If, for example, this kind of protection were afforded to the British sugar industry against French and German bounties, the farmers might reasonably demand like treatment for corn against the low rates of American railways, or "the unfair fertility" of superior foreign soil. Many similar claims could easily be sustained, for bounties are given in a variety of forms, the natural and artificial shade into one another, and cannot be clearly discriminated. Some countries give bounties in money, some in drawbacks or exemption from taxation, some in free grants of land; in some countries the state undertakes the organization of an export, as in the case of Australian butter; some give subsidies to steamship companies and to railways, which reduce the cost of transport. All in some degree, difficult to estimate, tell upon the price of the goods exported, and so far cheapen them to the importing country at the expense of the exporting country.

The principle of Free-trade is easily grasped; it interferes neither with producer nor consumer; its merits are obvious and can be followed; the perplexities of the tariff system are endless, and the injuries it inflicts are too serious to admit of any trifling with schemes which would lead to the possibility of their recurrence. Movements in that direction, however plausible, are only Protection in disguise.

Chapter VII.

Fifty Years of Free-trade.

The essence of the Protectionist contention is that articles excluded by tariffs will be produced *at home*, and thus home industries will be encouraged. The weakness of this contention, so far as it fails to recognize the advantage obtained from the exchange of products in foreign trading, is examined in the previous chapter. We shall deal with only one question here. Did the protective system, during the thirty years of its application to agriculture, feed the people of this country? The labourer who exclaimed, "I be protected and I be starving!" summed up the results of the Corn-laws on this point. The history of the thirty years from 1815 to 1845 is a continuous record of distress; periods of scarcity and privation, fluctuating prices alternately starving labourers and ruining farmers, bread riots and disturbances, in manufactures uncertainty and loss. At length a famine in Ireland, following closely upon manufacturing depression and starvation in Great Britain, terminated the system devised to secure an abundant home-supply of food at steady and profitable prices. No principle could have received a fuller trial, and none could have failed more completely. With a population less than half the present population of Great Britain, the condition of the people was such that multitudes, daily employed in the occupation of rearing cattle and growing corn, rarely tasted any meat except bacon, and many could not earn sufficient bread to maintain their own families in health and energy.

The test of a principle is in its *total effects*, not in any partial or peculiar advantage to individuals; every monopoly benefits the holder, but it does this at the expense of others; and if we inquire into the results of the Corn-laws, we find they were a cause of great misery, want, and suffering to a large proportion of the community, and of loss and injury to many others.[1] The abolition of the restrictions gave immediate relief, an era of prosperity began, and fifty years of free-trading show no such instances of suffering and distress as those which preceded it. On the contrary, the progress of the nation in comfort and material well-being has been continuous and marvellous. Fluctuations have accompanied the advance; the Crimean War, the American Civil War, and other misfortunes have imposed checks, but the outcome of the change is that Great Britain is the best-fed country on the globe, although it is the country which produces the smallest proportion of its own food. Common observation reveals the fact that the lot of the working-man has entirely changed, and that his economic condition in the present day would be an enviable one to those circumstanced as were the labouring classes of the early forties. Statistics of wages and prices show that, with easier work and shorter hours, a labourer gets now about 65 per cent, factory operatives 75 per cent, and a skilled mechanic 90 per cent more of necessaries than he did fifty years ago. Sir R. Giffen has stated that nearly the whole of the economic advantage of the last fifty years has gone to the working-classes, that is, their position has not only changed absolutely as regards the comforts of life, but relatively as regards other classes in their share of the general prosperity.[2]

[1] As already stated (chap. iii.), various causes of distress operated during the first forty years of the century—bad harvests, the war, with its burden of taxation and debt, the Poor-law, which, until 1834, fostered an idle and inefficient population—the rapid changes in manufactures also dislocated industry. The Protective system accentuated all the evils arising from these various causes, created scarcity of food, and prevented the means of profitable employment.

[2] " Hence, while capital has increased, the income from capital has not increased in proportion. The increase of earnings goes exclusively, or almost exclusively, to the 'working-classes'". . . . " What has happened to the working-classes in the last fifty years is not so much what may be called an

This wonderful transformation is of course not to be
assigned exclusively to the Free-trade movement; the
marvellous progress of science, the conquest of man
over the forces of nature, and their subjection to his
purposes, are features of the century which need no
detailed enumeration to remind us of their vast import.
But the reform of 1846 and the subsequent fiscal changes
were factors of the deepest importance in the scientific
development and industrial progress of this country; and
the Free-trade movement may be credited with rendering
possible the freest application of scientific discovery and
invention, so as to lead the nation to a standard of life
hitherto inconceivable.

As a self-supporting country Great Britain must have
continued to devote the chief part of her labour and
capital to obtaining food from her soil; and we have
seen what was the average of comfort when that was
attempted. Her population must have remained smaller,
and her resources in other industrial directions could not
have been utilized.   Under Free-trade she was enabled
to give full play to her mechanical and manufacturing
genius and reap the full advantage of her mineral wealth,
relying upon an abundant supply of cheap food in exchange for her other products. The abolition of hindrances to trade gave to the nation fresh possibilities,
and called into activity the energy and skill by which
they could be realized.   The scientific discoveries and
wonderful inventions which have enriched Great Britain
through her various industries, and have even made agriculture a mechanical industry to some extent, could never
have found an opening in this country; the vast industries of coal, iron, machinery, of cotton and wool, &c.,
could never have been developed under a system which
compelled the country to produce its own food, and excluded the agricultural products which are now purchased by means of these industries. Free-trade was
therefore a necessity prior to the full and profitable ex-

improvement as a revolution of the most remarkable description."—("On
the Progress of the Working Classes"—*Financial Essays*, vol. ii.)   See also
Labour in the Longest Reign, pp. 9–16, by Sidney Webb, for similar testi-
mony as regards men in organized trades.

pansion of those industries which have enriched Great Britain during the last fifty years. The industrial revolution, with its mechanical inventions, factory-system, and the steam-engine, began its operation more than fifty years earlier, but the masses were, notwithstanding, poor and half-starved until the advent of Free-trade.

The Free-trade movement really involved at root much more than the revoking of the Corn-laws and the reform of our fiscal system, though these were the actual matters about which it was definitely fought out and decided. It meant the adoption of the idea of enlarged opportunity for enlightened individual action, and for true freedom of contract, both as regards trade and labour, on the largest and fullest scale possible. Adam Smith had advocated "natural liberty" in this sense; he contended for the removal of all restrictions which operated injuriously, he urged the justice of workmen's combinations and the necessity for education as a means of conferring higher freedom and opportunity, as well as the removal of protective tariffs and bounties on food. Errors sometimes arise in regard to Free-trade among its most ardent devotees owing to a too narrow interpretation of its doctrine. Having for its aim the promotion of the wealth of nations, in principle it would apply to any measure, which, by removing obstacles to trade in any direction, makes for that end. Commercial treaties (in the absence of fuller measures) are consistent with the spirit of Free-trade, which is one of peace and good-will, displacing jealousy and warfare by means of friendly business relations. Arrangements between nations, involving " give and take " of many kinds, recognize mutual interests; in various ways the world is being educated to appreciate the advantages of improved intercourse and enlarged markets. International communication (through telegraph, post, travel, newspapers, and financial relations) all point to the advantages of diminished friction. It is difficult to believe that artificial obstacles to the full enjoyment of nature's products can be permanently maintained. So long as the pressure is not felt acutely the burden may be tolerated, but there are many evidences that sections of other nations smart

under a consciousness of the injury inflicted upon them
by tariffs on foreign merchandise.

Great Britain, with her growing population, found the
pressure of tariffs upon food intolerable in a time of
scarcity, and the lesson of the economic advantage of
free exchange was brought home to her by the most
impressive kind of teaching that could be conceived.
No other country has had the principle enforced in the
same manner, and those who in protective countries
fully realize its worth are confronted with the difficulty
of dealing with interests which would suffer loss if the
tariff-fed manufactures of those countries were suddenly
placed in competition with the products of other countries.   But the trend of events is towards universal
trading.   The boundaries of race and nation are being
effaced in the operations of exchange, and gradually the
economic area will expand to comprise the whole productive world.   Science cannot continue to bring nations
nearer together, bestowing fresh gifts of wealth and
power upon all, without at length the fact dawning upon
them that to resist nature's generosity, by imposing artificial limits upon the acceptance of her lavish productiveness, is much the same as to refuse to enjoy the use of
steam-power, or to deny themselves the fruitful discoveries of electricity.

Statistics of wealth, commerce, rates of wages, savings, consumption of food, &c., of shipping, revenue,
and of the expansion of the great staple trades, give
indubitable evidence of the vast advance in comfort of
the nation since the abolition of the protective *régime*.
In considering these figures we must remember that
though young countries, like the United States and
Australia, rich in natural gifts, and fed with streams of
emigrants from Great Britain, have advanced rapidly
during the past fifty years, their progress starts from a
comparatively recent date, while that of Great Britain is
the growth of a more mature and relatively populous
country.   To compare their progress in some respects
with that of Great Britain would be to compare the
growth of the child with that of the man.   Taking note
of like circumstances, no country has made the same

relative progress as Great Britain during the past fifty years.

In 1840 the population of the United Kingdom was 26½ millions, it is now nearly 40 millions, living at a vastly higher level of comfort. The population had grown rapidly from 1800 to 1840 under the stimulus of the new factory industries and under the influence of the Poor-laws, which practically gave a bounty on births, but the standard of living had not advanced; with the removal of restrictions on trade, improvement began, and it has proceeded at an accelerated rate. Meanwhile the nation has supplied the Colonies and the United States with some millions of its able-bodied offspring as emigrants, and has further provided hundreds of millions of capital from its savings to enable them to develop the newer regions in which they have settled. Although the population of Great Britain increased 50 per cent (from 12½ millions to 18¾ millions) between 1811 and 1841 the export trade made no progress: it declined from 1815 to 1836, and had barely recovered by 1844.[1] In 1845 our total foreign trade (imports and exports) only amounted to £160,000,000, or less than £5, 15s. per head of the population, and the exports were greater in value than the imports. The effect of the repeal of the Corn-laws was an immediate increase in our foreign trade; the exports for the twenty-five years following 1845 were nearly three times those of the preceding twenty-five years, though some of this increase must be attributed to the effects of the gold discoveries. By 1854 this commerce amounted to £268,000,000, and the imports exceeded the exports by £32,000,000. In 1896 the total foreign trade had grown to £738,000,000, being £18, 10s. per head of the population, and the imports were in excess of the exports by £130,000,000. This large surplus, which has been annually increasing for

[1] See Porter's *Progress of the Nation*, pp. 361-362.

DECLARED VALUE OF EXPORTS OF THE UNITED KINGDOM.

1815,	...	...	...	...	...	...	£51,632,971
1821,	...	...	...	...	...	...	38,870,851
1831,	...	...	...	...	...	...	47,020,658
1844,	...	...	...	...	...	...	58,584,292

more than forty years, is practically all profit to Great
Britain, arising from interest on foreign investments,
profits on trading, earnings of British vessels, &c.

The increase in money values of our foreign trade
does not fully represent, however, its real magnitude;
the general fall in prices during the last quarter of a
century should be taken into account, in which case the
business would need to be estimated at probably some
50 per cent more.   A better idea, perhaps, of the magnitude of our foreign trade is gained from the statement
that it is more than the total foreign trade of Germany
and the United States together, and that while it
amounts to £18 per head of the British nation, the
foreign trade of Germany is only £7 per head of its
population, and that of the United States is £4, 10s.   It
must be remembered that in this immense trade 70 per
cent of the exports are manufactures, and an equal proportion of the imports consists of agricultural produce
(food and raw materials), and that the industrial interchange has been stimulated by the removal of impediments to free exchange.   Great Britain possesses about
30 per cent of the commerce of the world in manufactures, while France and Germany jointly control about
an equal amount.

Consequent upon this enormous growth of business
with distant parts, and under the same stimulus of free
enterprise, another vast source of wealth has grown up
in our ship-building and carrying trade.   Great Britain
owns more than half the tonnage of the mercantile shipping on the globe, and does more than half the conveyance of goods by sea.   During the last fifty years her
carrying power has grown fourteen-fold, her sailing tonnage (2,189,000 tons) is only slightly greater than that
of 1840, but her steam tonnage has been developed from
an insignificant amount to more than 10,213,000 tons,
about 55 per cent of the steam tonnage of the world.
Her ships employ a quarter of a million of seamen,
ship-building has become one of her most thriving and
highly-paid industries, and during the last fifteen years
has annually added to her mercantile sea power some
600,000 tons.   It will be seen that this great expansion

has taken place *since* the repeal of the Navigation Acts in 1849, and it is under the system of free competition that the United Kingdom has become the general carrier of the world, and that her commercial navy has grown in so remarkable a degree. Meanwhile under protective tariffs the United States shipping has declined, until only 23 per cent of her foreign trade is carried in her own vessels. Out of a total tonnage on the globe of 25,907,451 tons the United Kingdom and her Colonies possess 13,482,876 tons, the United States comes next with 2,326,838 tons, Germany has 2,029,912 tons, and France with bounties on both ship-building and freights possesses only 1,162,382 tons.[1]

Railway development and home trade have run parallel with that of iron ship-building and foreign commerce. Railways were in their infancy when Queen Victoria ascended the throne. In 1845 only 2400 miles had been laid in the United Kingdom, fifty years later this had increased to 21,174 miles. The enormous traffic is one further proof of the prosperity of the nation; in 1896 the passengers conveyed numbered 981,603,296, the goods amounted to 356,468,009 tons. The British railways, created by voluntary enterprise, represent wealth valued at more than £1,000,000,000. No doubt the railways, roads, canals, may be said to be concerned with the internal development of the country; they have been necessitated, however, by the manufacturing expansion which received so strong an impulse from the new conditions of trade. Internal transport is a needful accessory to commercial development, with its elaborate specialization and localization of industry, and the extent of the machinery of transport is an indication of the degree to which this differentiation has been carried.

If we next glance at the textile trades (cotton, wool, flax, silk, hemp, and jute), we find our factories employing more than one million operatives, and manufacturing one-fourth of the raw materials produced in the world. Thus we provide about one-fourth of the clothing ot civilized races from materials which, with the exception

---

[1] Statistics from *Lloyd's Register of British and Foreign Shipping*, 1897–8, quoted in *Whitaker*, p. 728.

of wool and flax, are entirely imported from other
countries. In the interval since 1846 these various industries have increased not only in extent and value, but
in efficiency and output per man. During the last fifty
years the total value of the manufactured products of all
the textile trades has grown from some £90,000,000 to
about £190,000,000 per annum. Between 1854 and
1895 the import of raw wool increased from 104·9 to
771 million lbs. The cotton trade alone daily pays in
wages £100,000 and turns out 14,000 miles of cotton
cloth. At present we consume at home a little more
than half the cotton goods manufactured and export the
remainder.[1] With some vicissitudes due to various
causes, such as the American Civil War (which checked
the supply of cotton), to the construction of mills in
India, to the natural development of the cotton industry
in other countries, and to the fluctuations arising from
the dictates of fashion in dress materials, &c., this large
section of our staple employments has gone on increasing
its consumption and advancing in value and importance.
Wages have risen, the standard of living of the artisans
employed has considerably improved, and there have
been no such periods of depression as that of 1842, when
half the spinners of Stockport failed, and thousands of
operatives were standing in the streets. The cotton
famine of 1862–1863 has been the sole serious inter-
ruption, and this was due to a definite cause, beyond
the reach of economic foresight.[2]

The great expansion of the manufactures of Great
Britain has been accompanied by a proportionate development of her industries in coal and iron, as in turn the
prosperity of the manufactures are dependent upon these
natural resources. It is by means of their joint results
that payment is made for the enormous amount of food-
stuffs which annually enters the kingdom. In 1840 the
output of coal was about 30 million tons; in 1896 about
195 million tons were raised, this output being valued
at £57,231,000. The whole mineral wealth produced

[1] For some interesting statistical details of progress see Mulhall's *National Progress in the Queen's Reign.*
[2] Consumption of raw cotton by Great Britain in average periods of five

was worth £76,601,000, and 838,000 men were employed
in its extraction.   More than 40 million tons of coal are
now exported yearly.   The production of iron has increased between 1835 and 1896 from ¾ million tons to
8½ million tons.   Great Britain exports annually about
4 million tons of iron and steel goods.   The annual
value of iron and steel manufactures is £115,000,000,
and the increase in value continues in spite of the
enormous reduction in cost which has been caused by
recent inventions and new processes.   Machinery, cutlery, tools, steel rails, engines, and apparatus of various
kinds form a considerable part of our exports, as well
as of the provision for the demands of home industries,
and employ skilled artisans at several times the amount
they could possibly earn in agriculture if Great Britain
were a self-supporting country.   The only extensive
industry which has not advanced during the Victorian
era is agriculture; the causes of this exception are of
sufficient interest and importance to call for discussion
in a separate chapter.

years, and exports of piece-goods and yarns, from Ellison's *Annual Review
of the Cotton Trade* for 1895:—

CONSUMPTION BY GREAT BRITAIN.

			Export of Piece-goods.
1841–45.	521,300,000 lbs.	1840.	790,600,000 yards.
1856–60.	947,300,000 ,,	1850.	1,358,200,000 ,,
1861–65.	628,600,000 ,,	1870.	3,252,800,000 ,,
1871–75.	1,228,600,000 ,,	1890.	5,124,200,000 ,,
1881–85.	1,444,100,000 ,,	1895.	5,033,400,000 ,,
1891–95.	1,579,400,000 ,,	1896.	5,218,248,000 ,,

WOOL.

Raw Wool Imported.			Export of Yarns.
1854.	104,900,000 lbs.	1840.	118,500,000 lbs.
1870.	259,400,000 ,,	1850.	131,400,000 ,,
1880.	461,000,000 ,,	1870.	187,700,000 ,,
1890.	629,200,000 ,,	1890.	258,400,000 ,,
1895.	771,000,000 ,,	1895.	252,100,000 ,,

UNITED KINGDOM.

Coal Raised.			Pig-iron Produced.
1870.	110,431,000 tons.	1870.	5,963,000 tons.
1880.	146,969,000 ,,	1880.	7,749,000 ,,
1890.	181,614,000 ,,	1890.	7,904,000 ,,
1895.	189,661,000 ,,	1895.	7,703,000 ,,
1896.	195,400,000 ,,	1896.	8,660,000 ,,

There are many other proofs of the national prosperity and progress during the fifty years, that can easily be made visible by the use of statistics, a few of which may be indicated. It is computed by official statisticians that the capitalized wealth of the United Kingdom has increased since 1840 from about £4,000,000,000 to £11,806,000,000; that is, from £155 to £295 per head of the population, and many facts tend to show that the wealth is widely diffused. The value of house property alone has increased nearly fourfold; and since the character of its housing is a very real test of the comfort of a people, it is of interest to observe that the proportion of houses rented at sums above £20 has increased from 7 to 20 per cent of the whole in the same period. The income-tax, reimposed by Sir Robert Peel in 1843 as a means of remitting taxes on commodities, was then assessed on property and incomes valued at £250,000,000, and each penny then yielded £800,000 of taxation. In 1895 it was assessed on £700,000,000, and each penny produced £2,200,000.

Increase of business calls for an enlargement of the special machinery for effecting exchanges and payments. The expansion of banking thus forms an excellent index of the growth of commerce; the deposits and capital of the banks of the United Kingdom have advanced between 1840 and 1895 from £132,000,000 to £1,111,000,000; that is, from £5 per head to £28 per head of the population. In the same period the accounts settled by the Bankers' Clearing House have advanced from £950,000,000 to more than £7,000,000,000. With this great development of general banking there has been a corresponding addition to Savings-bank deposits; these increased between 1841 and 1897 from £24,500,000 to £176,000,000. In 1861 Post-office Savings-banks were devised to carry thrift to the doors of all classes, and there are now some eight million depositors in Savings-banks of all kinds in the United Kingdom. Meanwhile other openings for investments have been brought within the range of the working-classes, not only in building clubs, co-operative, trade, and friendly societies (the deposits in which, together with the Savings-banks

deposits, amount to more than £280,000,000), but the
system of joint-stock enterprise with limited liability,
which has proved a most potent instrument for converting labourers into capitalists, has enabled large numbers
of workmen to become owners of shares in municipal
stock, gas and water companies, railway companies, and
various industrial enterprises.

In the budget speech of 1897 the chancellor of the
exchequer stated that during the Queen's reign the
National Debt had been reduced by £175,000,000, while
the revenue had risen from £52,000,000 to £112,000,000;
meanwhile taxation had been so reduced and its incidence rearranged, that, while a labourer earning 13s. 2d.
a week paid 43s. 3d. a year in taxes in 1841, he would
now pay only 12s. 3½d. a year.

Perhaps in no way can the advance in the material
condition of the masses be indicated with more assurance than by their consumption of necessaries. As the
rich may be assumed to have had always a sufficiency
of necessaries, a reduction in prices would affect only
their consumption of luxuries, and not of necessaries;
any increase in the average consumption of ordinary
commodities therefore has arisen from a larger consumption by those classes who formerly had an inadequate supply; the addition, though spread over the
whole population by an average, is really in the lower
grade of incomes. Between 1840 and 1895 the average
consumption of wheat, corn, and flour in the United
Kingdom has grown from 290 to 360 lbs. per head, of
meat from 75 to 110 lbs. (and meat in 1840 was to the
labouring classes mainly bacon), of sugar the consumption rose from 15 to 88 lbs., of tea from 1¼ lbs. to
5¾ lbs., of tobacco from ·86 lbs. to 1·7 lbs. If Ireland,
which only consumes 40 lbs. per head of meat, be
omitted, the consumption of meat by Great Britain
becomes 120 lbs. per head, which is far in excess of
that of any other European country: Germany con-
suming 75 lbs., France 70 lbs., and Belgium 56 lbs. per
head. The consumption of imported butter, bacon,
cheese, and eggs has been multiplied tenfold in the
fifty years. If diet, as asserted by medical authorities,

be a chief determining factor in the endurance and efficiency of labour, there can be no doubt as to the advantage possessed by British workmen of to-day over those of the protective era, and also over the labourers of most other European countries at the present time.

It was on January 1st, 1840, that the penny post was introduced, taxes on advertisements were abolished in 1853, and on newspapers in 1855, the duty on paper was removed in 1861, the Education Act for England was passed in 1870. It is difficult to realize the full benefits of these measures, all of a character removing restrictions upon knowledge and communication, and all steps in the development of individual freedom. There was no daily paper published outside London in 1841, now the daily issue of papers in the United Kingdom is about seven millions. The average number of letters per head of population in the United Kingdom was in 1839 only three, and in 1895 it had risen to fifty-three, for England alone it was eighty per person. The mass of cheap literature, which now appeals to a reading public, speaks both for education and for leisure. A free press, untaxed papers and advertisements, free education, and means of extending those opportunities for gaining knowledge, which have formed so considerable an element in the progress of the nation, have removed some of the most effectual barriers between different classes, and have tended to promote a feeling of the common claims of humanity.

Among other significant changes, which have followed upon the improvement in material condition, is the steady diminution in crime, convictions having latterly fallen to about one-third of the number in 1840, although the population has increased fifty per cent; pauperism has also been reduced one-half. Better food, improved dwellings and sanitation, and reduction in the severity of labour under modern conditions have told favourably upon health and the duration of life; the death-rate has fallen materially, sickness is diminished, and human life has been prolonged. Very real evidences of the substantial improvement in the condition of the masses are to be found in the abbreviation of the hours of labour

(for British labourers work fewer hours than those of
any other country), in the increase of holidays and
excursions, and the dress and manners of the people.
We read, for example, in a recent Oldham newspaper:
"Holiday club subscriptions for seaside, &c., amounted
this year to £150,000. Nearly every factory and public-
house has its club, and the average takings are £750 a
year". The contrast with the descriptions of the same
district in 1842 is very significant. The multiplication
of free public libraries and newsrooms, of which there
are now more than 200 in the country, is a further
addition to the comfort and well-being of the industrial
classes.

Hospitals and dispensaries for the free treatment of
disease have increased, and subscriptions for their support, received from all classes, indicate not only the
growth of sympathy and social sentiment, but the existence of a surplus upon which the benevolent feelings
can operate. The Metropolitan Hospital Sunday Fund
alone has raised for this purpose some £900,000 in
twenty-five years. In Burdett's *Hospitals and Charities*
for 1897 we read that the working-men of Wigan contributed £58·24 per 1000 of the population to their
hospital, Wolverhampton £41·73, Birmingham and
Sunderland each £30·1. These are suggestive facts
indicative alike of material progress, regard for health,
and the increase of that consideration and sympathy
with suffering which mark an advance in refined feeling.

The amount expended by the working-classes upon
athletics is a proof of a different kind, but a forcible
one, that they have both energy, time, and money to
spare. A starving people has neither the spirit nor the
means for sport. During the first half of this century
our working-classes had little to spend on amusements.
The healthful pleasures of football, cricket, cycling, and
boating are no monopoly of the rich in this country; and
indeed the very extensive industries called into existence
by cycling alone are sufficient to demonstrate that a very
large proportion of the community is able to secure, not
only the necessaries, but some share in the luxuries of
life and in its amusements. Again, theatres and con-

cert-rooms multiply at a very rapid rate, especially those which cater for the working-classes. We learn from statistics that while, during the last fifteen years, teachers have increased 15 per cent, shopkeepers 27, bank-clerks 30, commercial clerks 34 per cent, the class of public entertainers has been augmented 50 per cent.

Thus in every field of observation there is most convincing evidence of the great and general advance in material prosperity, which has been made since the policy of restriction on commerce was abandoned. That the problem of poverty yet remains, and that there is a residuum of helpless, shiftless poor in our large towns, and that many classes are yet ignorant and struggling for a wretched subsistence, hidden away in back streets and alleys,—these, and facts like these, only prove that there are weighty social questions still unsolved, and that moral and economic reforms have to penetrate to a much lower level. Vicious propensities and ignorance are not eradicated by fiscal legislation. Free-trade is not an idol, nor is its adoption a charm to cure social diseases; there is neither fetish-worship nor miracle-working in the recognition of a sound economic principle. The whole doctrine is summed up in the liberty and opportunity for men to employ their labour and expend their earnings to the best advantage without let or hindrance. But liberty of purchasing will not make the ignorant skilled nor the idle industrious; it will not prevent the waste which arises from drunkenness or gambling, nor save a man and his family from the consequences of vice or imprudence. These evils demand other remedies; many efforts are being made to combat them and to reduce these dark spots on the social horizon. The progress of the last fifty years lends hope that the comforts and advantages which have been extended to so large a proportion of the community will, in time, penetrate to these lower strata also; meanwhile, to no class is cheap food a greater boon than to the struggling workers on the verge of bare subsistence.

Chapter VIII.

Why Free-trade is not adopted in other Countries.

One of the most frequent objections brought against the Free-trade policy of Great Britain is that other countries have not adopted it.   It is said, "We stand alone, and it is presumptuous to think that we are wiser than all other nations", "The verdict of the world is against us".   Much attention has been drawn to the sanguine but unfortunate prediction of Cobden that if England led the way other European nations, convinced by her example, would follow within five years.[1]   But fifty years have now passed, and not only have the European nations failed to follow the example of Great Britain, but some have increased their tariffs, while the United States have advanced still further on the lines of Protection, and even most of our Colonies have rejected the policy of the mother-country in its favour.   This constitutes apparently a weighty expression of opinion against the Free-trade doctrine, and calls for some examination.

In the first place, however, Cobden did not rest the argument for this policy upon its adoption by others. His prediction was no more than an expression of his own firm conviction that the merits of a doctrine, so clearly grasped by his own mind, would be brought home with equal force to others when its actual operation in Great Britain afforded visible evidence of its advantages. But he did not make sufficient allowance for difference of circumstances or for interested opposition.   Adam Smith had been more awake to these difficulties when he wrote; John Bright also had no expectation of the sudden conversion of Europe; and Peel distinctly stated

---

[1] Speech in the House of Commons, Jan. 15th, 1846: "I believe that if you abolish the Corn-laws honestly, and adopt Free-trade in its simplicity, there will not be a tariff in Europe that will not be changed in less than five years to follow your example".

(M 460)   K

that his action rested on the conviction, slowly and surely attained, of the necessity of Free-trade for Great Britain, and not upon any anticipation of its becoming the policy of other countries. Scientific doctrines are not settled by votes, and new principles have ever to fight their way to general acceptance; and when their application in practice proves adverse to the interests of particular classes there can be less hope of their speedy adoption. Moreover, as the circumstances of all countries are different, special reasons can be advanced to show why Protection has taken root so firmly in many countries. Yet it is not strictly true that Great Britain has no followers. In Europe several of the vigorous and flourishing smaller countries—Switzerland, Holland, Belgium, Denmark, and Norway—are all but Free-trading, and New South Wales has always been a staunch supporter of the policy of the mother-country.

Nor must we forget the nature of the trade of other countries. Great Britain is unable to provide herself with sufficient food; raw materials and food-stuffs together account for nearly 75 per cent of her imports, while manufactured goods are about 75 per cent of her total exports. This is the case with no other country. It is true that France and Germany both import some corn,[1] but their chief imports, and almost the entire imports of most other protective countries, consist of manufactures, materials for manufactures, and luxuries, on which the pressure of duties is less severely felt than would be the case if they were levied upon the immediate necessaries of life. While, then, different circumstances have fostered the protective principle in Europe, the United States, and the Colonies, in all of them the facility for collecting revenue by the customary method of duties on imports gave it an easy footing; and in all it has been maintained by the sentiment of supporting home industry, and the fallacy that more employment is found for labour in the country by excluding foreign competition.

The circumstances that have favoured the growth of

---

[1] France imported 99 million bushels of grain in 1894, 43 millions in 1895, and 35 millions in 1896.

Protection in the United States are its vast extent and large resources, great variety of climate, fertile soil, and abundance of minerals. While richly endowed by nature with a multiplicity of products, it has been supplied by Europe with vigorous labourers, and with abundant capital. Each such adult immigrant to the States from Great Britain, endowed with average strength and skill, has been estimated as equivalent to a gift of £200 in his personal capital. A unique concurrence of favouring conditions in the United States has made for wealth, in spite of the impediments raised by legislation, and has enabled the nation to maintain a high standard of living, and to bear its burden of taxation. It must further be remembered that the states comprising the Union, trade freely with one another, and this freedom extends over 51 states and territories differing so widely as New York and Texas, Florida, and California. The United States covers an area of 3,500,000 square miles, and includes almost every variety of climate and every kind of product. Were it severed from the rest of the world, its people might live in comparative affluence, and miss very few of the comforts and luxuries found elsewhere. It is not remarkable that they should be able to uphold a system of Protection in these circumstances. In no sense, however, can that system be said to be the product of healthy conditions. In its origin it was a reaction against the oppressive "colonial policy" and "sole-market theory" of Great Britain, which helped to provoke the War of Independence; partly in retaliation and partly for revenue purposes the American colonists began to tax our exports. In 1789 Secretary Hamilton advanced the plausible principle that "infant industries" should be protected as a temporary expedient in order to enable them to become firmly established, and that when they no longer required this safeguard, the duty would be abolished. With this object duties of 8½ per cent were adopted for seven years. The war between Great Britain and France led to complications with the United States, which then increased its tariff as an act of hostility. Reduced in 1815, it was again raised in 1816, and from that time its fluctuations have been

frequent.   Between 1847 and 1860 reduced tariffs were
followed by a period of great prosperity.   Then came
the Civil War, and the need for revenue led to greatly
increased import-duties, which rose to 47 per cent.
Some relaxation followed the war, but from that time
the tariff has been the sport of financiers and political
parties.   With every increase of duty fresh vested interests have been created, and tariff-fed industries call
for yet further aid.   What has happened to the "infant
industries" of a hundred years ago?   Without the help
of duties, ranging from 40 to 100 per cent, they are still
unable to compete with Great Britain, and the tariff is
perpetually under manipulation.   A "national policy"
was advanced by Mr. M'Kinley in 1890, by which duties
were still further augmented; the avowed aim of this
policy was "to encourage home industries", "to keep
money in the country", and "to exclude goods made
by *pauper labour*".   With all its natural gifts and extensive territory, the United States has, in consequence
of its inflated prices, become a most expensive country
to live in; yet American workmen apparently fail to see
that high prices do not necessarily mean high real-wages.
The bounty of nature is counteracted by measures which
end in the creation of monopolies and millionaires, while
labour troubles are frequent, and the contrasts of wealth
and poverty, sufficiently glaring in Old-world cities, are
enormously magnified in the New.

Tariffs have become recognized instruments for creating vested interests, politics are rendered corrupt, and
the newspapers complain that politicians combine in
log-rolling and in reciprocal voting with the object of
securing an increased share in the plunder of the community.   If the principle of stimulating infant industries
into striving and energetic adult industries ever had an
opportunity for fair trial it has surely been in the United
States, with all its magnificent natural resources; and
yet the duties, adopted for a brief seven years a century
ago, are still in existence, while the rate is enormously
increased and the period of operation is unlimited.

It might be expected that the cotton manufacture
would become a successful industry where the raw

material is a natural product and so many other causes
are favourable, yet the whole export of manufactured
cotton by the United States is less than £3,000,000,
while that of Great Britain, which fetches the raw
material 3000 miles, is £60,000,000.   In the States the
cotton manufacture has been a protected industry since
1816, when a duty of 25 per cent was imposed; yet,
after eighty years of fostering, this industry is protected
by a tariff ranging from 30 to 60 per cent *ad valorem*.
The iron industry is an even more telling example against
"the infant industry theory".   It was protected in its
early development by a duty fixed at 20 per cent in 1816;
yet, in order to avoid the competition of English iron
goods, the duty has been augmented by the Dingley
tariff to 60 per cent *ad valorem*, under the plea of the
"national policy", which is adopted now that the "infant industry" theory is no longer tenable.   If the iron
industry can compete successfully with British goods,
legislation imposing a duty of 60 per cent to exclude the
latter is surely superfluous.

The effect of the tariff of 1890 upon woollen goods was
to render them nearly three times the price of the same
article in Great Britain.   Mr. M'Kinley sustained his
protective doctrine with the remarkable dictum that
"cheap goods were a badge of poverty", and he found
a strong supporter in Mr. Jay Gould, the millionaire,
who supplied the additional argument that "high prices
would teach working men thrift".   Nor is the doctrine
entirely extinct in the United States, that commerce
between nations is war.   Only a few years ago Senator
Evarts declared in the United States that "trade between nations stands for war in a sense never to be
overlooked and never to be misunderstood".   President
M'Kinley's message on the occasion of his accession to
office takes somewhat different ground, and seeks to
combine the conflicting aims of securing high prices,
increasing employment by high tariffs, and "checking
deficiencies in revenue by protective legislation which is
always the firmest prop of the Treasury"; and yet these
ends are to be secured "by extending the reciprocity
law of 1890 under which a stimulus was given to our

foreign trade". This combination of aims will no doubt recommend the policy to different groups of Protectionists, but it displays an amount of confusion and contradiction which is almost hopelessly bewildering.

The tariff will no doubt succeed in creating high prices by the exclusion of foreign manufactures, but it strikes a blow at American farming so far as the latter depends upon foreign consumption for markets. In 1895, out of a total of £158,000,000 of exports from the United States, agricultural produce amounted to £110,000,000. If the United States renders payment for its exports difficult or impossible in foreign goods, the British corn-importing trade will naturally move towards freer markets. Argentina affords just such a market, and she is becoming a rival to the United States in the supply of wheat to Great Britain in exchange for British manufactures.[1] No measure could be more favourable to the extension of commercial relations with our Colonies also than that the United States, by pursuing a policy of isolation, should make it less easy to dispose of her wheat in Great Britain; and if at such a stage, the Colonies, following the example of Canada, reduce their tariffs to the mother-country, her trade will naturally flow to their shores, while the tide of emigration, both of labour and capital, will tend to set strongly in the same direction.

The duties on linen and sewing-thread supply another illustration of the waste and expense caused by the protective system in America. A duty of 35 per cent on linen has long existed, but the new tariff raises this duty by various additions ranging from 50 to more than 100 per cent. The duty on sewing-thread is also increased from 40 to 67 per cent. On the linen duties the *New York Journal of Commerce* thus comments:—"There is practically no linen industry in this country, and there

[1] IMPORTS OF WHEAT (GRAIN AND FLOUR) INTO THE UNITED KINGDOM.

| | From United States. | | From Argentine Republic. | | Total Imports. |
	Cwts.	Per cent.	Cwts.	Per cent.	Cwts.
1881.	45,699,956	... 64	31	... —	71,344,659
1885.	39,709,567	... 48	335,635	... ·04	82,331,552
1890.	33,903,563	.. 41	2,848,771	... 3·	82,381,591
1895.	45,322,801	... 42	11,432,721	... 11·	107,261,636

probably never will be. The conditions of our climate do not favour the growing of flax, even in parts of the country which seem best suited for it; and the industrial habits of our people do not favour attention to the mass of tedious and toilsome details that go to the preparation of this fibre for the loom." The loss incurred by forcing an industry in such circumstances is obvious.

The moral of the tariff system in the United States is, that the benefit to be derived from imposing a temporary protective duty is a delusion,—the weakly infants do not grow up to independence, but are always requiring additional nourishment. As in opium-taking, the doses have to be increased to maintain the unhealthy system. The tendency of the new tariff is towards prohibition, but the President's message also contemplated an extension of markets for American produce, although the fundamental fact in trading is that a nation cannot sell without buying. It is of the manufactures of Great Britain that the United States is most jealous. The tariff is not levied so much against the labour of inferior races as against the highly-productive labour of Great Britain. Through blindness to the fact that the object of trading, as of all work, is to satisfy wants, the tariffs of the United States are being pushed more and more towards a point where much of the labour of the country will be employed at an economic loss. Waste cannot increase wealth, and misdirection is a species of waste, since it causes capital and labour to be employed with a loss of efficiency.

New and unexpected difficulties are arising out of tariffs in America; both South and West are calling for Protection for *their* infant industries against the East. So long as they were agricultural and mining only, they adhered to the "national policy"; but some of the San Francisco papers now urge that the plea for protection against foreign products holds good equally against those from other parts of their own country. Consumers in California are advised to give the preference to the products of their own States, and to reject those of the Eastern States. Thus the fallacious principles so long upheld in international relations are beginning to

be applied at home between state and state. This is
consistent but serious, and should it be maintained it
promises to put an end either to protection against
foreign countries, or to the free-trading between the
States. The latter alternative would raise very weighty
problems. The latest alterations in the United States
tariff endeavour to give some of the privileges of monopoly to the wool-growers of the West; but no protective
duty can help the grain and meat farmers, who are
taxed heavily on every article of their consumption. So
also a duty has been demanded on imported long-staple
cotton by the cotton-growers of the South, and both
West and South are urged to fight for protection for
their young manufacturing industries. The Western
farmer has hitherto been too weak to resist Protection,
which has always told against him. Will the Western
manufacturer be sufficiently strong to carry it to its
logical conclusion of protecting every state and district
from every other, and if so, how will it affect the Federation?

In the Australian self-governing Colonies Protection
grew out of the system under which duties were levied
upon imported goods for revenue purposes. These
duties were, after a time, extended to foster infant industries, on the representation that *temporary* and
moderate duties would soon accomplish the firm establishment of manufactures, and give a desirable diversity
of employment. The duties have more recently been
advocated as a means of producing higher wages. The
Colony of Victoria has taken the lead in the protective
movement. It deliberately adopted Protection in 1865,
and duties of 10 per cent were then levied upon clothing,
furniture, boots, and woollen goods. As in other cases,
the duties, once commenced, were afterwards increased
to sustain the vested interests created, and the period
of operation was extended. But after thirty years of
Protection, Victorian industries, with duties of 30 per
cent, are as far from independence as at the beginning.

J. S. Mill's unfortunate, though somewhat guarded,
admission, that temporary Protection might be adopted
in a young colony to start new industries, is often

quoted in justification of such attempts. Mill, however, contemplated only a very brief period of support to enable an industry, in the success of which there were strong grounds for belief, to be started on a scale sufficiently great to overcome initial difficulties, and to prevent it from being crushed at the outset by the rivalry of old-established competitors. This policy might be theoretically sound, on the assumption that governments are omniscient, and can foresee what industries will soon be thus established so as to stand alone. In practice, however, this state of things is not realized. Governments are not endowed with this prescience, nor are political parties proof against the representations and demands of their supporters. The experience of a century of the "young industry" policy in the United States, and of more than thirty years in Australia, bears out what might have been anticipated—that such aid cannot be restricted to industries sure to succeed, and proves that the academic exception to free-trading has no practical application. Cobden in this matter showed more insight into the facts of politics than the philosopher. Sir Louis Mallet reports a conversation with him only a few days before his death, in which Cobden said with peculiar earnestness: "I believe that the harm which Mill has done to the world by the passage in his book on *Political Economy* in which he favours the principle of Protection in young communities has outweighed all the good which may have been caused by his other writings".[1] Without endorsing this remark as regards the impossible estimate of the value of Mill's writings, it must be admitted that the theoretical conditions contemplated in Mill's defence of Protection for young colonies do not seem really to exist, since in practice it is impossible either to predict what industries will become self-supporting, or to resist the claims which are made for the application of the principle of temporary succour to other fresh industries, or the plaintive appeal for further aid to save from ruin those already established by the aid of tariffs.

[1] Quoted in a letter of Sir Louis Mallet, given in the Appendix to Mr. Gowing's admirable *Life of Richard Cobden* (Cassell & Co.).

The argument that it is desirable to stimulate "diversity of employment" in young countries is one which seems at first sight to contain some force. It is undoubtedly desirable that the varied capabilities of every country and people should all find useful application and scope for development. Nor is economic gain to the community the sole consideration; there are many social advantages which may be well purchased at some sacrifice of wealth. But, on examination, it does not appear either that Free-trading hinders this diversity, or that Protection encourages it. New South Wales is not behind Victoria either in the number and diversity of its industries, or in its social development and educational advantages. Great Britain and Holland are both remarkable for the great variety of their industries and their social institutions, and they are not excelled in these respects by protective Germany or France. It has been shown that Protection has a cramping and narrowing tendency from its artificial methods and its want of enterprise. A country, by using its powers to best advantage, will inevitably soon develop towns, ports, and markets, with their special characteristics and many varieties of trades and employments; and such a country is able to afford (as New South Wales has done) both time and endowment for education and the higher aims of life. In a large number of cases the natural circumstances determine the chief local industries, such as mining, fishing, and shipping; again, many trades are subsidiary to others, and must be carried on in or near to definite centres, distance and cost of conveyance limiting the power of outside competition. In countries like Victoria and South Africa, where the discovery of valuable mineral deposits has led to rapid development and much wealth, many considerable industries inevitably spring up quickly near the seat of the prime industry, and civilization soon takes an advanced form. Building and repairing trades, printing of newspapers, &c., must of necessity be local, and numerous industries are thus bound to arise in any country with an intelligent population, which has the means of sustaining life in any degree of comfort. Experience suggests that extension

Protection in other Countries. 155

of freedom has been more fruitful in promoting diversity
of powers and variety of products than special and artificial stimulation. Under a protective system some
industries have even declined; of this result, ship-building
in the United States is a forcible illustration. The conditions are too onerous; it has been found more econo-
mical to purchase ships in Great Britain, or to hire their
services, than to build them in the States. It is sometimes urged that immigrants desire to practise in their
new homes the skilled trades acquired in the country
whence they came; but it by no means follows that
healthy diversity is gained by artificially aiding them to
do this. As openings occur, men of capacity or enterprise will utilize their acquired skill. There is always a
favourable field for exceptional talent in a young and
growing community; but it is not incumbent upon such
a community to find employment in his own trade for
every artisan-immigrant who comes from a country
differing in development and character.

If we study Protection on the Continent we find many
reasons to account for its survival. The older commercial nations, like Great Britain, inherited the belief,
handed down from "the mercantile period", that in
commerce between nations there was a hostile element,
and that in trading one country gained at the expense
of another. In France, Colbert's efforts in the seventeenth century to create a system of state-directed industry and commerce accentuated this belief, until
reaction provoked from a leading merchant the retort
of, "*Laissez-faire, laissez-aller*". At the close of the eighteenth century restrictions became universal and tariff
wars were constant. The military spirit generated by
Napoleon increased them by arousing national jealousy
and hostility. Gradually more moderate views prevailed,
and an advance was made towards unshackling commerce between 1850 and 1873. Duties were reduced,
and the commercial tariff of 1860 between Great Britain
and France gave great hopes of better relations. The
Franco-German war shattered these prospects; the
military spirit was revived; the cost of the war and
subsequent military defences caused immense expendi-

ture in both countries. Revenue was required to meet
it, and the method of indirect taxation was adopted, as
being least offensive and least easily perceived by the
taxpayers. On the pretence of assisting native industries
protective duties are levied, which curtail the foreign
trade and raise only a small revenue from the diminished
imports. This is a wasteful and expensive system, but
has the advantage of not being very obvious, while it
gains some popularity from its apparent encouragement
of home industry. These duties do not press heavily
upon food, since Continental nations are mostly self-
supporting as regards necessaries.[1] They do not therefore awaken the strong opposition which the duties on
corn did in England.

The case of Continental countries thus differs somewhat
from that of Great Britain, though Protection is not an
advantage to them any more than it was to this country.
The *economic* objections to Protection are equally cogent
in either case, but its real effects are not widely understood, and vested interests in the protected trades and
in the industries aided by the sugar and other bounties
support it; some revenue is realized from the system,
but at a great economic loss to the nation.

Nor can it be maintained that, in the endeavours to
extend their commerce and find a market for their products, these nations derive any assistance from their
protective system. Their efforts to develop an export
trade encounter at every point the difficulties created by
the limitations upon their imports, and also suffer from
the increased cost of production which is caused by a
protective system. Their attempts at colonizing and at
securing a colonial trade suffer from the same exclusive
methods. In commenting upon the very meagre results
to French trade, which have followed upon the immense
expense incurred in the acquisition of Tonquin and its
maintenance under French rule, M. Clemenceau lately
said that " France was paying 50,000,000 francs a year
to find a market for Manchester ". France has colonies,

---

[1]Though France imports some corn she grows an immense amount of
wheat, averaging nearly 35,000,000 quarters per annum; while the average
produce of the United Kingdom is less than 8,000,000 quarters.

dependencies, and protectorates with an area of 3⅓ million square miles. Her total trade with them in 1894 (excluding Algeria and Tunis) amounted to £8,500,000, while Great Britain's trade with these French possessions amounted to £1,750,000. Germany has about one million square miles of colonial territory, and her total colonial trade amounts to only £500,000; the trade of Great Britain with her Colonies exceeds £170,000,000.[1]

The colony of the Straits Settlements offers a very instructive illustration of the beneficial effects of Free-trading. These British possessions, comprising Singapore, Penang, Wellesley, and Malacca, less than 1500 square miles in extent, and with a population of little more than half a million, have few natural products of any commercial value; but there are no customs-duties whatever, and the freedom of the commerce, combined with the advantages of the situation as a convenient emporium for eastern trade, has stimulated enterprise, which has built up in fifty years a vast transit-trade amounting to £40,000,000 a year. The Settlements receive from the Dutch East Indies numerous products for re-exportation, notwithstanding the Dutch restrictions on that trade, and they form a centre for the collection and redistribution of the commodities of the East, coming from China, Japan, Australia, New Zealand, and the East Indies. The policy of Free-trade has created this flourishing entrepôt out of a small fishing village, and the trade of the Eastern Archipelago gravitates there because it can be carried on without hindrance. If the results of this experiment in Free-trading be contrasted with those obtained under the restrictions practised by the Dutch in their settlements, and by the French with even greater stringency in their attempts to develop and

[1] TOTAL FOREIGN TRADE (1895).

	Imports.	Exports.	Total.
	£	£	£
France, ...	148,725,000	134,480,000	283,205,000
Germany, ...	212,305,000	171,215,000	383,520,000
United States, ...	156,944,934	172,640,097	329,585,031
United Kingdom, ...	416,689,658	285,832,407	702,522,065

monopolize the trade of their territory in Cochin China, an object-lesson is provided from which the conclusion is inevitable, that in trade, as in the domain of physical science, movement follows the line of least resistance.

There is little weight, therefore, in the objection that neither the leading commercial nations of Europe, the United States, nor our own Colonies copy the example of Great Britain in free-trading. Their proceedings are explained by various circumstances, some of which are peculiar to each; and though the reasons for their policy are not economically sound, they are sufficient to account for their adherence to a system to which they have committed themselves, and their apparently slight appreciation of our policy forms no argument for condemning it, or for inducing us to modify it in imitation of the methods of our commercial rivals.

It has been noted in connection with the arguments first considered, that Protection has a tendency to stereotype the industries of a country and to check its natural development. A trade once established under the shelter of legislation has a claim to its continuance. It is shut in from the healthy play of competition, from the invigorating influence of new ideas, and from the necessity for keeping pace with the growth of science and the industrial advances of other countries. But the law of progress is one of change. A country inclosed by mountains, or shut out from the world by a species of Chinese isolation, does not display the most advanced forms of social or industrial life, and restrictions upon trade are apt to produce like results.

In all times there have been natural movements and changes in industry, although the forces which created them operated slowly in more primitive conditions. The family system of spinning and weaving in homes gave place to more complex production in factories. Village manufactures ceased and passed to towns; thus agricultural labourers lost their various other employments which had been subsidiary, but had now become specialized. Industries have frequently changed their localities. Norwich, Suffolk, and the valleys of Somerset and Gloucester have ceased to be the great centres of the woollen industry, which moved to the coal-fields of the North with the invention of machinery and the steam-engine. Similarly the iron industry left the forests of Sussex for the coal-fields of Yorkshire, Lanark, and other counties. Coventry, once the leading centre of the silk industry, turned to watch-making; and when the American machine-made watch destroyed the trade, with ready adaptation it took up the bicycle industry, and is now much more prosperous than at any previous period. Under a protective system the silk industry might have remained its staple trade, and we might still be having distress among protected weavers instead of a prosperous and increasing population of mechanics. Paper-making and printing have found suitable settlements at certain rural towns in Buckinghamshire and Kent, within easy distance of the metropolis. Great Britain about 1770 was exporting corn to the Colonies and to Russia; a century later she is dependent upon them for part of her own supply; in the interval their agriculture and her manufactures have been developed. India has long been one of the most considerable markets for Lancashire cotton goods. She is now setting up cotton mills, and is creating a demand for English machinery and the products of Yorkshire ironworks.

A few extracts from a recent speech by the Japanese minister in London pointedly illustrate the effects of progress upon the character of industry and commerce from the case of a country which has been open to the influences of Western civilization, science, and commerce only some forty years. After alluding to the alterations in the industrial aspects of the country wrought by the introduction of machinery, and referring to the great progress of the manufacture of silk piece-goods and of cotton-spinning, His Excellency remarked, that " whatever Manchester might lose would be more than made up by Oldham, Birmingham, or Sheffield; the British nation, taken as a whole, would thus have nothing to regret in the industrial development of Japan. Woollen fabrics were unknown to the Japanese until foreign commerce introduced them, no sheep having been reared in Japan; but the army, the navy, and the police force were now clothed in wool, and many civilians now wore raiment of the same material.   The industry was as yet in its infancy, but in all probability it would become an important one in spite of the fact that all the raw material had to be imported.   This afforded an opportunity for Australian wool-growers.   The production of iron is exceedingly limited, and the bulk of iron and steel required was obtained from abroad. . . . Great Britain had an excellent customer in Japan in these commodities, and would have for many years, provided Japanese demands were met in an intelligent manner. . . Foreign trade, which was valued in 1886 at yen 81,000,000 rose in 1896 to yen 289,000,000.   Comparatively large as the commerce of Japan was already, it was sure to grow rapidly, and the country might assuredly be regarded as full of hopes for Western manufacturers and merchants.''

These examples are sufficient to show that it is a natural law that industries tend to move to, and flourish in, the localities best adapted to their requirements; and that owing to discoveries, the spread of science, and the rise of new conditions, this locus is not permanent, but is ever changing to take advantage of more favourable circumstances.   By artificial obstructions, such as protective tariffs, we may attempt to direct and retain industries, but only at a considerable loss, and waste of natural productiveness.   Progress is a product of the combination of the two universal laws of unity and variety—of persistence and change.   Free commerce avails itself of both; restraints on commerce tend to destroy some of the advantages to be derived from change, and so far retard national progress.

Although, for reasons adduced, Free-trade has not been adopted by other countries or by most of the Colonies, yet there is strong indirect evidence for the soundness of the principle of commercial freedom in the *internal* fiscal arrangements of large states and federations of states.   In all cases of the extension of the boundaries of a country, or the inclusion of a new member, fiscal federation is adopted.   The United States place no restrictions on the trade between the several states, and every new territory admitted to the Union is placed on the same footing; the same principle is adopted in the Dominion of Canada, and in Russia and Germany. But if Protection has any economic advantage, its virtue would not cease with the political inclusion of a territory in a country; the local industries should require the same defence as formerly. It is found, however, that the larger the country the greater is the gain from the removal of these restraints. The reason is plain, the field of commercial intercourse is greater, and there is a nearer approximation to complete free-trading. If a country is of vast extent and its climate and products very varied, and if it possesses minerals as well as abundance of land, such a country is most favourably situated for industrial independence, for it has within itself resources of all kinds, and it will suffer less than others from attempts at being self-sufficing. On the other hand, the smaller the country and the more specialized its products, the greater is the advantage which it gains from contact with others. Relations of mutual interchange with countries differing economically from themselves become essential to small and populous countries, and such in an eminent degree is the case of Great Britain.

Under a natural system of trade, industries adapt themselves to wants; under Protection they are apt to be either abnormally stimulated and to over-produce, as is the case with the sugar industry in France; or the privilege tends to develop them into strong monopolies, often sufficiently powerful to completely control an industry. In all protective countries the interests of some classes thus become an obstacle to the adoption of Free-trade, a difficulty seen very clearly by Adam Smith. In free-trading Great Britain few syndicates have succeeded in maintaining high prices;[1] foreign competition, sooner or later, comes in and defeats attempts at artificial monopoly rates. The United States, the country in which Protection has had its strongest hold, have become the home of trusts and corners. There are

---

[1] This is true at all events of necessaries and articles of general consumption; no doubt the prices of some articles (diamonds, iodine, quicksilver, &c.) with a very limited supply are controlled by monopolies.

some twenty of such gigantic trusts, many of them
erected upon the exclusion of foreign competition, which
control the most extensive industries and fix prices at
monopoly rates.   The sugar trust has already been
mentioned; a glass trust flourishes under the shelter of
a duty of 120 per cent on foreign window-glass, while
another trust in mother-of-pearl buttons is protected by
1400 per cent tariff against foreign competition.   The
iron, copper, nickel, and tin industries are all monopolies
in the United States, and have become mines of wealth
to their proprietors.   The latest of these is the tin
monopoly, which was created by the M'Kinley tariff,
not only to the great injury of the British tin industry,
but also of some other American trades.[1]   Minerals
could be worked at a reasonable profit in the States,
but the effect of the monopoly created by a tariff is,
that under the plea of developing the home industry
and national resources, syndicates are formed which
secure duties almost prohibitive, and enable the owners
to obtain exorbitant prices and profits.[2]

A further serious evil attaches to the tariff system as
regards the internal trade of a country.   Tariffs are at
best a clumsy machinery for regulating trade, but their
frequent alterations make them most potent instruments
for disturbing trade and creating depressions and crises.
It is now understood in the industrial and commercial
world that steadiness is a desideratum of healthy business,
and that violent fluctuations, however created, lead only
to uncertainty and injury in the long run.   The latest
tariff bill in America illustrates the action of such interference with trade.   From the time it was proposed it

[1] "The Ruckel Company are large dealers in iron and tin. They have
just reduced the wages of their workmen by five per cent. Messrs. Sher-
man S. Jewett & Co. are among the largest stove manufacturers in the
United States. They employ in Buffalo upwards of a thousand men.
They have just given notice to their men of a reduction of wages, owing to
the increase of the duty on tin-plates, of which the firm use hundreds of
tons yearly".—Note from American Correspondent of *Pall Mall Gazette*.

[2] The proprietor of the nickel monopoly has become a millionaire, and
has founded a Chair of Finance and Economy at Philadelphia to teach
Protection; by the deed of gift the professor has to show how by suitable
tariff legislation a nation may keep its productive industry alive, cheapen
the cost of commodities, and oblige foreigners to sell to it at low prices.···
See Mr. Wise's *Industrial Freedom*, pp. 283–293 (Cassell & Co.).

created disturbance and dislocation; speculations based on its probable results disordered the markets, some imports were vastly increased in anticipation of its prohibitive effects, while other industries held back to await its promulgation. The bill was frequently altered to meet the demands of the representatives of different trades.[1] During the whole period it was under consideration the utmost uncertainty prevailed, business hesitated, industry languished, and trade was stagnant. Many interests were involved, and none could forecast the issue. And this gratuitous injury to trade is a consequence of a system which professedly organizes trade for the benefit of the community.

While, then, various reasons can be adduced for the maintenance of the protective system in other countries, it is plain that the strongest impediment to its abolition is self-interest—a principle which finds abundant illustration everywhere, but which, in the case of protected industries, is enlisted very widely in a cause economically injurious to the community as a whole. By a mistaken policy many industries have been started in those countries, which can only flourish through the exclusion of competition afforded by the tariffs; those interested fight therefore for the maintenance of the tariffs, and their influence is great in the Legislature. The principle, being admitted, gains wider application, monopolies are built upon it, and interests are created embracing powerful sections of the community, hence its abolition is difficult; strong defences are sought and plausible arguments created on its behalf. In Great Britain the repeal of the

[1] An interesting side-light is thrown upon the working of the protective system by the indignation and protests against the Dingley Tariff in the United States coming from Americans visiting Europe. This latest fiscal device has not only intensified the ordinary effects of Protection, but represents the American Government as agent of a "New York Tradesmen's League", composed mainly of tailors and milliners. The Act prohibits Americans from bringing home more than $100 worth of personal effects, all excess being charged at about 60 per cent duty. The measure inflicts annoyance and inconvenience upon some 60,000 or 70,000 American citizens who visit Europe in the year, and is calculated to yield some £50,000 excess duty, while it entails increased expense in customs-officials, and has created a system of spies on board ship and detectives in the Custom-house in the interest of the so-called "Merchants' Board of Trade".—See *The Times*, 19th October, 1897.

Corn-laws was opposed by only one large interest, and its resistance was weakened by the allies of famine and misery which came at a critical moment to join its opponents. It was a question of food and sustenance in Great Britain which drove home the economic argument; the like conditions do not exist in any other country.

***

Chapter IX.

British Agriculture and Free-trade.

The problem of the relation of our Free-trading system to British agriculture is of such importance as to merit separate consideration. In most countries the demand for protective duties comes more especially from manufacturing industries, but in Great Britain protection has chiefly been invoked during this century on behalf of agriculture. The explanation is, that other countries are for the most part self-supporting as regards food; in this respect the case of Great Britain is exceptional. In the United States and most of the Colonies the farmers are Free-traders, and the Protectionists are manufacturers, who wish to keep out British competition. In Great Britain the manufacturers are mostly Free-traders; it is the agricultural interest that is most desirous of excluding foreign competition. In 1896 our imports were valued at £441,807,000, of which £154,315,000, or 35 per cent, was on account of agricultural produce in competition with British farming. The table (on page 165), from the Board of Trade returns, indicates the nature of these imports.

Farming has been undoubtedly the least progressive of our great national industries during the past fifty years. In 1846 agriculture employed 3½ millions of labourers in the United Kingdom, while in 1895 only 2½ millions found work upon the soil. Agricultural capital, which increased up to 1879, has since fallen to nearly the same value as in 1846. The introduction of

IMPORTS.			1895.	1896.
Animals living (for food),	...	...	£ 8,966,000	£10,438,000
Meat (for food),	...	...	23,762,000	24,753,000
Wheat, Flour, and other Cereals,		...	49,723,000	52,792,000
Butter, Cheese, and Eggs,	...	...	25,480,000	26,926,000
Lard and Milk,	...	...	4,025,000	3,440,000
Fruit and Hops,	...	...	2,033,000	2,728,000
Potatoes, Onions, and other Vegetables,			3,144,000	2,874,000
Poultry and Game,	...	...	605,000	605,000
Wool (sheep and lambs),		...	26,026,000	24,958,000
Other Articles,	...	...	4,618,000	4,801,000
			£148,382,000	£154,315,000

machinery into farming, by which means two men can do as much as three formerly, accounts for some reduction in the amount of labour; but the fact remains that a large part of our food supply is now obtained from abroad in exchange for our manufactured goods; farming has become less profitable than other industries, and has during the past twenty years tended to decline. The question we have to consider is whether Protection would provide a remedy for depressed agriculture.

After the repeal of the Corn-laws until about 1876 agriculture flourished, more land was brought under cultivation, farmers prospered, and rents rose; increasing population, thriving manufactures, and growing commerce created a greater demand for agricultural produce; the standard of living advanced considerably, and classes who had subsisted mainly on bread and vegetables became comparatively large consumers of meat, milk, butter, and cheese. The repeal of the Corn-laws did not operate injuriously to agriculture; the thirty years which succeeded were a period of exceptional prosperity for the agricultural classes, and falsified all the predictions of the opponents of Free-trade. Between 1853 and 1860 Mr. Gladstone removed the import duties on butter, cheese, &c., and on half-manufactured goods, and further, considerably reduced the taxes on imported commodities, leaving only forty-eight dutiable articles. The railway mania and crisis of 1847 retarded progress for a time; the general upheaval in 1848, the year of revolutions, turned men's minds to political rather than to social reform, and

Chartism once again became temporarily a disturbing force; but trade progressed, the harvests were good, and the farmers had a prosperous period until about 1862, due mainly to the improved standard of living of the industrial classes. Meanwhile food, especially wheat, came in abundance from other lands, yet rents rose steadily to 1873, and land values increased 27 per cent. The cotton famine, which threw Lancashire into idleness, checked the general prosperity somewhat, and the disastrous commercial crisis of 1866 marked an epoch of severe trial for trade, yet agriculture flourished. The impulse to foreign trade gained by the opening of our ports, and the gold discoveries which developed Australia gave an unwonted period of activity. Agricultural imports increased during the seventies, but demand kept pace, and, excepting corn and wool, prices did not fall materially for some years.

In 1879, however, severe depression set in, and from that time agriculture has not recovered. A series of bad harvests culminated in 1879 in failure of crops, but the more enduring causes of the decline in agriculture are to be found in an intensity of foreign competition previously unknown. Prices fell with the influx of all kinds of food, rents were gradually reduced, but not until much farming capital had been lost and farms were going out of cultivation in some counties. It is perhaps not remarkable that agriculturists should have turned to the State to relieve their distress. Two facts only were patent to them; prices had fallen to an unprofitable level, and the importation of foreign food at low prices was becoming immense.[1] Farmers, unable to meet their expenses or obtain sufficient relief from lower rents, sought aid from a rise of prices, or something which would remove the intensity of the competition which oppressed them. They also began an agitation for a modification of burdens upon land, that is, for a reduction of local rates. This last has been granted. It

---

[1] Estimated value of agricultural produce of the United Kingdom in 1891: £222,915,000. From the same quantities, at prices of 1874, the estimated value would be: £298,997,000, showing a decline in money values of £76,082,000, or 25 per cent.

cannot be doubted that the act of 1896, which made this remission, will confer no permanent advantage upon farmers. If rates are a deduction from rent, as has been argued from both sides of the House of Commons, the gain must accrue ultimately to the rent-receiver, although this will not be accomplished until the competitive principle has had time to work out the adjustment.

Of the various remedies proposed for the restoration of agriculture none have been regarded with more hopefulness than Bimetallism and Protection. The former of these involves questions much too large and intricate to be here discussed, but its special bearing upon agricultural prices may be touched upon briefly. Prices of agricultural produce have fallen generally, though not equally in all the different products; meat has fallen least of all, while poultry has actually risen.[1] The fall in prices is not, however, peculiar to agriculture, it applies equally to most other articles of general consumption. The comparison of prices by means of the index-number system, taking forty-five articles of ordinary use, shows that the buying power of money as regards those articles has changed during the last quarter of a century, so that £62 will now purchase as much as £100 would have bought of these commodities at the former period. This means that where money earnings have been constant their purchasing power has increased about 50 per cent; as just stated, this applies to manufactured articles as well as to food. Now a cause which is general, that is, one which would act upon all prices in much the same manner—such as an alteration in the standard of value—would be as potent in its influence upon the prices of articles on which the farmer *spends* his earnings as upon the price of corn or other produce he has to sell. It

[1] A comparison of the prices of agricultural products (1893-1896) with the prices which ruled (1865-1875) when they were exceptionally high, shows a fall as follows:—

	Per cent.		Per cent.		Per cent.
Wheat, ...	... 50	Butter, ...	... 10	Mutton, 1st quality,	8
Barley, ...	... 32	Hay, ...	... 16	,, 2nd ,,	15
Oats, ...	... 25	Beef, 1st quality,	16½	,, 3rd ,,	20
Wool, ...	... 26	,, 2nd ,, ...	19	Straw ...	... nil.
Cheese, ...	... 15	,, 3rd ,, ...	28	Poultry,...	... *risen.*

could only be in money-payments of rents or fixed
charges that he could reap a benefit by an alteration in
the standard.   Would it affect the competition of other
corn-producing countries?   Now our chief imports of
corn are from the United States, Russia, Argentina,
and Canada, and not from silver-using countries.   Out
of £50,000,000 worth of cereals imported, only about
£3,000,000 worth, that is, 6 per cent, came from silver
countries in 1895, and a large proportion of this was
from India.   It is asserted that the divergence between
silver and gold places India at an advantage in exporting grain.   There are, however, other special reasons
why India should be expected to become an exporter of
grain.   For some forty years past the policy of developing the resources of India by British capital has been
powerfully advocated, both in the interests of the natives
and also as a means of increasing our commerce.   It
was maintained that India would thus become a producer of corn, tea, and other valuable crops, and would
yield a profitable return on the capital sunk in her
development, while she would also become a purchaser
of British manufactures.   This has now been partially
achieved; British capital flowed to India for both public
and private undertakings.   Roads, railways, irrigation,
planting, and cultivation have followed.   By these
means, and under a strong and capable government,
India has enjoyed peace and prosperity.   The anticipated results have only been partially realized as yet.
But India has become an exporter of tea and of grain,
for labour there is cheap and transport is now easy;[1]
railways, steamships, and the Suez Canal (opened in
1873) put Indian produce on British markets at low
rates; yet the wheat exports fluctuate greatly and the
average is small.   Between 1872 and 1891 the export of
wheat to Great Britain rose from 394,000 cwts. to
30,000,000 cwts ; but it fell to only 7,000,000 cwts. in
1894, and owing to the triple disasters of drought,

---

[1] In 1868 the United Kingdom consumed 107,000,000 pounds of tea, of
which it obtained 100,000,000 from China and 7,000,000 from India.   In
1896 the consumption was 227,000,000 pounds, of which 203,000,000 came
from India and Ceylon, and 24,000,000 from China.

famine, and plague, was almost a nominal quantity in
1896.   Without entering, therefore, upon the difficulties of the currency controversy, sufficient reasons
can be adduced to show why India should tend to
become a producer of grain and a rival of the British
farmer in the market for wheat.   It seems useless, then,
to look to bimetallism as a remedy for agricultural
depression.   British farming is affected only in a limited
degree by the competition of silver-using countries.
Of these India is the most important, and its capacity
to send wheat to Great Britain has been determined
much more by the circumstances just narrated than by
any influence of the currency.

We turn next to the other remedy—Protection.   It
is in the highest degree improbable that any statesman
will venture to propose the renewal of tariffs upon the
necessaries of life; for good or for evil Great Britain
has become dependent upon imported wheat to the
extent of more than 70 per cent of her consumption.[1]
Cheap food is essential to her industrial supremacy, and
only by free importation can an adequate supply be
obtained.   Under thirty years of exceptionally strong
Protection food was dear, and at the same time the
farming classes complained frequently and bitterly.   It
is a remarkable fact that during these thirty years of
systematic effort to protect agriculture there were no
less than five parliamentary inquiries into agricultural
distress; and at those times, we read, both operatives
in towns and agricultural labourers were half-starved,
workhouses were crowded, farmers were ruined in
numbers, and the burden of poor-rates was overwhelming.   Other causes contributed to the distress, but the

[1] FOR THE YEAR 1895 THE WHEAT SUPPLY WAS:

From	Bushels.
United Kingdom,	51,000,000
United States,	87,000,000
Russia,	46,000,000
Argentina,	23,000,000
India,	17,500,000
Canada,	9,500,000
Other countries,	26,500,000
	260,500,000

WHEAT IMPORTED 1893-1895.

From	Per cent
Russia,	16·6
Other European countries,	4·7
United States,	50·3
Canada,	5·2
India,	6·8
Argentina,	11·0
Other countries,	5·4
	100

evidence as to the operation of the protective laws upon
the supply of necessaries proved conclusively the failure
of the system.   From 1846 to the present time there
have been but two inquiries (1880 and 1893) into agricultural depression, both subsequent to a series of bad
seasons; meanwhile the country has been constantly
advancing in comfort, and the agricultural decline did
not set in until some thirty years after Protection had
been abolished.

Agriculture presents four distinct interests or aspects
for consideration: namely, as it concerns the labourer,
the farmer, the landlord, and the consumer.   We have
seen that at no time has the last and largest class
(which also in a sense comprises all the rest) been so
favourably situated as at present.   Low prices rule, and
the consumer's table is loaded with abundance and
variety.   Let us turn to the condition of the agricultural labourer, the second largest class.   According
to the reports of the Royal Commission on Labour in
1894 the money-wages of agricultural labourers have
risen generally, though not equally, and least in corn-
growing districts; but the buying power of their wages
has everywhere vastly increased, and altogether there is
an estimated improvement of about 40 per cent in the
cost of living of this class during the last thirty years;
meanwhile free education for their children, and allotments have indirectly added to the material comfort of
the labourers.[1]

[1] From an analysis of the reports upon thirty-four districts, Mr. Little
shows that money-wages (exclusive of harvesting) averaged: In 1867–1870,
12s. 3d. a week; in 1879, 13s. 9d. a week; and 1892–1893, 13s. 3d. a week;
with harvesting the average wages in 1892–1893 amounted to 15s 11d. a
week.   The average cost to a labourer's family of five persons in flour,
butter, cheese, tea, sugar, is stated by the same authority to be:—

1860–1867 = 50·41d.
1868–1875 = 48·4.
1876–1883 = 36·21.
1884–1891 = 31·62.
1892–1894 = 29·2.

Writing in 1878, Sir James Caird (*Landed Interest*) estimated that the
wages of the agricultural classes had risen 60 per cent since the repeal of the
Corn-laws; and Sir Robert Giffen, in a paper on *The Progress of the Working Classes*, read before the Statistical Society in December, 1883, made a
similar statement.

Mr. Little, who summarized the reports of the commissioners, concludes: "It is no exaggeration to say that in the last quarter of a century a great economic revolution, accomplished with little aid from legislation, has transferred to the labourers from one-third to one-fourth of the profits which the land-owners and farmers previously received from the cultivation of the land".

One commissioner reports: "The agricultural labourers were never so well off as they have been during the last few years in spite of the depression which has caused serious distress to most of their employers".

Another writes: "The labourers are better off than they were; all things taken into account, their wages are higher, cottages more commodious, hours of work shorter, and resting time longer". Again: "Women no longer go into the fields as formerly, excepting a little in harvest or fruit time; children are at school getting a free education, which is an indirect addition to wages; young women go to service or regular occupations; and altogether the lot of the labouring class has been vastly improved; its chief drawback being the lack of rational recreation".

At the same time several commissioners speak of the decline in the efficiency of the labourers. One says: "They are less interested in their work and far less skilled than the older men who are dropping off; modern conditions unsettle them; they look less to agriculture as their life work, and take less trouble to acquire the special arts connected with it".

Turning next to landlords, we find that during the war (1793–1815) rents were more than doubled, and the Corn-law of 1815 raised them still higher. Immediately on the repeal there was a fall, but this was followed in a few years by a rise, which continued until about 1878.[1]

[1] Sir James Caird, in *The Landed Interest*, gives the following table for *England*:—

	1770.	1850.	1878.
	s. d.	s. d.	s. d.
Rent, ...	13 0	27 0	30 0
Labourers' wages, ...	7 3	9 7	14 0

From that time rents have declined in amounts estimated
in different parts at from 10 to 50 per cent. The fall has
been greatest in the corn districts, and in some parts of
Essex corn-land has gone out of cultivation. The fall is
least in districts where cattle, butter, and cheese form
the chief products. Over a large part of the country
the landlord-interest has suffered considerable loss:
land-owners large and small, corporations, and all institutions which were dependent upon rents, in the parts
most affected—*i.e.* where it has become unprofitable to
continue corn-growing—have experienced a serious diminution in their finances. This has been strongly exem-
plified in the case of some of the Oxford and Cambridge
colleges, whose revenues are derived from land in the
eastern counties, and also by instances like that of Guy's
Hospital, the income of which fell one-half from depreciation in land values. Clergy dependent upon the rent
of glebe-land or upon tithes, which have fallen with the
price of corn, have suffered acutely. The Duke of Bedford's book, *The Story of a Great Agricultural Estate*,
proves conclusively that purely agricultural outlay has
in some cases yielded only loss in recent years; and if
rent be regarded as the return to capital invested in improvements during the past twenty years, it has in such
cases proved a bad investment. Estates purchased about
1873, when rents were about the maximum, have been
offered for much less than half the amount given for them.

To rent-receivers, then, the fall in prices of agricultural
produce has yielded a serious loss of income, and the
contraction of the spending power of this class has
affected industries and classes which were dependent
upon their expenditure. Local employment has suffered,
and local institutions have lost some of the support
which was accorded from this source.

As pointed out, the fall in agricultural rents is very
irregular, and has been determined by the character of
the soil and products. Pastoral counties like Cheshire
have suffered little; and in many districts, where town
population has been increasing, the net result to rents of
land from all sources has been an increase, owing to the
extension of building.

While money-rents have fallen, the same general fall in prices, which has benefited all consumers, must be set against the fall in the matter of ordinary expenditure of incomes derived from rent. A fact of great importance in some cases as an off-set to the fall in agricultural rent, is the increase in ground-rents of houses, shops, and manufactories. The growth of population and of industries has created a steady demand for building land, thus augmenting the incomes derived from land which is diverted from agriculture to building, while house-rent has formed an increasing item of expenditure for all classes of the population. Agricultural rental in the United Kingdom is estimated at about £50,000,000,[1] and the ground-rental of houses, &c., at a somewhat larger and increasing amount. Professor Marshall writes: "Taken altogether the *money* rental of *England's* soil is probably twice as high, and its *real* rental three or four times as high as it was when the Corn-laws were repealed".[2] The rise in ground-rents and the fall in agricultural rents are both in conformity with the economic principle that rent is a surplus profit, and varies with price under the play of free competition.[3]

[1] The Reports of the Commissioners of Inland Revenue give the gross annual value of lands (including tithes) for Great Britain as follows:—

	Gross Annual Value.		Decrease.	
	1879–80.	1893–4.	Amount.	Per cent.
England, ...	48,533,340	36,999,846	11,533,494	23·7
Wales, ...	3,265,610	3,065,985	199,625	6·1
Scotland, ...	7,769,303	6,251,898	1,517,405	19·5
Great Britain, ...	59,568,253	46,317,729	13,250,524	22·2

[2] *Principles of Economics*, book vii., chap. 13, first edition, 722, note.

[3] Under free competition rent follows, and is determined by price; the poorest soil worth cultivating pays no rent, since it only just recovers the expenses of cultivation; all land superior to this "marginal land" pays rent in proportion to its superiority. The working of the theory, however, depends on perfect competition; in actual fact many farmers go on paying a customary rent, and rent is often treated in practice as if it were a first claim upon the land and part of the cost of production, instead of a surplus profit dependent upon price (rising and falling with it). Rent, as surplus profit, measures what is left from average farming after all average expenses

Coming last to the farmers, the only remaining interest, profits have undoubtedly fallen with prices, especially in districts devoted to corn; of this the decline in agricultural capital, and the failures and withdrawals from farming, are proof only too apparent. The Report of the Royal Commission on Agriculture, 1897, finds, that " the farmers whose accounts have been furnished have for twenty years past received on an average only 60 per cent of the sum which was in past days considered an ordinary and average profit". The chief explanation is found in the vast influx of food from Western America, produced under conditions of nature more favourable than those which prevail at home, and transported by the aid of modern science at trivial cost.[1] South America also is becoming a serious rival in wheat; in 1896 from Argentina and Chili alone we received wheat valued at £2,000,000. Rich virgin soil, a fine climate, cheap labour, low freights, and quick transit seem to promise indefinite and almost limitless possibilities of supply from these new sources for many years to come.

In the matter of British corn-production the change in the last twenty-five years has been marked. In the year 1871 there were 11,833,243 acres under corn and 22,525,761 acres under pasture in the United Kingdom. In 1895 corn covered only 8,865,338 acres, while 27,831,117 acres were devoted to pasture. The reduction was mainly in wheat, the price of which fell from 57s. a quarter in 1872 to 22s. 10d. in 1894, though it rose again to 26s. 2d. in 1896, and to 33s. 4d. in September, 1897. The home-grown wheat in 1895 was worth £8,400,000, the imported £30,700,000. The decline of arable land, and the increase of pasture, point to an

are paid. In practice many special circumstances modify this principle in particular cases. The theory is very visible in the case of ground-rents, which notoriously rise with the superiority of the site.

[1] At the present time (1897) wheat comes from the United States to London at a cost of 3s. 2d. per quarter (of 480 lbs.), but 2s. is considered a fair freight, and corn has been sent to Liverpool as ballast at 20 guineas for 2000 quarters; that is, at 2½d. a quarter. To put the matter simply, the transport of the flour in a 4-lb. loaf from the Western States of America to London costs about one halfpenny. In his speech in the House of Commons, 12th March, 1844, Cobden stated that the average cost of transit from Dantzig over ten years was 10s. 6d. a quarter.

important change which is taking place in agriculture.[1]
British farming, not for the first time, is undergoing an
experience common to all industries when new discoveries and inventions modify the methods of production and disturb either supply or demand; something of
the nature of an agricultural revolution has taken place
since 1877, comparable in importance to that which took
place in the period of enclosures (1790–1820), or to the
transition from tillage to sheep-farming in the sixteenth
century.   Manufactures have been revolutionized in
Great Britain by successive scientific discoveries yielding
new mechanical appliances or powers; each occasion
has called for some fresh adaptation, and has given a
shock to some old-established method of industry.   But
while there has been dislocation there has been also
constant advance; and the gains, not only to society
but to industry, if intermittent, have been permanent
and sure.   The changes in ship-building from wood to
iron and steel, and in artificial lighting from candles to
gas and electricity, the transformations in industry
effected by steam, electricity, and chemistry will serve
to illustrate the benefits to society from the rapid advances of science.   Wages have gone up, improved circumstances have followed; new products, new modes of
transport, and fresh industries have arisen, while the
development of the engineering trades and of the iron
and coal trades has been enormous; though these rapid
evolutions may have brought loss to some, who are
crushed out by the advance in special industries, they

[1] Total area of United Kingdom and Channel Isles=77,671,319.

AREA UNDER CULTIVATION IN UNITED KINGDOM.

	1870.	1895.	1897.
Corn, ...	11,755,053	8,865,338	8,890,092
Pasture, ...	22,085,295	27,831,117	27,924,710
Green crops, ...	5,107,135	4,399,949	4,327,568
Other crops, ...	7,550,740	8,514,198	6,726,183
Total, ...	46,498,223	49,610,602	47,868,553

During the period the largest area under corn was in 1871, under green
crops in 1871, under pasture in 1897, other crops in 1893.

have conferred greatly increased comfort upon the nation as a whole, and especially upon the classes of manual labourers.

In agriculture a similar transition is going on. Science has modified the conditions of production and exchange very greatly during the past twenty years, and success in this sphere of industry now demands knowledge of the most recent scientific and business methods, and a readiness to profit by the latest information. It is probably due to slowness in these respects, and to an adherence to old-fashioned ideas and methods, that British farming has been outstripped in some directions by its younger competitors in the States and in the Colonies, and even nearer home.

The fact must be admitted that wheat-farming has suffered a decline in Great Britain. Notwithstanding a temporary revival in prices, we cannot compete in cereals with the rich virgin soils of the almost boundless plains of North and South America. Ultimately, no doubt, these countries will consume their own crops, but for a considerable period we may count on large and cheap supplies from their fertile soils, which will undersell corn from the inferior lands in Great Britain. In 1895 there were in the United Kingdom[1] only 1½ million acres under wheat,[2] while oats occupied 4½ million acres, and

[1] The latest official figures attainable are as follows:—

AREAS UNDER CORN CROPS IN THE UNITED KINGDOM
IN 1897 AND IN 1896.

Crop.	1897.	1896.	1897 compared with 1896.	
			Increase.	Decrease.
	Acres.	Acres.	Acres.	Acres.
Wheat, ...	1,938,956	1,734,118	204,838	—
Barley or bere, ...	2,213,529	2,285,933	—	72,404
Oats, ...	4,226,231	4,303,697	—	77,736
Rye, ...	89,621	88,634	987	—
Beans, ...	230,429	252,983	—	22,554
Peas, ...	191,326	196,973	—	5,647

[2] France has 17,000,000 acres under wheat, and also imported 35,000,000 bushels of grain in 1896.

barley 2⅓ million acres. Cattle-rearing and dairying are taking the place of wheat-growing. Pasturage has increased 6 million acres since 1868, and there is an addition to cattle of 2⅓ millions. Horses and pigs are more numerous, while sheep have decreased in number. It is obviously more profitable to provide for increased demands for meat and dairy produce than to grow corn. But even here competition has arisen. Improved transit brings cattle from America in greater numbers; the tinned-meat trade, which grew up some thirty years ago and threatened rivalry from Australia and South America, was followed later by the discovery of a process by which frozen mutton was shipped from New Zealand.[1] No fall in meat, however, took place until 1884. It was feared that these imports would be a serious blow to British farming, but the most marked effects have been a great increase in the consumption of meat and of trade with the Colonies, which take our manufactures in payment for food. The cheaper and more abundant supply of meat rendered possible a better standard of living among some classes, while the demand for the superior British meat has remained as strong as ever.[2] It cannot be said that foreign beef displaces British beef, for the Royal Commission reports there is no diminution in the absolute quantity of meat produced in the United Kingdom; and though the wholesale price of British meat has declined 30 to 40 per cent, the price of superior British meat has not fallen appreciably to buyers in retail markets.[3]

In yet another direction has the farmer found himself tried by modern progress. Butter, cheese, and eggs to the value of £26,000,000 are imported annually. The factory system of making cheese, which was quickly adopted in the United States, introduced a serious com-

[1] Quite recently a vessel has been built for the Australian trade with cold storage for 90,000 carcasses of sheep, besides accommodation for other cargo and passengers.

[2] Imports of meat (live and dead) into the United Kingdom have increased from 22 lbs. per head in 1876-78 to 40 lbs. per head in 1893-95.

[3] The Duke of Bedford writes (*Story of a Great Estate*): "A recent Blue Book shows that the profits of the grazier are principally absorbed by the middleman and the railways".

petition with English cheese; this was followed by the application of the freezing process and cold-storage system to butter, which, combined with the co-operative system of dairying, have led to large exports from Australia in ships specially constructed for the purpose. The co-operative dairy system was speedily copied in other colonies.   Meanwhile in Europe, Denmark and Sweden had turned to dairy-farming and the co-operative system of butter-making with great success. These countries have adopted the most recent improvements in the methods of production and in the organization of the sale, with the result that they are underselling Great Britain in her own markets.   Butter worth £6,250,000 came from Denmark alone in the year 1896. At the International Congress on Technical Education, held in London in June, 1897, Sir William Windeyer of New South Wales read a paper in which the following remarks occur:—

"As a visitor to England I have been somewhat surprised at the absence amongst English farmers of *that co-operative organization* in the dairying industry which is so conspicuous amongst the farmers of New South Wales, and which enabled the Australian Colonies in 1896 to send you, at a profit to themselves, 17,000 tons of butter; whilst the dairying industry of England seems to me to be languishing for want of the diffusion of that *scientific teaching* of the best methods of producing a uniform quality of butter which has given Denmark and other countries so large a control of the English market".[1]

This extract points to one serious cause of the depression in British agriculture, namely, that it is falling behind other countries in scientific and technical knowledge and in business organization.   Whilst farming is being conducted in other countries on the most modern business principles, and with the utmost skill in the application of science and economic methods, it is being

[1] In 1895 there were 155 butter and cheese factories in Victoria, which exported 21,000,000 lbs. of butter.   The Government has given no bonus since 1893–94, but the butter may be stored in the Government refrigerating works free.   There is a bonus on exported cheese of 3*d*. a lb.

pursued in England far too much on the old traditional lines. British farmers have a natural protection in the expense of carriage from distant parts; and, with the application of the highest science to their industry, and of the principle of combination to the disposal of the product, they ought to be able to hold their own in matters like dairying against the world. There is no remedy for this defect but progress, and it is useless to ask for prohibition or restriction, which would only encourage greater inefficiency. Large production has been a great factor in the success of manufactures, and it is secured in the matter of butter and cheese in a country of small farmers like Denmark by co-operation. The same system, if adopted here in conjunction with the most approved methods of manufacture, would secure the pre-eminence of home-made butter, for there is a natural prejudice in favour of home products.[1]

The British Dairy Farmers' Association was founded in 1866 to promote this kind of knowledge by conferences, exhibitions, and experiments. It has established a Dairy Institute and Dairy Farm, Schools, and Colleges, it encourages butter factories and creameries. Yet its representatives admit that they make converts very slowly, and they complain bitterly of the want of technical education and of interest among those most deeply concerned—both farmers and labourers.

Cattle and dairy farming, supplemented by the rearing of fowls, would seem to be at present the most paying side of British farming, and in all these branches British produce is admittedly superior to foreign pro-

---

[1] The small French-Canadian farmers adopt the same system of co-operation for dairying and other matters. The writer, when visiting Canada, noticed on the roadside not many miles from Quebec stone slabs projecting from the walls in front of each little farm; on inquiry he was informed that the peasants placed on these their cans of milk, which were then collected by a common cart and carried to the butter factory. Contrast the economy of this joint action with the perverse individualism of the British farmers, who persist in making their own butter in the old-fashioned way, and finding their own market, and also in sending their individual milk-cans to the railway-station. The writer once asked a small East Anglian farmer why he and his neighbours did not make some attempt at co-operation; the reply was, that "he had once suggested it, but without success; they were all jealous of one another, and each supposed the other wanted to make something out of it".

duce, while the same cannot be said of corn. It is a question of expense and method, and improvements in the latter will diminish the former. If Great Britain falls behind the United States and Germany in efficiency, or in the knowledge of chemical and other sciences, she pays the penalty in injury to her manufactures; the same applies to the agricultural industry. It is necessary that those engaged in agriculture shall be made familiar with the best that is known respecting their art, and all that the sciences of chemistry and mechanics, that commercial and economic methods, can contribute, be regarded as essential to its success. The plain fact is, that the conditions under which agriculture can be successfully carried on have been transformed by modern science, and the only mode of meeting the competition of those who have adapted themselves to the changed circumstances, is to adopt the same or superior methods.

Experts in agricultural matters and in the science of farming are loud in their lamentations over the apathy of practical farmers, and the want of co-operation and mutual trust which would enable them to emulate their rivals in methods which depend largely upon union. We read that farmers trust too much to experience, often gained personally at much loss and labour, although it is out of date in the presence of ever-advancing science; they have much manual skill, but little technical knowledge; only a minority avail themselves of the opportunities offered for acquiring the principles of their art.[1] Labourers are not as a rule skilled except in routine work; they are wanting in observation and, above all, in knowledge of the scientific basis of their work; and they require more training in the principles of agriculture. Some technical agricultural schools in this country afford encouragement by their results, but those who attend them constitute, as yet, a very small percentage

[1] A young intelligent farmer known to the writer (and son of a farmer who was a strong Protectionist), after attending lectures given by the County Council completely changed his practice and views, and has become convinced that he can make farming a success, yet he cannot succeed in inducing other farmers to attend the lectures ; a typical reply being that of one of them, who said of the lecturer, "What I don't know he can't tell me".

of the classes interested in the industry.   When the knowledge has penetrated so as to reach all small farmers and labourers, market-gardeners, and allotment-holders, there will be a revival in the affairs of agriculture, and much produce now imported may be expected to be plentifully supplied at home.   In short, there is a great consensus of opinion among experts that scientific knowledge is more backward in farming than in other industries, and that among the large body of practical agriculturists the prevalent adherence to traditional methods is adverse to the success of the industry under the conditions of modern competition.

As a minor branch of agricultural industry, the rearing of fowls has been much neglected in this country in comparison with continental countries where peasant farming prevails.   There seems no reason why it should not rank higher and form at all events a valuable supplement to other branches of farming.   Recent experiments in Sussex, where fowl-farming and feeding have been systematized, appear to prove that it has peculiar difficulties where it constitutes the sole industry, but as an addition to small dairy farms it demands more attention than it receives.   The revenue to be derived is not a negligible quantity, since the demand for eggs in every town and village is constant, and good prices are obtainable.   If it pays to import eggs and poultry of the value of £4,750,000, it would certainly pay to raise more at home.   Facilities are now being provided by some of the principal railways to send farm-produce to towns on easy terms in a convenient manner and in small quantities.   A century and a half ago, according to Defoe, the rearing of geese and turkeys was a considerable industry in East Anglia; the birds were then driven to town on foot from remote parts of Norfolk and other eastern counties, often in droves of a thousand or more.   The system of capitalistic farming, which began to grow up in the eighteenth century, has driven out fowl-farming among large farmers, who have been trained to look to corn, cattle, and roots as their sole produce.   The Corn-laws are largely responsible for this, since they inculcated the doctrine that Great Britain should be self-

supporting as regards bread, and that the chief end of
farming should be the production of corn.   Statistics of
consumption, however, prove that the demand for eggs,
fowls, and rabbits is such as would find employment for
a considerable rural population.   There is no presump-
tion in arguing from the above facts that a section of
the agricultural community might find in the smaller
products a profitable adjunct to the other branches of
their industry, one which would involve no great capital
or risk, and which would at the same time satisfy a
constantly-increasing demand.   The difficulties of transit
are being removed, and business organization, which
would dispose of the produce without handing over the
profits to middlemen, seems to be the chief thing wanting to enable considerable additions to be made to the
incomes of many small farmers from this source.

The Report of the Royal Commission on Agriculture,
issued in the autumn of 1897, gives no support to Protection as a remedy for low prices.   It points out that
agricultural depression is general all over the world, and
is even felt severely in the countries which, like the
United States, are large exporters of corn.   The conclusion of the Commission is, that for some time past
there has been general over-production of corn.   Rapid
increase in the conveniences for cheap transport has
brought more distant lands under cultivation, and has
over-stimulated production, especially of wheat; and
until supply and demand have adapted themselves there
will be excess in production and unprofitable prices.
Though prices fluctuate with each year's total harvest,
or expected supply, on the whole there is little hope
of any material *permanent* rise in prices for the present,
in the face of the extraordinary fertility and extent of
corn-land in Argentina, and the slight cost at which she
can raise wheat and send it to Europe.   The direct
remedy for the farmer is in a reduction of rent, which,
however, comes but slowly, and transfers the loss to the
land-owner; other palliatives are in the direction already
indicated.   On this report Sir Robert Giffen has put
forth an interesting speculation, based upon comparative
statistics of British consumption of meat and corn.   He

finds that while the consumption of meat has vastly in
creased, that of wheat has fallen off. He concludes
that improved resources have converted bread-eaters
into larger meat-consumers, and have thus reduced the
demand for bread. The over-production of corn is thus
translated into a falling off in demand: "cereals have
been subjected to a new indirect competition of meat".
This fact is matter of congratulation to the community,
as it bespeaks a higher standard of living, but it presses
hard meanwhile on the producer of corn. No doubt
both events have occurred, *i.e.* the supply of wheat is
increased from new districts, and the demand relatively
to the population has yielded to meat; in any case it is
by the adjustment of supply and demand that the price
is fixed, and the temporary conditions affecting supply
and demand have yielded a low average price.

The whole official inquiry supports the conclusion
already arrived at in this work, that in the immediate
future the success of British agriculture must be looked
for rather in the supply of superior meat, dairy produce,
vegetables, and fowls, &c., than in the growth of cereals.

One matter concerning markets possibly calls for
regulation in the farmers' interest: this is the question
of railway rates, which are said to operate seriously to
the disadvantage of British agricultural producers. The
transit of produce from some rural parts to markets is
difficult, and the cost is in excess of that from foreign
countries, which succeed in negotiating low "through-
rates". No doubt the railway companies find difficulties
as regards the smaller quantities forwarded, irregularity
of supply, and imperfect packing, all of which could be
removed by some system of organization and co-operation
on the part of farmers. But the grievance calls for investigation, and some arrangement by which British
industry shall not suffer to the advantage of a foreign
rival. This is probably a proper subject for Government
inquiry and intervention. It would not be a case of
artificial aid; for the protection, if any, is on the side of
the foreigner. At all events, in the interests of British
agriculture it is necessary that the railway companies
and farming interests should combine their powers and

arrive at some satisfactory solution.   Doubtless both
would ultimately profit by such a scheme of rates and
such an organized trade as would materially increase the
facilities for placing British produce in British markets.[1]

Many other questions enter into the complicated problem of agricultural decline.   Such are the conditions of
land-tenure, and the expense and difficulties of land-
transfer.   Free-trade in produce did not bring Free-
trade in land, and in this country there are still many
obstacles attending the sale and transfer of land that do
not apply to other forms of wealth, and that do not exist
in the countries which are its rivals in agricultural production.   Competent writers on this subject have long
pointed out much-needed reforms affecting ownership,
transfer, and tenure.   These should tend to direct capital
to the land as a commercial venture, and enable it to
be easily acquired by those most desirous and able to
develop it; they should give greater security to agricultural capital, and stimulate various kinds of investment
that would utilize the land most profitably in different

---

[1] By the courtesy of the secretary of the Great Eastern Railway Company,
I am enabled to state the results of an experiment commenced by that Company on 1st December, 1895, for forwarding farm and dairy produce to
London and other towns at low rates.   The railway company supplies boxes
of various sizes for a few pence at the stations, and charges at the rate of 4d.
for 20 lbs. weight, including delivery in town.   The Company also has
collected, and distributes gratis, a list of 1100 farms from which produce can
be obtained.   During the thirteen months ending Christmas 1896, the Company carried 61,412 boxes; in the eight months to end of September, 1897,
this was increased to 82,000 boxes.   The contents of the boxes are valued
at an average of 7s. per box; this gives in the last eight months a value of
£28,700 of farm-produce transmitted by the Company direct from farmer to
consumer at a very cheap rate.   The result is most encouraging, and doubtless co-operation and a little organization by farmers may carry the economy
and profit still further.   The farmers obtain by this means about double the
price for eggs which they receive when they are collected by middlemen.
On the other hand, it should be stated that an attempt to introduce a somewhat similar system by the London & North-western Railway Company was
not successful.   The Company sent out agents, who interviewed 1000 farmers,
and endeavoured to induce them to combine so as to guarantee truck-loads
of not less than 2 tons at low rates.   The official report states that the movement met with scant encouragement, and that (a) the number in favour of
combination was exceedingly small, (b) that more that one-half showed
absolute indifference, (c) that generally there does not appear to be any really
acute depression in the farming industry in their district, and (d) most of the
farmers did not seem to look to railway rates as a cure for any depression
there might be.

localities.   Some improvements in this direction have
been effected by Lord Cairns's Act, the Agricultural
Holdings Act, the Allotments Act, and others; but these
measures have not yet accomplished that degree of freedom which is essential to the fullest development of the
soil.   This is not the place for a discussion of these suggested reforms, they can only be alluded to as essential
factors in a complete investigation into the complicated
question of the backwardness of agriculture in a country
progressing so rapidly in other directions.   The tendency
of the reforms already made supports the conclusion
that it is the removal of restrictions to the free application of capital, knowledge, and skill, and not any reimposition of restraints, that is required to advance this
most important branch of national industry and source
of national wealth.   Protection can afford no remedy,
and could only intensify the evils which existed before
its abolition.

In connection with the agricultural problem, a few
words may be devoted to the question of rural depopu-
lation, *i.e.* the tendency for country labourers to flock
into towns, and for urban population to increase while
rural population is diminishing.   The phenomenon is
visible in all progressive countries—the United States,
France, Germany, and the Colonies—though in a less
degree than in Great Britain.   Several causes contribute,
and chief amongst them that progress in science and its
applications which have enabled man to be fed at less
cost and to devote more labour to manufacturing industries.   Owing to discoveries and improvements in
the methods and tools of agriculture, to the application
of machinery (steam-plough and thrasher, self-binding
reaper, &c.), fewer labourers are required to supply the
demand for food, and a large number are set free to
minister to other wants.   In our own country the importation of corn, and the conversion of arable land
into pasture, have had an additional effect.[1]   Meanwhile
the growth of manufactures and the spread of railways

---

[1] The Duke of Bedford writes: " For every 200 acres of arable land converted into pasture, we may assume that five labourers are displaced ".—
(*Story of a Great Agricultural Estate*, p. 196.)

find employment at higher wages for a continually increasing number. Improved education, newspapers,
post, cheap travelling, open up new possibilities and
more attractive industries to villagers, and the sons of
agricultural labourers become artisans earning much
higher wages than their parents. The railways and
police draw away many vigorous young men. Others
find employment as carters, porters, &c., in towns,
where their superior strength often displaces weaker
town-bred labour. From Mr. Booth's investigations in
East London we learn that these countrymen usually go
to places provided for them by friends in towns, and
that in the "submerged tenth" are to be found very few
genuine country labourers. Again, modern progress has
accentuated the attractiveness of towns, and brought it
into contrast with the dulness which often characterizes
the village life of the labourers. Thus intelligent and
enterprising young men seek towns to improve their
chances in life, and to enjoy the greater interests which
towns offer them. Further, with the growth of machine-
industry, by-employments for women and the children
of rural labourers have declined; for their daughters,
service in town is the only field, while towns provide
subsidiary employment by which the incomes of families
may be augmented.

Thus the movement of population is largely explained
by those forms of progress which have effected economies in the methods of producing food, which have
made communication easy, and which have called into
existence innumerable kinds of new industries—the advent of steam, railways, mechanical inventions, &c.—it
is one of the effects of the transition to a mechanical age
of large industry. To the labourer it means generally
higher wages and other advantages, together with the
stir and excitement of town life. Important questions
arise as to the influence of town life upon the stamina
of the nation, and its future effects, which are more
speculative. It is not improbable, however, that with
further scientific advances, especially in the direction of
applying electricity for the distribution of motor-force
and for lighting, many industries may establish them-

selves in country towns and villages, and again restore the balance.   Much has been written on the subject of drawing the agricultural labourer back to the land.   The problem is partly one of the system of farming and of land-tenure.   Where the peasant-property system obtains, the country is covered with small farms; and in earlier times, when agriculture was the principal occupation in this country, and the peasants had large allotments with their cottages, they could live in comfort on the land according to the standard then prevailing. But the industrial revolution has changed all that; it has found other and more profitable employments for labourers, it has introduced machinery into agriculture, and farming is now an affair of large capital, large production, and fewer labourers.

To revert to a system of small farming is not easy if it be found desirable, and it would demand a large outlay upon farm premises; the only means of keeping men upon the soil is to give them some interest in its cultivation, either by purchase or by hire, so that they shall be encouraged to look to it as a means of profit and not merely of wages.[1]

The Allotments and Small Holdings Acts have done something to foster this idea; but market-gardening, allotment and small farming, on any considerable scale, would demand great changes in land-tenure, and many primary difficulties must be met in providing houses and farm-buildings, in securing markets, and in organizing the industry on a different plan.   Still, much might be accomplished by such a system, especially on suitable land within easy reach of a town population affording an assured market for produce.   There must be a great potentiality of success for such a class of agriculturists within some zone surrounding large towns.   It has been questioned whether a century of mechanical industry has not diverted the genius of the British nation from agriculture; but it may be urged that there is much versatility in the race, and its abilities

[1] In France 17,500,000 persons are employed in agriculture; in England, by the census of 1891, there were 1,360,000 persons engaged in agriculture; in the United Kingdom, 2,500,000.

are soon applied to that which is proved profitable; also
there is a large agricultural population still to be retained
upon the soil; and it is highly desirable for many reasons,
social as well as economic, that facilities should be made
abundant, and encouragement given to every possible
form of cultivation, which can succeed by natural
methods and the application of the fullest knowledge,
so as to obtain the maximum advantage from the cultivation of our own soil.

Chapter X.

The Reaction against Free-trade.

In recent years there has appeared a kind of reaction
against the Free-trade doctrine, which was so strenuously
upheld during the first thirty years following the repeal
of the Corn-laws.   This seeming desire for a return to
protective legislation is manifested in various ways—by
the growth of Fair-trade societies, occasional motions in
the House of Commons of a protective character, various
proposals for measures to provide against scarcity of
food, such as bounties on land under wheat cultivation,
demands for countervailing duties against foreign bounties, attacks upon Cobden and his political views, articles
dilating upon the progress of other countries, and so
forth.
    Several causes have lately conspired to give a certain
vitality to this retrograde tendency.   The expectations
of those who believed that an era of universal free-trading was at hand have not been realized; France and
Germany have both gone back upon the lines of national
protection; the United States has extended and increased
its tariffs; and most of our Colonies continue the policy
of promoting the encouragement of "infant industries".
The apparent isolation of Great Britain in her commercial
policy has caused some wavering on the part of those
who conceive that a doctrine, if sound, must gain

general adhesion.   The truth of scientific doctrines is,
however, not determined by popular majorities, and still
less by a majority of countries, in each of which there
may be a large minority of the opposite opinion; the
value of such principles must rest upon evidence.   Nor
is political practice always the exact counterpart of conviction; a nation might be convinced of the wisdom of
Free-trade and yet hesitate to adopt it because of the
practical difficulties in dealing with the vested interests
which have been created by the existing system.   In
every protective country there is a free-trading party,
but it is generally less powerful in politics than its
opponents.[1]   Again, only a limited number of any community gives any time or thought to the question, fully
understands its bearings, and takes an active part in
deciding upon it as a public policy; the majority has no
economic conviction on the subject, but is swayed by
considerations of narrower interests and by prejudices.

It cannot be said, therefore, with truth that the public
opinion of other nations is entirely adverse to Free-
trade; the utmost that can be maintained is that a
majority in each protective country is, in existing circumstances, opposed to the change.   In a previous
chapter the economic and other reasons why most
nations do not adopt Free-trade are separately discussed,
and are shown to have no weight towards reversing the

---

[1] It is a common practice to ignore this fact, and assume that the whole
of the people of France, Germany, &c., are in favour of Protection because the government has adopted it. Mr. M'Kinley's speech of February
12th, 1891, affords an illustration of this mode of argument, though he was
constrained to admit that some Americans were Free-traders. He denounced
these as wanting in patriotism on that account. "The weight of nations
is overwhelmingly on our side. Which is right—the British Government
whose Colonies and dependencies, with two exceptions, have protective
tariffs, applicable not alone to other nations but operative against England
itself; or all the rest of the civilized world? Let us call over the roll of
nations. Which are for Protection? Germany, France, Italy, Spain,
Mexico, Canada, South America, Portugal, Denmark, most of Australasia,
Switzerland, Austria-Hungary, Sweden and Norway, and the United States.
Which are against Protection? England, New South Wales, New Zealand.
It will be noted that tariff for revenue only, or tariff reform, is almost
exclusively English.   But *how stand the people of the world on this question?*
At least 430,000,000 people are in *favour of Protection*, while against it there
are 38,000,000 of Britons, to whom must be added those Americans, whose
numbers are not known, who, living under our flag, seem to follow another.
This is how the jury stands."

British policy; little therefore remains to be added with regard to that particular objection.

The reaction in Germany and France arose after the Franco-German war; both countries previously looked favourably towards Free-trade. Influenced by the success of the repeal of the Corn-laws in Great Britain, and the treaty of 1860 with France, Prussia made a similar treaty with France in 1865, and also with Britain, both of a very liberal character. After the successful issue of the war in 1871, Germany further imitated Britain in finance by copying her banking system and her commercial law, and by adopting a gold currency. The expenses following upon the war, and the increased expenditure upon armaments and naval equipments, called for fresh revenue; meanwhile a fall in prices and incomes, consequent on a general depression, made demands for further taxation burdensome. A reaction then set in; it was found easier to raise taxes by indirect means, and the protective system gained favour with some classes because it appealed to their particular interests or appeared to support national industry. Prince Bismarck, who was perhaps at the time the greatest political force in Europe, cast his influence into the Protectionist scale, and this determined the national policy in Germany. New duties were imposed upon agricultural produce and upon iron goods, machinery, railway plant, and manufactures. The sugar industry received special encouragement by bounties, and the nation gave itself again to a protective policy. The successor of the great chancellor endeavoured to return to more moderate measures, and by commercial treaties to modify the severity of the Protectionist reaction, and to a slight extent he succeeded.

German example told upon her military rival France. Similar circumstances called for great expenditure upon military equipment and made demands for increased taxation, and France began again to pursue a policy inimical to Free-trade. The commercial treaty with Great Britain was not renewed, increased tariffs were adopted, and the bounty system for aiding the sugar and shipping industries was strengthened.

In political and social movements there has been discerned something of an epidemic character.   The action
of two powerful neighbours could not be without effect
upon Great Britain; and, both from a tendency to imitation and a desire for retaliation, a revival of protective
sentiment was awakened.   The depression in British
agriculture, and the injury wrought to cane-sugar refin-
ing by the continental sugar bounties, aided the reaction
among certain classes, and a demand arose for countervailing duties on continental sugar.   An ineffectual
attempt was made by the British Government to induce
the continental nations to abandon their system of
bounties; but it was not easy to throw aside a system
in which so many interests had been created under the
stimulus and practical guarantee of the State.

The Protectionist feeling in Great Britain thus excited
has adopted the form of a demand for " Fair-trade " or
Reciprocity, and since we cannot succeed in inducing
our neighbours to abandon their policy, we are urged
to follow their example.   It is clear that the revival of
Protection on the Continent is due mainly to the expense
caused by a military and aggressive spirit, which has
led to large unproductive outlay, and that it has no
economic *raison d'être* other than that protective duties
are the most convenient form of disguising the evils
which an increased burden of taxation involves.

Probably the most powerful cause of the revival of the
Protectionist feeling in Great Britain, however, is the
depression which has overtaken agriculture during the
past twenty years, and which has been indicated by
a considerable fall in prices of agricultural produce, in
rents and in farmers' profits; at all events the largest
expression of Protectionist sentiment comes from those
interested in this industry, and they are both numerous
and influential.   Further, the losses incurred by land-
owners and farmers make themselves felt in their expenditure, and are thus in part transmitted to other
classes—the traders and those who in various ways are
dependent upon the expenditure of the agricultural
section of the community; hence there is a large amount
of sympathy with the sufferers.   Agriculturists look to

a rise in prices as the only means of recovery; they see no hope for a permanent restoration in the face of the extensive and ever-growing competition of other countries, and they naturally revert to the traditional "exceptional treatment of the land", and call for "moderate duties" and other modes of making their industry lucrative through a rise in price.

The whole community is profoundly interested in the problem of an adequate supply of food, and many persons seem to see cause for alarm as well as regret at the alleged decline of our oldest and largest industry. Sentiment also attaches to agriculture in a manner which no other industry awakens; hence many are prepared to hold that this industry should be maintained at any cost, and that some sacrifice by the nation would be worth making to prevent its decay. Others have maintained that special burdens attach to land, and that these should be met by special legislation. From many quarters, then, arise demands for some intervention to improve prices. The various methods suggested resolve themselves generally into some form of protective duty, or into changes in the system of currency. The bi-metallic remedy does not admit of adequate discussion in the limits of this book, nor does it properly come within the scope of a work on Free-trade. The application of the protective method to agriculture is discussed in another chapter, where some of the causes of agricultural depression and its remedies are set forth. It remains only to deal with some special points which have lately been prominently put forward.

Some advocates of Protection express great concern as to our dependence on foreign countries for food, in which they foresee the possibility of great disaster in case of war. We are told that other European nations are increasing their armaments and naval forces, and that this constitutes a menace to the very existence of Great Britain; should they combine against her they could stop her supplies of provisions and starve her into surrender in a few weeks. Other nations, it is said, are, or can be, self-supporting; Great Britain alone is dependent on external supplies. The remedies sug-

gested take various forms: (*a*) a deliberate return to
Protection; (*b*) bounties on land under corn to stimulate
the production of grain; (*c*) preferential treatment of
our Colonies to enable them to provide our external
supplies of food, &c.

A bounty on land under corn differs in no sense from
a protective duty except in the *mode* of protection.   It
would amount to a tax on the community to enable land
to grow corn which cannot at present do so, and would
become an element in the cost of the corn, that is, a tax
upon necessaries.   The dependence of Britain upon other
countries for food is undoubtedly a fact, but a review of
the history of the past fifty years and of our present
naval standing does not seem to give any occasion for
fear as to the failure of foreign supplies, but rather to
indicate that we are in a stronger position to secure
them than at any previous time.   In no circumstances
known at present could this country feed her enormous
population of 40,000,000 people at their existing standard
of subsistence; to be self-sufficing as regards food, a
portion of the population would need to emigrate, and
of the remainder, the majority must betake themselves to
agricultural pursuits.   Is the nation prepared to put
back its progress and revert to that position in order
that it may be self-sustaining, when by means of free
exchange it is able easily to maintain its vast population
in considerable comfort?

Our dependence upon other countries has a counterpart; if we take food from them, they take from us
manufactured goods; they seek our products as eagerly
as we desire their grain, and in case of war they would
be no less desirous to dispose of their produce, which
would directly or indirectly reach our shores.   The
decrees of Napoleon did not put a stop to the trade
between Great Britain and the Continent; French merchants sent their corn to Great Britain, while French
soldiers were clad in English woollens.   A world-wide
free commerce now brings us abundant and cheap food
from all quarters, and even a deficient harvest at home
causes no suffering.   Many countries compete to gain
our markets for grain, and in all quarters of the globe

vast quantities of corn are annually grown for British consumption, for which no market could be found if we ceased to provide one; and so suitable are many newly-accessible districts for corn-growing that there seems to be little cause for anxiety as to the supply, provided that Great Britain is capable of protecting the food in transit. In the case of such an undesirable event as a war with any country which sends us food, the rise in price would call forth additional supplies from all other countries capable of increasing their export. One conclusion is very obvious—an island nation must depend ultimately upon her naval defences; to such a people a powerful fleet is as essential for national existence as for the protection of commerce. We may then rest with more assurance upon obtaining adequate supplies of food from other countries than upon our own capacity to produce them, and ironclads are more efficient for that end than bounties on land growing corn at an economic loss. To attempt to provide our own food-supply from British soil would, with our present population, only precipitate the very evil of famine the alarmists dread. France affords an example of the folly of excessive precaution; she spends nearly three-quarters of a million annually to provide her own salt, for fear there should be a deficiency in case of war. The greater part of this outlay would be saved by purchasing her salt abroad.

The remaining suggestion is that the Colonies should be encouraged by preferential duties to supply our wants. The objections to such a course are discussed in a later chapter. Canada has set an example of giving preferential duties to the home-country in return for the defence she affords, and this without making any claim for special treatment of Canadian exports: by this step Canada will secure greater advantages from the home trade, and we may hope to see much further development on these lines. The Colonies may be expected to provide a continually-increasing proportion of our food-supply. It is highly desirable that this should be the case, and so far as it can be promoted without any departure from Free-trade principles it should be encouraged. But, to a Protectionist, food from the Colonies must appear to be a very inadequate and unsatisfactory solution of the problem of dependence.   Further, the Colonies are very remote, and whatever danger a war with European powers could create to food for Great Britain crossing the ocean, would apply to food coming from distant Colonies.   National defence by powerful fleets would still be a matter of the first importance to Great Britain, and it is to this that she is constrained to look, as much on account of her insular position and the wide separation between the various parts of her empire as by the necessity for securing an adequate supply of food.

It has been already pointed out that the intercourse, relations, and interests, which are created by mutual trading, constitute a powerful argument in favour of peace.   In every trading community a large section becomes interested in the maintenance of markets and supplies.   It is a fallacy to start with the assumption that hostility is a permanent attitude of trading nations, and that nations arming for defence are necessarily preparing for *offensive* operations.   This is not implied by the precautions of Great Britain and the increase of her navy, though other nations might suspect it; why then should it be necessarily assumed to be the object of other nations?   The old maxim, *Si vis pacem para bellum*, implies that possible dangers are reduced by powerful defences.   But defences are not necessarily threats; if so, British fleets have long threatened the peace of Europe.   The aim of a commercial nation should rather be to encourage a better understanding between nations, to settle international difficulties by arbitration and concert, to increase the amity of nations, and decrease the probabilities of war.   Mutual economic relations, which imply an extension of the principle of the division of labour, mean co-operation, progress, increase of wealth. But some risks must attend the application of this principle, whether among nations or in communities. For example, some 5,000,000 of people pursue their daily avocations in the metropolis without any anxiety as to the means by which they will be satisfied with food and other necessaries on the morrow.   They each rely upon the co-operation of others, whose interest it is to

serve them, and they are not disappointed. It was in
this sense that Adam Smith recognized the identity of
public and private interests. Governments should rather
seek to reduce the risks contingent upon trading and
mutual dependence than, by placing restraints upon the
operations of exchange, to lose the advantages and conveniences which they confer, or to diminish the good
feeling they promote.

The Protectionist reaction has received some countenance from a very different quarter. If agricultural
profits have fallen, so also have business profits (both
industrial and commercial) declined during the last
quarter of a century, and among the classes dependent
upon this source of income much discontent has arisen.
This finds ready publicity with the capitalist class.
Without very profound investigation of the causes of
the decline in profits, some of the sufferers fall in with
the suggestion offered on behalf of agriculture, that
Protection may provide a remedy by stimulating home
industry.

Various circumstances have contributed to the decline
in profits. If, as has been maintained, the chief cause
be an alteration in the standard of value, Protection can
provide no remedy. Two other factors, however, enter
unmistakably into the explanation of low profits: (1)
the great increase in the supply of capital which has kept
pace with the prosperity of the country, and which,
being more rapid in its growth than the demand, has
forced down the rate of interest; and (2) the sharper competition of foreign countries in the markets formerly held
by British produce, which has sprung up of late years.

Formerly capital was saved only by the rich landed
classes from rents, and by the merchant traders. The
industrial revolution brought in new wealthy classes,
the manufacturer and dealer, to whom the term *capitalist*
came to be applied. These made fortunes rapidly, and
accumulated wealth. Time has wrought great changes
in this field also. The joint-stock system, banking, and
all the machinery of modern investment stimulated saving among the professional and middle classes, and
opened up new sources of income. As education and

prosperity extended, capital was augmented from the
thrifty shopkeeper and artisan class; the openings for
fresh investments were made easily available to all classes
by new developments of the loaning and company system,
so that the term "capitalist" is no longer capable of
restriction to any particular class.   The joint - stock
system is tending in some industries to drive out the
private employer, and capital is brought into the reser-
voirs of trade from tiny rivulets of saving over the whole
field of industry.   Two events have followed, which are
specially relevant to the present matter.   Although the
field of loaning has been enlarged so as to cover the
whole industrial world, capital has increased so much
more rapidly than fresh openings for its investment that
the rate of interest has declined; and owing to the
facility with which it can be borrowed the competition
of employers of capital has been greatly intensified by an
accession to the class of controllers of industry, of men
who live, not on their own capital, but by the skilful
employment of borrowed capital.   Both facts have tended
to depress profits.

Another not less potent influence in the fall of profits
is the increased knowledge and power of the working-
classes, who now, with better capacity for bargaining
and strength gained through their trade-unions, succeed
in obtaining a larger share of the product than formerly,
while legislation on behalf of labour tends to throw
greater expense upon the employer.   Meanwhile keener
competition among employers hands over, in reduced
prices, an increasing portion of the commodity to the
consumers of their products, and tends to keep down
profits by "cutting rates".   On all sides circumstances
seem to have been combining to reduce ordinary profits;
fortunes are rarely made now with the rapidity of bygone
times; men have to remain longer in business, and be
content to earn a living instead of making a fortune.
While the general standard of comfort has advanced
and prosperity has been more widely diffused, capital
has suffered a reduction in value.   The so-called depression of trade in recent years would seem to be more
correctly described as a fall in the value of investments

and capital employed in industry; it is a genuine depression as regards capital and profits, but wages on the whole have advanced, and goods have been cheapened. From business men complaints of dulness in trade have been frequent. The real fact is, that trade has been quieter but steadier than formerly; while there have been no periods of violent excitement and huge profits, commercial crises, once frequent and very acute, have been fewer and less disastrous in their effects during the past twenty-five years, and the interference with industry from these causes has been diminished. Profits, however, have steadily declined, and among the numerous causes to which this has been attributed, our free-trading system has, without any reason, been included. If profits were determined by Free-trade, the fall should have commenced from its adoption, but the contrary was the case; profits rose and were maintained for thirty years after 1846. The decline has taken place during the last twenty years, and must therefore be accounted for by causes which have made themselves felt in that period.

The other factor contributing to the fall of profits is the competition of other countries, which has lately become so keen and intense. On this account some persons favour protective proposals as a species of retaliation or defence. Our rivals have gained a firmer footing in neutral markets, and their rivalry has reduced prices. Time was when Great Britain had sole command of many markets, she was in the van of mechanical invention, and early succeeded in spreading the products of her industries over the globe; but she could not hope to retain this monopoly. There is no "corner" in scientific knowledge or industrial skill; other nations are rapidly developing their powers and extending their industries, and their commercial activity is increasing; their competition is inevitable, and has hereafter to be recognized and reckoned with. Its tendency is, however, to lower profits. This fact has naturally excited some concern; it is not the sole, nor yet the chief, cause of the fall; profits, as we have seen, have fallen from causes at home which are independent of foreign competition. But it is the commonest of errors to mistake a part of the cause for the whole; and since in this case self-interest seems opposed to foreign interests, undue emphasis is placed upon this factor. Many persons dependent upon interest on capital have suffered from reduced incomes without understanding the economic grounds for the reduction; such persons are naturally attracted by any proposal which promises a remedy; they cannot demonstrate the effects of that exclusion of foreign goods from which they are told to anticipate a revival of vigorous trade and large profits, but join in the demand for Protection, in the vague hope that it may resuscitate their business profits and restore the prosperity of a past period. There is, however, no basis for any such expectation by the method of trade regulation.

Prediction is dangerous; but the course of events seems to justify the inference that a low rate of profit is likely to prevail in the future, unless the present system of industry should undergo some very radical change. The growth of intelligence and skill, the increased habit of thrift, better means of communication, higher refinements in the machinery of finance and commerce, all point rather to an increase of competition and of the forces which have been lowering profits.

Another cause of the apparent relapse towards commercial restriction is probably to be found in the change which has come over public opinion as to the proper scope of governmental activity, and the enlarged views now prevalent in regard to the general functions of the State. A considerable reaction has taken place on this subject during the past fifty years. Many duties are now undertaken by the community which were formerly left to private enterprise, while the active interference of the State on behalf of the industrial classes by Factory and Mine legislation, Truck and Shipping Acts, Compulsory Education, Employers' Liability, Compensation for Injury, and many other measures, has tended to create a belief in the omnipotence of governments, and has led to a more distinctly socialistic kind of legislation. The extension of the functions of government by judicious regulations, imposing beneficial restraints in certain directions, has been misconstrued as a return to a general faith in Government control.   There are, however, different kinds of restraints, and they need discrimination; one class may be compatible with freedom, and another with its loss.   It is not always perceived that the character of modern interference differs entirely from that which was attacked by Adam Smith; that while the intervention in former centuries imposed disabilities, the aim of modern legislation has been to remove them, and to secure the greater freedom of the majority by curbing the power of minorities (whether individuals or classes); that the protection that is secured by Acts regulating mines and machinery is different *in kind* from that which conferred a monopoly upon a favoured industry; and that compulsory education is an interference which gives benefits to many, while protection for native industries takes something from all.   To place restraints on adulteration, or on the power to enslave young children in mills, is not the same thing as to prevent a nation from buying its food at a cheaper rate.

The problem of the proper functions of Government is a standing topic for each generation of politicians, and a fertile field of debate.   No absolute solution is attainable; much depends upon the nature of the government, and much upon the governed.   But the stage of development, the standard of education, the material prosperity of the nation, the degree of political freedom, the capacity for organization, the morality of the people, are all factors in the problem.   The meaning and nature of true liberty is open to various interpretations; opinions have fluctuated from the pole of an extreme individualism, which would leave to Government nothing beyond the protection of life and property, to that of an advanced and absorbing socialism in which the individual is totally merged in the citizen.   The movement of public feeling in the direction of socialistic legislation has distinctly aided the Protectionist reaction by its exaggerated beliefs in the power of the State to remove economic evils, and its tendency to substitute State action for individual enterprise, and to refer many questions to Government which can only be ultimately resolved by the conduct of men themselves.   There is an element of confusion both as to the field in which Government intervention can avail, and as to the characteristics of the intervention which is beneficial; but this confusion has, for the time, contributed to uphold the wave of Protectionist sentiment.

A cause somewhat related to that last considered, and yet differing from it, may also have assisted the reaction. This is the attempt occasionally made to identify the economic doctrine of Free-trade with a general policy of *laissez-faire* and with the political opinions of some of the early advocates of Free-trade.   This is unjust.   Peel certainly did not adopt Free-trade as part of a larger measure of non-interference; he was seriously convinced of its specific application to the facts of the time, and he was very earnest in his desire to reform taxation.   Cobden's views on general politics and foreign affairs were widely at variance with those of Peel, and they are not germane to the question of Free-trade, though they are often dragged in to its prejudice, as if the Free-trade doctrine were Cobden's peculiar invention, and summed up all his political ideas.   To attack his general politics or his business capacity is not to overthrow the validity of his arguments against the system of protective tariffs upon commerce.

Although, however, such a method of controversy is illogical, it is probable that public opinion on the Free-trade policy has been affected by the circumstance that its chief exponents and ardent advocates, between 1839 and 1846, were mainly men engaged in manufactures, who were personally interested in the issue of the agitation, since the removal of the Corn-laws would increase their export trade, and would also provide cheap food for their employees; while its chief opponents were landowners equally interested in maintaining high rents and high prices.   Of course the true judgment upon the merits of the case is unaffected by the interests of either, and depends upon the effects of the policy upon the welfare of the people as a whole.   From this stand-point the manufacturers were on the right side in advocating Free-trade, as their opponents were equally in the right when they supported factory legislation.   It is interesting to note that both conflicts worked out to the advantage of the people. The resistance of the "Manchester school" of politicians to factory legislation has, however, been employed to bring discredit upon the Free-trade measure, which they were mainly instrumental in passing, by suggesting that it was their private interests alone which they were pursuing in both cases.

The two questions are, however, distinct, and there was even no absolute identity between their supporters; some large land-owners were Free-traders, and some manufacturers were amongst the factory reformers; and it ought also to be remembered that Cobden gave it as his opinion and desire "that no child should be allowed to work in a cotton-mill earlier than thirteen years of age". Also, with whatever motives the agitation against the Corn-laws was originated,—and there can be little doubt that depression in the cotton trade was the fact which first suggested it,—the movement developed into a great national movement for a reform which benefited most of all the poorer classes, and which exacted immense service, devotion, and sacrifice from those who conducted it.

The views of Cobden on India and the Colonies, and on foreign relations generally, are no part of the fiscal doctrine under consideration; we are not concerned with the whole of his opinions. He doubtless had his limitations; his political horizon was probably narrowed by his experience, and by a tendency to look at public affairs rather from a commercial point of view. There was possibly a lack of grandeur in his political philosophy and conceptions, quite out of sympathy with the imperial idea, now so easy of acceptance after fifty years of colonial expansion. It was difficult then to foresee the rapid development of the Colonies, and their possible future consolidation. Our only considerable experience of colonization had been in America, where a policy of intervention had entailed disastrous consequences. It was not unnatural that with such a warning some well-meaning persons should push to an extreme the opposite principle of non-interference. Cobden, moreover, had exaggerated notions of the effects of commerce in pro-

ducing universal peace, and in his continual attacks on
the expense of the army and navy he seemed to forget
that it was "the strong man armed that keepeth his
goods in safety", though on one occasion he stated that
he would not object to an expenditure of £100,000,000
on a navy if Free-trade were adopted.[1] He was unconsciously influenced by the prejudices of his class and
occupation, and though his patriotism was sincere, it
was perhaps not sufficiently comprehensive to embrace
all the important factors of national greatness. There
was not an equal breadth of view in his treatment of
questions relating to land and manufactures. He could
see the injustices relating to the one industry more distinctly than those relating to the other. But nothing of
this detracts in any degree from Cobden's treatment of
the Free-trade question. He was honest, candid, and
clear-headed; he grasped the doctrine of free commerce
in all its bearings, and he devoted the best years of his
life to the removal of a national grievance, with a tena-
city of purpose and ungrudging self-sacrifice which
deserve the fullest gratitude of all, whether or not they
adopt his views on general politics, or join in his optimistic anticipations of an era of universal peace. After
fifty years of rapid development it may be as easy to
criticize the colonial views of Cobden as it is to discern
the defects of the colonial policy of a previous century,
but this is altogether beside the question of Free-trade,
which rests for its validity upon the soundness of its
economic principles and the tests which half a century
have applied to their adoption in practice. At a time,
however, when our social institutions are being scruti-
nized with no reserve, when *laissez-faire* ideas are specially unpopular, and the opinions of the "Manchester
School" find little favour, undiscriminating criticism
has succeeded in identifying the political views of this
school with Free-trade doctrines, in creating confusion
as to the real meaning of the Free-trade movement, and
in raising some doubt as to its beneficial tendencies in
the minds of those who do not clearly grasp the issue,

[1] Speech at Rochdale, June 26th, 1861.

or who have not studied the history and effects of restrictions upon commerce.[1]

Chapter XI.

Recent British Trade and Foreign Competition.

The progress in manufactures made by foreign countries, and especially by Germany and the United States,
has been so marked in recent years as to arouse concern
in some quarters about the future of British industry
and commerce.   The manner in which attention is sometimes drawn to this fact seems to assume that these
countries are outstripping us in our national industries,
that their progress has been aided by their tariffs, and
that the Free-trade policy of Great Britain is somehow
responsible for their success.   It is suggested that German goods in particular are taking the place of British
in many foreign markets, and are even "flooding our
country" to such a degree that things "made in Germany" are the chief articles of common use, and that
meanwhile our produce is being excluded from their
markets.   Hence a very gloomy forecast is made as to
the future of British trading.   It is necessary to examine
the value of these opinions in order to determine whether
the progress of other countries in industry and commerce
does in any way modify the free-trading position of this
country.

The questions of comparative trade in neutral markets,
and of the progress of other countries relatively to our
own, with the causes thereof, are so important as to
have elicited public inquiry; and we have the advantage

---

[1] See "Cobden and the Manchester School" in Mr. A. J. Balfour's *Essays
and Addresses*, which may be regarded as the counterblast to Mr. Morley's
eulogium on Cobden.   In this essay Mr. Balfour passes many strictures
upon Cobden as a political philosopher, but fully admits all that is necessary for this argument—his merit in bringing about "the change in our
fiscal policy, which was the most important work of his public life, and with
which his name will for ever be connected".

of recent official reports and statistics on this subject. Early in the year 1897 the Board of Trade, in response to a request from Parliament, issued a lengthy Memorandum giving comparative statistics of our home and foreign trade, and those of some leading foreign countries, and in the autumn an important Blue Book was issued by the Colonial Department on the growth of foreign competition in our Colonies. From these documents, consular reports, and other public sources reliable facts can be gathered.

The advance in manufactures made by other countries in the last quarter of a century is indisputable: in Germany the progress in population, industry, and commerce since the consolidation of the empire has been very great. Eleven millions have been added to the population since 1872, and the increase has been mostly in towns and manufacturing localities; meanwhile the United Kingdom has increased 8 millions, France only 2 millions, and the United States 31 millions. The population of Germany now exceeds that of the United Kingdom by 12 millions, while the population of the United States is estimated at 70 millions. All these countries have now reached a much more advanced industrial position than that which they occupied thirty years ago. It was the good fortune of Great Britain to attain a high level in manufacturing industries at a much earlier date; the products of her mines and factories long held the markets of the world with ease, since she had practically no serious rival, and under the *régime* of Free-trade her commerce expanded rapidly. More recently other nations have been developing their resources of coal and other mineral wealth, and have been increasing their scientific knowledge and mechanical skill; and they are now well equipped as competitors in many of the fields of manufacture and of commerce. It is not remarkable that their relative progress should appear rapid in comparison with that of a country which attained industrial maturity at an earlier period, and that it should even give rise to erroneous views as to its real nature and magnitude, and the causes to which it should be ascribed. It is inevitable that, at an earlier stage, growth may proceed at a greater pace, but it does not necessarily follow that the *absolute* increase is really greater, or even that it is an amount of vital significance. If a business earning £5000 a year increases 10 per cent, while a younger rival earning £500 a year increases 20 per cent, the absolute increase of the first (£500) is five times the increase of the latter (£100), although the relative progress of the latter is greater. Statistics prove that, for the present, Great Britain retains her pre-eminence as the leading manufacturing and commercial country.[1] Other countries are advancing, but as yet they have not overtaken British foreign trade.

VALUE OF EXPORTS OF DOMESTIC PRODUCTS PER HEAD OF POPULATION OVER TWO QUINQUENNIAL PERIODS.[2]

	United Kingdom.	Germany.	France.	United States.
	£ s. d.	£ s. d.	£ s. d.	£ s. d.
1870–1874.	7 7 3	2 16 7	3 15 0	2 9 11
1890–1894.	6 2 11	3 2 9	3 11 4	2 19 0

Similar Table for Domestic Imports.

	United Kingdom.	Germany.	France.	United States.
1870–1874.	9 2 4	4 6 3	3 15 8	2 18 7
1890–1894.	9 7 3	4 2 2	4 8 0	2 11 11

From these figures it appears: (*a*) That the imports and exports of the United Kingdom, per head of population, are nearly double those of any one of the three great progressive countries; (*b*) That British imports per head have increased in money values, while the exports have fallen slightly in value in the twenty-five years; that German *exports* have increased, but the *imports* have diminished in the same period (a general fall in prices has taken place since 1873, but, since it affects all the countries, it can be ignored for purposes of comparison); (*c*) The most important conclusion,

[1] For comparative total foreign trade see Chapter VIII.
[2] "Comparative Statistics of Population, Industry, and Commerce in the United Kingdom and some leading Foreign Countries", Memorandum by Board of Trade, January, 1897.

however, to be drawn from the tables, is that while a change in the magnitude of the trade is clearly going on, Great Britain retains her leading position. Germany, for example, with a larger population and a much greater extent of country, exports a little more than half as much *per head* as the United Kingdom, and receives in return, as imports, *less* than half the amount per head received by Great Britain.

Following up the comparison between Great Britain and Germany, two points—(*a*) the trade between Britain and Germany, and (*b*) their competition in neutral markets—require fuller illustration; and these two points, as involving different considerations, must be taken separately. As to (*a*) we learn from the Board of Trade Memorandum that the imports of Great Britain from Germany between 1880 and 1895 increased from £24,400,000 to £27,000,000,[1] while the exports of Great Britain to Germany in the same period grew from £16·9 millions to £20·6 millions. This means that the two nations have been doing a larger business with each other, a fact indicative of increased prosperity to both. That the imports and exports do not balance is a matter of no importance, since much trade is indirect and cannot therefore be assigned; indeed, a considerable amount of German trade passes through Holland and Belgium. There is also a certain amount of transit-trade which creates discrepancies in different statistics. The figures are sufficient, however, to dispose of the statement that German goods are displacing home manufactures in Great Britain, and are crushing out our industries. The trade is mutual, each takes more from the other than formerly. While the intercourse between the countries has grown "there has been no material displacement of home manufactures in our home market by Germany"; indeed, as the Memorandum continues, "on the figures of 1896 we seem to be increasing our market in Germany more rapidly than Germany is increasing her market here".

By limiting the comparison to selected industries, and

[1] It is worth noting that of this sum sugar amounted to £9,393,890. This is bounty-paid, and is sold to Great Britain at a loss on production.

by ignoring the *total amount* of trade, it may be made to appear that one country is encroaching upon the industries of another, and some alarm has been created by applications of this method.   Countries, however, like localities, specialize in their manufactures when it is found that they can do so successfully.   Special adaptation to circumstances enables one industry to develop in one country, another in another.   Germany has thus made great advances in certain trades, of which dyes, paper, chemicals, and electrical machinery are the prominent examples; in these industries she has been employing much scientific research, and has made important discoveries.   Other nations purchase these commodities from her with their manufactures, and thus German progress in these arts becomes a gain to the world.   To represent such new developments as injurious to British manufactures *as a whole* is to misunderstand the nature of progress as well as of trade.   With every new development, whether at home or abroad, some industries are disturbed until matters have been adjusted to the new conditions of improved efficiency: this is a factor in progress and not an injury to mankind.

Localization of trades on a large scale leads to great economies in production, and yields a natural advantage which is expressed scientifically by the Law of Increasing Return.   All the important industries in our own country have been thus localized, and this association of an industry with a particular district has been regarded not only as a sign of its success, but also as a factor contributing to its general development. The economic advantage to the world is in like manner much increased when the specialization is spread over a larger area and embraces different countries.   Dyes, paper, glass, alkalies, and musical instruments have thus come to be included among the leading industries of Germany; but if Britain buys dyes, &c., from Germany, she pays for them with machinery, yarns, and other manufactured goods (which are the products of her own specialized industries), as the figures already quoted demonstrate, and both countries profit by the arrangement.

Countries may also go on adding to their production of articles in general demand without necessarily encroaching upon one another's foreign trade. Their own wants absorb an increasing supply, and there are also possibilities of indefinite expansion in the demands of other countries. The coal and iron industries of the United States and Germany have advanced enormously since 1870, and yet the output of Great Britain is greater than ever.

COAL PRODUCTION (Board of Trade Mem.).

	Annual average, 1870–1874. Million tons.	Annual average, 1890–1894. Million tons.	Increase per cent.
United Kingdom, ...	120	180	50
France, ...	15	26	73·3
Germany, ...	32	73	128·1
United States, ...	42	153	264·3

PIG-IRON PRODUCED (Board of Trade Mem.).

	Annual average, 1870–1874. Million tons.	Annual average, 1890–1894. Million tons.	Increase per cent.
United Kingdom, ...	6·4	7·3	14·1
France, ...	1·2	2·0	66·7
Germany, ...	1·8	4·9	172·2
United States, ...	2·2	8·1	268·2

It will be noticed that the output of the United States and Germany has increased much more than that of Great Britain. This is not wonderful; their industrial development began later, and their mineral wealth is at the base of their manufacturing progress. Whether these countries will ultimately take the lead in manufactures remains yet to be seen: the probable future seat of many industries will be affected, among other causes, by recent scientific discoveries, such as the application of electrical agency derived from water-power. Both in the matter of coal and water-power the United

States promises to become a much more formidable
rival than Germany. However, the present point is
whether our foreign trade has been injured by the
progress of other nations, and if so, *whether Protection
can help to maintain our supremacy or arrest the advance
of rivals.*

Following up the comparison with Germany, it is
obvious that her home industries will consume an increasing amount of her coal and iron, and though her
exports have increased, there is no evidence that this
has been at the expense of the trade of Great Britain;
the total amount of the iron export of Germany is about
one-fourth that of Great Britain. Yet it is growing,
and the causes and methods of this increase afford
matter for reflection.

TOTAL EXPORTS OF IRON AND STEEL GOODS.			TOTAL EXPORTS OF MACHINERY OF ALL KINDS.		
	Million tons.			Millions of £'s.	
	1884.	1894.		1882.	1894.
United Kingdom,	3·5	2·6	United Kingdom,	11·9	14·2
Germany,	·8	·9	Germany,	3·1	3·9

The table shows a decline in the export of British iron
in the less highly manufactured form, and an advance
of 25 per cent in the value of exports of machinery,
which is the form involving the largest amount of
skilled labour.

Because a country is developing her natural resources,
adding to her skill and efficiency, and extending her
manufactures, it is not to be inferred that she is of
necessity driving other manufacturing nations out of the
field, for there is room for great industrial expansion in
a progressive world. No fallacy is more misleading
than that the growing prosperity of one country is
necessarily a menace or an injury to the trade of others.[1]

---

[1] "The sneaking acts of the underling tradesmen are thus erected into
political maxims for the conduct of a great empire. By such maxims as
these nations have been taught that their interest consisted in beggaring all
their neighbours. Each nation has been made to look with an invidious

If foreign trade is to exist at all it can only be carried on among nations that can afford to purchase one another's goods, that is, which have products to offer, and the amount of their trade will be determined by their prosperity. No trader desires his clients to be poor if he himself wishes to attain success in business. So, too, if nations increase their wealth by new industries, they can afford to purchase the products of their neighbours. Australia, when settled by industrious whites, became a productive country and a profitable market for British goods, and South Africa is now undergoing a similar transformation. The prosperity of these colonies has been reflected in that of Great Britain. The truth, which is so obvious in the case of new and distant colonies, loses none of its import when applied to near and more highly-developed countries. Since trade consists in exchange, and the capacity to exchange depends upon the power to purchase, any increase in this power must come from increased prosperity. The progress of any nation in civilization gives rise to the demand for the products of other nations; such we have seen to arise from the recent development of Japan, which has created a considerable trade with Great Britain, while in some directions the Japanese have become competitors with British producers. It is quite as possible to contemplate a simultaneous advance in the wealth of different nations as in that of the different members of the same community. Jealousy of the progress of other countries is as foolish economically as it is ineffective: we cannot stay their advances, while if our own progress is real, we may by commerce participate in their increased productiveness and power to purchase our commodities.

That German progress (which is very real) has not been inimical to the mutual relations of the two countries is illustrated by the following table (from the Board of Trade Memorandum), which shows the proportion of our total foreign trade with four of the leading commercial nations.

eye upon the prosperity of all the nations with which it trades, and to consider their gain as its own loss " (*Wealth of Nations*, book iv. chap. 3).

	Germany.	France.	Holland.	United States.
1880.	5·92	10·21	6·30	26·04
1895.	6·48	11·39	6·82	20·77

PROPORTION OF BRITISH EXPORTS TO THOSE COUNTRIES

1880.	7·60	6·99	4·15	13·83
1895.	9·11	6·14	3·26	12·37

Whence we see that the *relative* amount of our trade
with Germany increased during this period of fifteen
years, and that exports to Germany increased more than
imports from Germany.

Statistics relating to a particular trade, or selected
for a particular area or period, may be very misleading
if no explanation be offered of the circumstances necessary for their interpretation and for a true comparison:
such an example is afforded by the wool trade between
Great Britain and Germany.

It has been pointed out as a proof of decline of the
British woollen industry in consequence of German competition, that the total British exports of woollen manufactures have fallen in the ten years ending 1895 from
£273,000,000 to £242,000,000. In the interval German
woollen goods have been much in evidence in Great
Britain in the form of Jaeger underclothing, and also as
ready-made jackets for women, &c., whence it has been
concluded that German woollens are ousting British
products in the home market. But what are the facts?
Neglecting the decline in money values, which alone is
sufficient to explain the fall in export values, we find
that our imports of raw wool in the last twenty years
have increased from 342,000,000 to 475,000,000 lbs.;
and the employees in woollen mills from 234,000 to
297,000. Wool has become much more fashionable,
and its consumption has greatly increased *at home.*
French and German woollen cloths of special make, as
well as British cloth, are consumed in Great Britain,
but a large quantity of the yarn used for the manu-

facture of German worsted cloths is spun in Bradford, and the export trade of Bradford in yarns has flourished greatly since the German demand sprang up. In such matters as Jaeger underclothing we have a new invention which has added greatly to the comfort of mankind; it can scarcely be said to displace any other branch of the woollen trade, and it has called into existence similar industries in Scotland and England, which promise to become permanent and increasingly successful rivals of the German product. And while in 1895 Great Britain received from Germany wool and woollen manufactures valued at £1,676,000, Germany received from Great Britain wool, yarn, and manufactured woollens worth £5,000,000.

It should be observed that many imported articles, such as tin-plates, sheet-metal, wire, alkali, nail-rods, and paper, are rather the raw materials of other industries than finished manufactures; they represent a stage in the operations, and illustrate that mutual dependence of nations which is daily becoming more apparent. The quickness and cheapness of transport render it easy to distribute the operations of production over several countries, and to promote co-operation among nations on a scale not possible until recent times; and such international joint-production is one form of that specialization in industry which adds to its total efficiency. To such co-operation tariff restrictions upon trading only create hindrances; they place limits to the advantages that can be realized when several countries contribute, as each best can, to secure the maximum utility by conducting different branches or stages of production. We may ask, In what sense could protective duties which excluded German goods avail to increase British industry? So far as these were effectual, they could only yield a loss to both countries by diminishing their total trade and reducing the advantages which both gain from the higher efficiency of each in some special direction favoured by the interchange of goods. The fallacy has a twofold origin: it arises from limiting the observation to special industries and ignoring the total effect, and it also assumes that German

goods would be sent to Great Britain without an equivalent in British produce.

Turning next to competition in *neutral* markets, there
can be no doubt that other countries (and Germany in
particular) are making great efforts to gain new markets
for their manufactures, and are displaying much enterprise and energy in pushing their wares both in British
colonies and in foreign lands.   To all this Great Britain
can offer no resistance except the competition of her
own enterprise and efficiency: no form of Protection is
of the least avail.   Great Britain is in the position of an
old-established firm which has for a long time experienced little competition, but has now to encounter the
opposition of a young and enterprising rival.   To retain
her predominance in such circumstances she will have
to rely upon her skill and efficiency, business capacity
and energy; she will need to be vigilant, skilful, enterprising, and active to meet the desires of her customers
and anticipate their wants.   She can afford to neglect
no form of economy that arises from improvement or
discovery either in mechanism or in processes of manufacture; she must adopt the most efficient commercial
methods, and   study   the   requirements   of   different
countries.

The competition of progressive countries in many
branches of manufacture is very real, and will become
more acute as each year adds to their skill and capital.
Great Britain cannot retain permanently the advantage of
her earlier start, inasmuch as there is a general levelling
up of capacity and effectiveness, and a tendency towards
assimilation of the circumstances governing both labour
and capital in progressive countries.   The contest has
begun, and it will become increasingly keen in the
future.   Whilst it is necessary to recognize this fact as
a comparatively new element affecting British commerce,
there is no occasion for despondency, and still less
rational would be recourse to measures of a retaliatory or
hostile character, which could only lead to further dislocation.

As yet Germany has not encroached very seriously
upon the markets which our goods find in India and our

Colonies, though she is pushing steadily in that direction.[1] The proportion of German export trade with
British possessions is, according to recent statistics:—

To India,... ...	Germany £1 to £65 from the United Kingdom.
To Australasia, ...	,, £1 to £30 ,, ,, ,, ,,
To Canada, ...	,, £1 to £11 ,, ,, ,, ,,
Total British } ...	,, £1 to £20 ,, ,, ,, ,,
possessions, }	

The Memorandum previously quoted concludes "that
the greater portion of the trade in non-European countries, and in British possessions everywhere, is carried
on with the United Kingdom.   Germany runs us close
in some European countries, and especially in Russia
or Northern Europe, but with this exception our pre-
ponderance is manifest."
There is nothing, then, in the facts to indicate that
Germany, France, and the United States have been
assisted in their industrial development or foreign commerce by the protective reaction of the last twenty
years.   Their progress can be traced to very different
causes, and has been attained rather in the face of disadvantages imposed by their tariffs and bounties, both
of which are a tax upon the whole community wherever
they are imposed.   A report published in Berlin in 1882,
embodying the views of eighty-five chambers of commerce on the new tariff, found it "a cause of depression", "an injury to the working-classes", and a "burden upon national labour".   In the trade with neutral
countries, tariffs (with the exception of the recent
Canadian tariff) which do not differentiate between

[1] From a Foreign Office Parliamentary paper, prepared by the secretary
to the British embassy at Berlin, and published October, 1897, we learn
that in the whole of the German colonies (which have an extent of
1,000,000 square miles) the German population numbers 1803 persons, of
whom one-half are officials and soldiers, and the non-German white population is 1778; that the cost of these colonies is estimated at £402,000, and
that since the German colonies were founded 1¼ million German emigrants
have settled in non-German countries.   The *exports* from Germany to her
colonies in 1896 were £337,150, and the *imports* from her colonies £230,250.
The trade of the United Kingdom with her colonies and possessions was in
1896: imports from colonies, £93,208,000; exports to colonies, £90,650,000.
As German trade is practically *nil* in her own colonies, it naturally seeks an
outlet in British colonies and neutral markets.

countries, are not an important factor in determining
the proportions of trade secured by Britain and the rival
manufacturing nations.   Tariffs are obstructions in all
cases, and while commercial treaties and favoured-nation
arrangements secure small gains by their bargainings,
they may involve indirectly greater losses through their
restrictions.   In the long run the competition with rivals
in foreign commerce must depend upon the methods
indicated in the Memorandum: " The commercial position of the United Kingdom has been attained and must
be kept up by the untiring zeal and energy of the
industrial community.   The work of seeking out customers, providing commodities that customers will buy,
exploiting new markets, and elaborating new methods,
rests with the individual.   What Government can do is
to facilitate the supply of accurate and carefully-collected
information."

A complaint may here be discussed, that Great Britain
has aided the competition of other countries by the free
export of her machinery; and it has been suggested that
a prohibition of, or restraint upon, such exports would
retain the manufacture of machinery as a monopoly for
Great Britain.   For example, it has been urged on behalf of the cotton industry, that we have created rivals
in Germany and India by supplying them with British
machinery, which they now employ to the detriment of
the Lancashire trade.   Scarcely anyone, however, would
be found deliberately to maintain that a country can, in
these days, reserve to itself the monopoly of any art or
process, which other countries have capacity to practise
and utilize.   The scheme, moreover, has been tried, and
without success; for export duties on machinery were
levied early in the century as a kind of protection, and
with the idea of preventing the development of foreign
industry.   The result was, that machines were smuggled
out of the country, and that skilled artisans were
tempted over to other countries to make the machinery
there, and start industries which became our rivals.
Thus attempts to monopolize an industry resulted in
setting up opposition elsewhere.   It was under this
system that the famous firm of Cockerill at Liege, and

others in France were founded by Englishmen. The
law which prohibited the export of instruments of industry was found to be futile, and was repealed in 1844.
Fifty years have not made it more possible to monopolize
skill and knowledge. Capital and talent flow easily to
any country, enterprise is ever seeking new openings,
and these forces only require security for their application. Great Britain imports both machinery and ideas
from other countries at the present day; and she owes
the establishment of many of her staple industries, like
wool, silk, glass, hats, and paper, to the circumstance
that Flemings, French Huguenots, and other foreign
artisans were either invited to settle in this country, or
found an asylum here when exiled from their own land.

It is idle therefore to imagine that foreign competition
could in these days be affected by any such restraints,
though it was characteristic of the Protective period that
the attempt should be made. But what would be the
result if a measure prohibiting the export of machinery
for the cotton industry could be effective? At the present
time the manufacture of cotton-spinning machinery for
export employs about 30,000 British artisans, not including the large number engaged in the subsidiary
industries of coal and iron. These are skilled workmen,
earning good wages in the pursuit of a lucrative industry. To check this machine trade by destroying its
market would throw these men out of employment and
drive the industries to other countries, which would
eagerly seize the opportunity of developing them. The
foreign demand for machinery would be met from other
sources, our own cotton-spinning industry would receive
no new impulse, and we should only have handed over
a valuable industry to another nation by ruining it here.
If other countries are able to set up cotton-mills, nothing
that we can do will prevent them, but we can profit by
their orders for machinery. British mills may still compete with the foreign mills by their superiority, or there
may be sufficient demand for the products of all, as
population and civilization are constantly increasing;
but it would benefit no branch of British industry or
commerce that an embargo should be placed upon a pro-

fitable industry for which we have a special fitness, and
for the products of which there is a real demand.

Whatever inroads are being made upon British commerce by continental competition may be explained by
two circumstances unconnected with tariffs. The first
is the rapid advance of foreign countries in scientific
knowledge and research, together with their highly-
organized systems of technical education, which have
been developed within the last quarter of a century.
The second circumstance is the superior energy and
enterprise of their merchants and commercial agents,
who are sparing no effort in their eagerness to gain
markets for their products. On the latter subject the
recent Blue Books, dealing with foreign and colonial
trade, give very conclusive evidence. From the Australasian Colonies the opinion is unanimous as to the apathy
" and indifference on the part of British traders to the
wishes of their customers and a disregard for suggestions ", while "foreigners are willing to comply with
the wishes of even small buyers ". " British manufacturers are unwilling to alter their patterns or styles,
their manner of packing, and their terms, or to make
concessions in their inflexible rules, and the foreign
competitor reaps the benefit." Abundant evidence of
these defects will be found also in the reports of our
consuls abroad. The British makers of tools (axes,
hammers, saws, &c.) and agricultural implements will
not, we are told, modify the styles of their strong and
heavy products, and hence the trade goes to the United
States and Germany, which offer "light, well-finished
articles, more suitable to the circumstances, and at a
lower price". In South America the German traveller
is everywhere able to speak the language of the people,
to present samples and offer goods in terms of weight,
measure, and currency of the country. He studies the
taste and convenience of the customer in every way.
The push, initiative, and energy, and the accommodating
methods of the newer competitors are making way
against the obstinacy of English merchants, who are
less complaisant, adhere to old-fashioned methods, and
are prone to dictate to their customers the kind of goods

they should buy. The conservative element in British commerce, which adopts "the take it or leave it" form of business, is, according to all these authorities, a factor favourable to foreign competitors. British commercial travellers able to speak the language of foreigners are few, while Germans are producing trade-lists even in Japanese and Chinese.[1]

The other serious charge against British industry is that it is not keeping pace with continental countries in the application of science to industrial ends, and that the technical training of our workmen is inferior. In some departments of chemistry and electrical engineering, we are told that continental nations are far in advance of Great Britain, and that we must go now to Germany or the United States for the latest appliances and the best machinery for certain purposes. A Commission of Inquiry by British experts brings home a like complaint against our inferior equipment in science, and the smaller esteem in which scientific research is held by our manufacturers. Trained experts are largely employed at great cost by foreign manufacturers in their works, and the highest scientific knowledge is thus devoted to their service. Sir Henry Roscoe states, for example, that "he visited a colour works near Frankfurt where 100 trained chemists were employed, many of whom had devoted years to original research with a view to making discoveries. One of these men, who received £1000 a year, had worked for several years without producing any result, but eventually made a discovery which repaid the firm ten times over, and placed an entirely new branch of manufacture in their hands." Nothing of this kind is to be found in Great Britain.[2]

Public and private encouragement of research as a commercial speculation is asserted to be a chief factor in the success of these continental industries. This competition seems to be literally a competition in the

---

[1] See also *Trade of the World*, by Charles H. Gastrell.
[2] At the General Congress of Engineers held in Germany in 1896, many British engineers expressed themselves as surprised at the superiority of the German processes and methods.

application of scientific knowledge to industry, and in business aptitude for commercial operations. The field of Government action in these matters is limited but important, its aid can only be indirect. The State cannot secure markets, for purchasers must be tempted and cannot be coerced.

It is by the encouragement of science, by technical training, and by the diffusion of knowlege that the Government can best aid private enterprise. It can also help by procuring full and accurate information, some of which is constantly being published in the Consular reports, as to the needs of Colonies and foreign countries, and by issuing such information in a cheap and accessible form,—a kind of knowledge which is especially lacking in regard to the Colonies. The consular agents of other countries are said to be particularly active in informing their governments on all matters of price, fashion, demand, freights, &c., such as will aid business men in adapting their operations to the special circumstances of the markets for which they are competing. Great Britain is very inadequately represented in this respect in many countries.

There are minor ways in which Government can assist trade, as by relaxing administrative rules where they impede some desirable end, and where the modification would conflict with no established principle. The following case will illustrate this:—Alcohol is taxed for revenue in this country, and whether it is imported or home-produced there is no drawback on its consumption for scientific purposes. In Germany, however, the duty is reduced to a trifling sum in such circumstances, the consequence being that 1s. will purchase as much pure alcohol *for experimental purposes* in Germany as 6s. 6d. in Great Britain, to the manifest advantage of chemical research in Germany. Other examples may be found where the working of an inflexible administrative rule operates so as to sacrifice a greater good for the sake of departmental convenience or stereotyped system.

Sensational alarms as to the decay of British industry and commerce have been seen to be baseless, but sufficient ground exists for anxiety that the nation should realize the nature of the competition to which it will in future be subjected, and that it should recognize its own defects. Continued success has a tendency to dull effort, while competition sharpens it by enforcing the need for alertness and energy.

There are other dangers to our trade and manufacturing supremacy which originate nearer home. These are the industrial conflicts that from time to time check production, paralyse industry, and dislocate the export trade, thus giving an opening to foreign competitors. The complete stoppage of a great industry, such as coal or ship-building, or the interference with trade caused by a vast railway or dock strike, or an engineering dispute, presents far more serious difficulties and grounds for concern than the competition with foreign skill and energy. These conflicts, when they reach the stage of industrial warfare, are a calamity of the first magnitude; they inflict suffering and loss at home, and not infrequently end by losing the foreign market and handing it over to a rival producer. No other country has suffered so disastrously from these industrial wars as Great Britain, though their tendency has been seen in the United States, Belgium, and even in Australia. This is not the place to discuss the remedies, but the importance of the subject cannot be overrated in its bearing upon trade and foreign competition. A break in continuity of supply may be fatal to a business connection. The complexity of modern trade is so vast and delicate that large issues depend upon the steady working of its machinery. The economic aspects of industry are as vital as the strictly scientific and technical. The losses to the nation incurred by these struggles of labour and capital are apt to be lost sight of in the heat of a conflict. The dangers from this quarter are only to be averted by the exercise of great forbearance, and by an appeal to the common-sense of those directly concerned. If British industry be made thoroughly efficient, it may hold its ground against the world, but both workmen and employers cannot be too fully impressed with the fact that their skill, ingenuity, and industry are now pitted against those of the most intelligent and progressive nations in the same classes of employment, and that there is no form of Protection which can avail them in the struggle for superiority.

Yet one other complaint against foreign competition remains to be considered. It is said that the products of foreign " sweated labour" compete unfairly with those of English labour and tend to drive them out of the market. It is difficult to come to particulars, and identify the kind of commodity which can be properly labelled "sweated" in our imports. So many circumstances control the rates of wages and standards of living in different countries that a common standard for comparison cannot be obtained. The corn exported from India is raised by labour paid at only a fraction of the British rate, and yet it cannot be termed sweated; it is the rate customary in a backward and populous country among natives apparently contented with their standard of living. The same objection might be raised to the importation of Turkey and Persian carpets in competition with Axminster, &c. It is inevitable that so long as the conditions of life and production are so various there can be no uniform standard of wages over the whole globe, and that a cheap article by no means implies a sweated industry. In like circumstances higher-paid labour is the more efficient, and can easily maintain its ground. In Great Britain wages and efficiency have advanced together. The best-paid labour is found in the superior factories and shops, and inferior workmen gravitate to the lower class of workshops. British miners show a larger output per hour than lower-paid workmen on the Continent, and British workmen boast that their production is greater than that of lower-paid labour abroad. It may be taken as an established fact, that sweated labour will not permanently compete with, and undersell better-paid labour in the production of the same class of goods; nor will inferior goods drive out superior if the capacity to purchase be not diminished; indeed the converse of this statement has been so widely accepted as to have been generalized into an economic law, with only one exception; this is money, which, as the standard of value, occupies a peculiar position.   Inferior goods may co-exist with superior when they appeal to different classes of consumers; they are then not really in competition at all; and goods, such as Indian and English carpets, produced by labourers existing in wholly different circumstances, may both find a market owing to qualities and style peculiar to themselves; but it does not follow that their competition is in any sense unfair.

The problem of the competition of British produce with that of other countries, whether in our own or neutral markets, is finally one of *skill and efficiency*, of adaptation to circumstances, and of wise economic arrangements; but it is not a matter which Government interference or regulation by tariffs can determine in our favour.[1]

[1] The seven months' strike of the engineers (1897-1898) has revealed another serious danger to British industry. If the evidence which it has called forth be true, the restraints imposed by trade-unions upon the efficiency of labour in this country are able more than any foreign tariffs to destroy British supremacy in manufacturing, and to render British labour less efficient and more expensive in competition with the United States and Germany—countries almost free from these ruinous methods.

The chief points alleged are, that these countries are gaining upon Great Britain in engineering trades in consequence of the better and fuller employment of machinery and the absence of trade-union interference with the full exercise of each man's skill and powers. In the *Engineering Magazine* for December, 1897, Mr. Hiram Maxim writes: "It was only a few years ago that any one equipping a machine-shop obtained the greater part of his metal-working machinery from England, but to-day the obsolete, awkward, and comparatively high-priced English tools have been completely driven out of the market by the German-made American tools". From a large Russian dealer he learns that, "Formerly nearly everything came from England, but at the present time all the rough and coarse tools we make for ourselves. Moderately good tools come from Germany; very fine instruments of precision, such as squares, scales, micrometers, lathe-chucks, twist-drills, &c., from America." "It may be said that the greatest bugbear in England, the labour question, is practically non-existent among the manufacturers of high-class metal work in the eastern part of the United States. I do not believe that one per cent of the highly-skilled mechanics in the great workshops of New England belong to any sort of a trade-union." "The pay of the American metal-worker is about one-third more per hour than that of the English. Nevertheless a great variety of the better class of metal work can be produced in the United States at a considerably lower price than in England." "The American workman commences work at seven o clock in the morning, promptly on the stroke of the bell; he works steadily until twelve o'clock, recommences at one, continuing until six. On Saturdays he leaves off at one."

Mr. A. Basil Wilson, M.I.C.E., M.I.M.E., writes to *The Times*:—"At works in Elsass, now engaged on a contract for delivery of machinery in Great Britain, one man receiving 25s. per week of 60 hours attends to eight machines, producing a special article largely used in spinning machinery.

Chapter XII.

Imperial Federation.

The principle of Free-trade has, within the last few years, come up for reconsideration in a new and interesting connection. The movement for the federation of Great Britain and her Colonies in a close and firm union which shall at once strengthen the empire in its defences, call forth a closer sympathy between the inhabitants of the scattered regions of which it is composed, and advance their industrial and commercial interests, is one which has grown very rapidly and has been occupying much of public thought. The grounds on which the movement rests are political, sentimental, and economic. Community of kindred, language, traditions, religion, and free institutions unites the Colonies with the mother country by ties of mutual sympathy; the possible encroachments of military and ambitious nations impress the importance of a closer union for common defence and security upon a nation largely dependent upon her commerce with remote parts of an oceanic empire; while the purely economic advantages to Great Britain and her Colonies to be gained by increased trading are in themselves sufficient to furnish an argument for any practicable form of union which will promote those advantages in the interests of all. The idea of forming some kind of federation has taken strong hold of the popular imagination, and the problem seems to be coming within the range of practical politics. It is a hopeful sign for peace and the development of

Each machine completes one article in 2½ hours; the wages of the attendant come therefore to approximately 1¼ d. a piece. In this country, making the same article one man works 54 hours per week, and attends to one machine only, thereby naturally turning out the article at a very much enhanced price."

Free-trade cannot guarantee to a nation advantages which may not be destroyed by other causes.   If the supremacy of British labour yields to that of other countries, it is obvious to what causes it will be due, and for this there is no remedy in any kind of Protection.   Great Britain is dependent upon foreign markets for the sale of her goods; if her efficiency declines, her exports must decline also.

free institutions. The question is, on what basis the desired consolidation of the empire can be secured, and whether it is possible at all upon purely commercial and fiscal lines.

It has long been a dream of some statesmen that a Customs Union, or common system of taxation of imports, might at some distant time prevail throughout the empire. There are many obstacles, however, to this project, arising out of the very different fiscal systems adopted by the Colonies, most of which involve Protection against the mother country and one another. A simple Customs Union based upon the existing British system of taxation for revenue only would be an immense advantage; but such a scheme would necessitate the adoption of Free-trade by the Colonies, and for this they are not yet prepared. Another suggestion, based on the protective idea, is that Great Britain and her Colonies, following the examples of the German "Zollverein" and the United States, should adopt Free-trade within the empire, with a common protective tariff against the other nations. This policy, as involving the adoption of the protective principle by Great Britain, is open to the same objections on her part as the former proposal was on the part of the Colonies.

As a middle course, it is proposed that "some arrangement should be made for placing trade within the empire on a more favourable footing than that which is carried on with foreign countries"; in other words, that the Colonies should reduce their tariffs on imports from the mother country, and that she in return should place high differential duties upon all goods from foreign countries which the Colonies are able to produce. This policy also rests upon the application of the protective idea in a modified form by the mother country. It will be seen that all the schemes for commercial federation involve difficulties in detail.

The federal sentiment is a natural evolution of the civilization and circumstances of the nineteenth century; it is abundantly illustrated in other countries, and its success in the Dominion of Canada suggests its application more widely to British Colonies. The case of

Great Britain and her Colonies presents peculiar aspects and difficulties, but with corresponding advantages foreshadowed. Time has wrought great changes in the relations of the Colonies to Great Britain and to one another. The mercantilist conception of last century regarded Colonies merely as a source of profit to the mother country, to be kept in due subordination, and exploited for its own purposes. The war of American Independence demolished that idea, and led to a reaction. This time public opinion went to the opposite extreme, and on the false analogies that as ripe fruit falls from the tree, and that as children grown to manhood become independent and leave their home to found another, so it was held that Colonies, following the example of the American States, would separate themselves from the mother country when they had attained the vigour of maturity.

At the time of the Corn-law repeal, when Cobden's hopes of universal peace as a result of free commerce were high, this separatist doctrine was widely prevalent. Fifty years' experience of colonial expansion, and of unbroken good relations between the Colonies and the mother country, has led public opinion to form a very different and much grander conception of the destiny of the empire. The policy which made the experiment of placing the Colonies upon a footing of equal rights and liberties with the mother country has been attended with the most salutary results, and has justified the wisdom of its principles. Responsible government was conferred upon the larger Colonies as they grew to be capable of its exercise—it was first accorded to Canada in 1840, to most of the Australasian Colonies between 1850 and 1860, and to the Cape Colony in 1872. Legislative self-rule carried with it the control of their own fiscal arrangements. The extent of this liberty is measured by the fact that, with the exception of New South Wales, all the Colonies adopted systems of taxation, which, though differing in details, agreed in involving Protection against the mother country.

Under the stimulus given to their enterprise by freedom, the Colonies have in fifty years made rapid progress

in wealth, in population, in commerce, and in importance. Their trade with the mother country is now very
considerable. Great Britain forms the chief market
for their exports of raw produce and food, and they
take a large return in her manufactures;[1] indeed, the
Colonies and British possessions jointly obtain 77 per
cent of their imports from Great Britain, and less than
10 per cent from France, Germany, and the United
States together, although the States, by reason of
their easy access, naturally do the largest trade with
Canada.

Our trade with the Colonies only amounts to about
25 per cent of our whole external trade; but per head
of population their trade with Great Britain is vastly
greater than their trade with other countries. While
Germany and France each take from Great Britain less
than 10s. per head of their population, Australia imports
from Great Britain £8, South Africa £3, and Canada
£2 per head of population.

Financially also, Great Britain is deeply interested in
the Colonies, and they have found a convenient loan-
market in the mother country. The public debt of
Australia to Great Britain is about £200,000,000, of
Canada some £60,000,000, while India has borrowed
£350,000,000, and the remaining parts of the empire
£100,000,000. Thus intimate business relations of
many kinds between the various parts of the empire
constitute a bond of common interest, and a factor
favourable to consolidation. There are circumstances
outside the British Empire that indicate the desirability
of some closer political union. Germany has become a
powerful empire, and the "Zollverein", or commercial
union of small German states, commenced by Prussia in
1834, has been extended to comprise the whole of Germany. As the United States have expanded their territory, they have maintained their fiscal union so as to
confer Free-trade over the whole of their extensive
federation, and they have sought, though unsuccess-
fully, by commercial relations to bring Canada within

[1] In the year 1896 imports from the British Colonies and possessions
amounted to £93,208,000, and exports to £90,650,000.

the scope of their fiscal union.[1] On the other side of
the globe the movement for federation is growing, and
there is little doubt that the whole seven colonies of
Australasia will at no very distant date be brought under
some common scheme of political and financial union.
Meanwhile the federation of the South African colonies
has been postponed indefinitely by recent unfortunate
events.

Federations are formed between countries from various
motives, but in all cases of federation, projected or
accomplished, the advantages to be gained from the
extension of the area of trading have been prominent
amongst the benefits, either anticipated, or claimed as
having accrued from the union. The fact is a strong
indication of latent discontent with the system which
imposes limitations. It constitutes a kind of protest
against the unreasonable restrictions which the protective system creates, and betrays an unconscious leaning
to the Free-trade principle. The countries joining such
unions look for some additional outlet to their export
trade, and they find it unattainable except upon terms
of mutual concession. They seek by treaties and federations to escape from the consequences of their self-im-
posed limitations. The whole of such expedients are a
condemnation of the protective principle. The policy of
Canada since 1867, and especially in the year 1897,
gives ground for hoping that intercolonial federation
will generally tend towards a more liberal commercial
policy.

The notion of an imperial inter-trading federation with
a zollverein appeals strongly to those who feel the strain
of an ever-increasing competition with progressive rivals.
A feeling of resentment against those nations that, by
their increasing tariffs, threaten to reduce our export
trade, provokes a desire for retaliation, which seems to

---

[1] The denunciation of their treaty with Canada in 1864 amounted to an
attempt by commercial pressure to bring her within their political union.

find possible satisfaction in the exclusiveness of a British and Colonial prohibitive tariff scheme.

It is argued that an empire on which the sun never sets is capable of yielding almost every species of product, and of becoming self-sustaining and self-contained. It is also maintained that the consequent internal development would compensate for any losses which might be incurred by narrowing down the limits of commerce to the boundaries of the empire, while the political and other advantages of consolidation would count as considerable assets in the balancing of accounts. It should be observed that the latter part of this argument assumes (what requires proof) that commercial union can be a satisfactory basis of federation, and also that it will yield the political and other advantages alluded to. Some supporters of federation lay stress upon the importance of federation for defence, and consider that fiscal autonomy is quite consistent with such an arrangement. On the other hand, it is argued that a policy which would convert Great Britain and her Colonies into a self-sufficing empire is merely a return to an earlier stage of civilization, with an amplification of the area occupied by the State; that it is retrogressive, and entirely antagonistic to that principle of evolution which has developed the commerce of modern times; and that it is opposed to the progress of science, which, by enormously reducing geographical distance and the cost and time of transport, tends to make the products of the whole globe accessible to every nation.

The common proposal is, that Great Britain shall meet the Colonies half-way and effect a compromise by placing differential duties upon the goods of other countries, in order to give preferential trade to the Colonies, in return for which they are to reduce their tariffs on British goods.

Now British trade with the Colonies and India amounts to about one-third of her total commerce with foreign

countries.   From the United States alone we took
goods to the value of 106⅓ millions sterling in 1896,
an amount equal to our imports from the whole of the
Colonies (93¼ millions in 1896), although the proportion
of trade with the United States has been diminishing,
while that with the Colonies has been increasing.   The
total of British imports in 1896 amounted to £441,808,904.
The effect therefore of this proposal would be to tax
75 per cent of our imports, in the hope that these may
be ultimately supplied from colonial instead of foreign
sources.   This would raise the price of these commodities to all British consumers, who would accordingly
suffer loss, and it would be equally disastrous to British
industry by raising the cost of raw materials.   A further
effect would be to reduce our exports to those foreign
countries, and to injure the industries which manufacture
those exports.   As an act of commercial warfare, dis-
ordering trade and damaging foreign industries, it would
call forth unfriendly feelings, and perhaps even acts of
political hostility.   The tendency of modern times has
been by foreign trade and exchange to increase mutual
dependence, friendly intercourse, and good relations.
Many of our industries depend upon other countries for
their half-manufactured materials, while they find in
those countries the largest markets for their finished
products.   The complexity which has grown up in manufacturing and trading is immense.   All this established
order would be dislocated.   The policy of isolation, if
achieved, would leave us equally liable to attack; and
foreign nations would have less occasion to consider us,
when their commercial interests were severed from ours,
and one of the forces making for international peace
would be removed.   As regards the proposal for preferential duties, it should be remarked that, had Great
Britain in the past retaliated upon all who placed hostile
tariffs on her goods, the Colonies would have been among
the chief sufferers; and it is unreasonable now to expect

Great Britain to impose duties in their favour by which she would incur loss, while they are free to tax her goods and to buy in other markets. Equally difficult is it for the Colonies to abolish their duties against Great Britain. In fact the prime difficulty in the way of any form of commercial union resolves itself into a conflict of commercial interests. The Colonies are mainly producers of food and raw materials; they send to Great Britain vast quantities of corn, beef, mutton, butter, cheese, &c., and it is desired that they should increase these exports until they become our chief external sources of supply. This form of progress, however beneficial to the country, is in competition with British agriculture, which desires protection against external supplies; and, to the British farmer who believes in that means of sustaining his industry, it will be no consolation to know that the supplies come from the Colonies. On the other hand, the Colonies have nearly all adopted protective tariffs against manufactured goods, with the aim of establishing manufactures in their own lands. They are committed to the principle, and the duties are in full operation; capital and labour have been diverted to manufactures dependent upon duties. Preferential treatment on both sides will therefore require that the duties imposed by the Colonies on manufactured articles shall be reduced in order to admit the goods of the mother country, which are already the chief competitors of the colonial goods. Are the colonists engaged in these fostered trades willing to make such a sacrifice, to reduce their manufactures, and betake themselves to agriculture in order to improve (as it is assumed they would) the relations of the empire?

Again, if Great Britain is to take from the Colonies exclusively all the commodities they can produce, by placing prohibitive duties upon like articles from foreign countries, she must continue to pay the Colonies for them by means of her manufactures; she will have no

other means of quittance, since circular trading through
other countries will be cut off or greatly hampered; yet
it is to this method of payment that colonial manufacturers are opposed, so far as it interferes with their industries and profits.   The difficulty of a common basis
for trading in such circumstances is a great stumbling-
block; it has arisen out of Protection on the part of the
Colonies, and cannot be remedied by a return to Protection on the part of Great Britain, however it may be
disguised.   It is not easy to reconcile the interests of
consumers and producers at home with those of manufacturers in the Colonies.

The Australian Colonies recognize the difficulty, and
while recently demonstrating their loyalty and attach-
ment to the mother country, some of them have, through
their premiers, declared their adhesion to Protection, and
laid stress upon the impossibility of its speedy discontinuance.   The remarks of Sir G. Turner, Premier of
Victoria, on this subject show no ambiguity: "Victoria
is a heavily protected colony, and I do not suppose our
people are prepared to give up Protection. . . . We
cannot afford to relinquish our duties, because we derive
two millions annually, principally from *ad valorem* duties."
So the Premier of South Australia: " In South Australia
they do not believe in Free-trade; it is contrary to the
established industries, which rest upon Protection ".

Great Britain already possesses the greater part of
the colonial trade, and it is only by expansion of the
colonial mining and agricultural industries that trade
can be increased.   But the colonies are not content to
grow merely in agriculture, they wish manufacturing
industries to develop, and their policy has been directed
towards this end.   As time goes on, they are unlikely to
have a surplus of agricultural produce equal to our
wants, because their growing town population will consume an increasing part of their agricultural produce.
In 1896 Great Britain imported wheat and flour worth

nearly £31,000,000, of which the Colonies supplied only £2,500,000, or 8 per cent, Russia 16·7 per cent, and the United States 55 per cent. If the Colonies are to supply Great Britain with food and raw materials they must alter their policy and modify their industries, they must cease to give artificial encouragement to manufactures, and devote themselves to the development of their natural resources, *i.e.* they must gradually drop Protection, which artificially directs capital and labour towards manufactures, and give full play to those forces which would make naturally for a supply of the produce required by the home country.

Had they never adopted protective measures in the desire to foster their own manufactures they would now be supplying a much larger proportion of our wants in food and raw materials. For with free play and open competition it would have been only worth while to develop the industries which were profitable without artificial aid. It is by agriculture and mining that their wealth has been obtained; their natural course of development is in that direction, and it is only by following it that they can increase their commercial intercourse with Great Britain.

We may conclude therefore that neither Great Britain nor the Colonies can without considerable injury to many interests suddenly adopt the principle of preferential trading. It is the exclusive and fostering policy, unfortunately begun in the Colonies under a mistaken idea, which has raised impediments. If the tariffs aimed at British manufactures be gradually modified, more British goods will go to the Colonies and will be paid for of necessity by colonial produce. The same movement towards natural development will cause the trend of colonial industry to be towards the development of the soil, and there will be a consequent flow of capital and labour to the land. The credit of the Colonies will advance, and British capital will flow by preference to their safe investments. These are the forces which incline in the direction of the desired *commercial* union by natural means, and they would involve no violent fiscal change or departure from sound principles of trading.

Canada has indicated the line of safe procedure and sure progress by lowering the tariffs on British goods, and her action has excited warm reciprocal feeling in Great Britain, which will tell upon commercial relations and upon the development of Canadian soil.

Adoption of preferential duties by Great Britain would amount to a departure from the principle of Free-trade, which was adopted only gradually and after much consideration, which has stood the test of long experience, and more than fulfilled the anticipations of its effects. It could not be without strong reasons that a policy so deliberately developed and so successful in its issues would be reversed. The injury to industry and to the community at large would alienate vast numbers in the home country and excite feelings adverse to the Union. Neither can the Colonies be expected to abolish their protective tariffs at once, for such a course would ruin the industries built up by such extraneous aid, and would raise bitter antagonism from all those adversely affected by their abrogation.

Even the sacrifice of trade and commercial interests might, however, be justified to secure the stability of the empire or maintain its integrity. When the existence of the country is threatened, or her destiny is at stake, all considerations give place to those of national security. But no such critical juncture has arisen, and there is no evidence that the safety or stability of the empire would be strengthened by exclusive trading between its scattered parts.

To enforce a Customs Union would be a violent proceeding, which would inflict grave injury, and cause much discontent and possible reaction. No man can see why his particular interests should be sacrificed for an idea. Very gradual and tentative measures may possibly lead up to the application of some common fiscal system in time, but it can be attempted only very gradually, if it is not to provoke strong resistance.

The federation of a group of Colonies, such as the Australasian, with a common tariff, would be a considerable step towards further federation. It presents the same difficulties on a smaller scale. The tariff of each colony differs from others in its details, and the various tariffs range from the revenue tariff of New South Wales to the highly protective tariff of its neighbour Victoria. To assimilate these systems and reduce them to one acceptable to all is no simple undertaking; public revenue will be affected and private interests will incur loss by any plan which secures uniformity. To balance these interests, and devise the most expedient system, is a difficult task; much more so is the construction of a scheme which will embrace an empire.

Federation on a fiscal basis seems to be impracticable, and likely to be defeated by the resistance of the interests concerned. Australia has declared against it in the words, "No hope that way; interests too weighty against it". The *Melbourne Argus*, writing on behalf of Protectionist Victoria, holds that "federation on a Protectionist basis is outside the range of practical politics". Some other basis, therefore, must be sought for.

So vast and various, then, are the interests involved in any attempt at a common tariff that the project must be indefinitely postponed. A common principle might be adopted, that, so far as possible, the Colonies should gradually modify their tariffs in favour of the mother country. As Sir Wilfrid Laurier said, "She has given all, she imposes no tariffs on our goods, and it is for us to draw nearer commercially by seeking her markets and the reciprocal advantages which will ensue from her trade"; and again, "A Zollverein must mean Protection, and Protection is the greatest of all mistakes".

Canada has vast territories undeveloped, and great potentialities for the production of all the requirements of life. There is no better market for her products than the home country. Canada wants population, and her chief future source of wealth is in agriculture. Great Britain can take Canadian products, and can supply her with labour, capital, and manufactures; this is reciprocity in the best sense. Her premier summed up the whole doctrine of free exchange in a sentence, "We know that, buying more goods from England she will buy more from us, and so develop trade, and thus Canada will be benefited". The United States seem to offer a nearer and more natural market, but the tariff shuts out Canadian produce, and the States have their own agricultural interests, which, under a Protective system, claim first consideration. Meanwhile Canada finds in Great Britain an easy and sure market, and many advantages are gained by her closer union with a strong naval power and a rich commercial country, which offers no barriers to trade, and is able to pay with manufactures which Canada can consume. Sir Wilfrid Laurier says: "There are parties who hope to maintain the British Empire upon lines of restricted trade. If the British Empire is to be maintained, it can only be upon the most absolute freedom, political and commercial. In building up this great empire, to deviate from the principle of freedom will be to so much weaken the ties and bonds which now hold it together."

Difficulties have been anticipated on account of the commercial treaties made by Great Britain with Belgium in 1862, and with Germany in 1865. These have properly been denounced as inconsistent with the fiscal freedom which the Colonies have long enjoyed, and as involving results never contemplated. Further, by this step no injustice is done to those countries, since a like reduction of tariffs is offered by Canada to them on the same terms as to Great Britain. If they accept, it will be a step in the direction of Free-trading, and can only help forward a more general adoption of the principle. The denunciation of the treaties is perfectly in harmony with the spirit of Free-trade.

There is yet another argument. The Colonies owe something to Great Britain for what they have cost her in the past. The great war of the eighteenth century for colonial expansion ended in the possession of Canada and other vast territories, which have become the fields for British emigration, and the home of English-speaking people living under her free institutions. The existence of the Colonies is mainly due to large national outlay both in blood and treasure. Great Britain has defended them with her army and navy, and has protected their commerce. They received self-government and free institutions, and they have profited by their relation with Great Britain, by her supplies of labour and capital, and her open markets. In many matters they even now influence the foreign policy of Great Britain, since in various ways they are open to attack and injury: foreign nations are their near neighbours,—Germans in New Guinea, French in Newfoundland, all the European powers in Africa,—and their contact raises many delicate and difficult problems for the home Government. Not only is there some gratitude due from the Colonies to Great Britain for past services, but their future destinies are intimately interwoven with hers. It is to the interest of all to maintain this unity, and consolidate the imperial strength. Self-preservation demands it, and it concerns the future of civilization and progress.

The amount voted by the Cape House of Assembly of £30,000 as an annual subsidy to the Imperial Navy for common defence is a distinct recognition of these facts, and that so substantial a contribution to imperial defence should be voted spontaneously and unanimously by the Cape Parliament argues well for imperial federation on a basis of common defence and unity of interests.

The almost simultaneous action of Canada and the Cape, coming at a moment when the sentiment of loyalty to the sovereign and the principle of free government which she represents found a unique opportunity for its display, have not only intensified the sympathy between the remote parts of the empire, but have suggested the lines on which federation can be firmly and surely accomplished.

It is beyond the limits of this work to discuss the methods by which it has been proposed that imperial federation should be carried out; but in considering the present position of Free-trade the subject of *commercial* union is necessarily discussed, since it has been suggested that the federation should be made upon a commercial basis, and since at the Ottawa conference on the subject of colonial federation preferential duties by Great Britain were advocated. The difficulties and dangers of that course have been pointed out. There are few, however, in the careful and tentative step taken by Canada. The Cape policy points to the more pressing aspect of the question. The immediate need for federation is on grounds of defence of the empire, and its interests in every quarter of the globe. Federation, so far as it concerns a common political policy in our relations to foreign nations, and a system of representation by a supreme council, and the duties which it should undertake, are matters which need not wait for the solution of the commercial question. The latter is not insuperable, but it is a question not to be precipitated, and many present difficulties will disappear with the natural development of the resources of the Colonies Under conditions drawing them into closer relations trade will increase, especially if the Canadian precedent be adopted; and in time the difficulties will be so diminished that the problem may be approached in a way not at present possible.

Free-trade was attained only late in the history of our

own country. It should not be prematurely forced upon
the Colonies in their present circumstances, but its
evolution may be anticipated. Federation on any basis
must not curtail the liberty of the Colonies, and it must
interfere as little as possible with existing interests;
changes must be gradual, and must be demonstrated
to yield advantages lasting and more than sufficient to
compensate for the temporary losses they may inflict.
A guarantee for peace having been secured by a powerful combination, and a strong motive for increasing
intercourse having been established, a way is opened
for progress and development of resources, which will
tend to work out the problem of commercial relations.

If self-taxation be retained (and both Australia and
New Zealand seem firm on that point) a Customs Union
is not possible, and inherent differences in the conditions
of production of Great Britain and the different Colonies
render it desirable, if not necessary, that each should
arrange the details of its own tariff. Unity does not
always imply uniformity in detail, but adherence to
common binding principles, the application of which
may vary with local circumstances, and may permit of
much elasticity.

One distinction between Great Britain and the Colonies is most marked. In an old and densely-peopled
country with much accumulated wealth the tendency is
to make direct taxation contribute more and more of the
revenue; in an agricultural and scattered community
living upon the produce of its labour direct taxation is
less possible, and revenue must be raised upon commodities in a larger degree. The difficulty of propounding
an equitable common system for the two sets of circumstances is practically insurmountable.

The scheme of an Imperial Zollverein on any basis
thus appears to bristle with difficulties. But imperial
federation based on a closer political organization of the
numerous elements of the scattered empire is not a

Utopian idea. There are indications that consolidation, on defensive and political grounds, and on the basis of many common interests and sympathies, is a possibility of the near future. The fiscal problem can wait. There have been various forms of federation in the past; but the federation of the British Empire presents a problem unparalleled in history.   The case of a vast oceanic empire has never before arisen: the magnitude of the conception, the variety of the conditions, and the difference in the character of the elements to be combined, the peculiar and sporadic nature of the whole, all render the problem as interesting as it is unique.   But while the circumstances are exceptional, the ideal is the natural result of the evolution of a great empire built upon the foundation of free institutions; and the principle of liberty which has guided its development may encourage us to look forward with confidence to its final consummation.

Chapter XIII

Preferential Tariffs (June, 1903)

The events of the last few years have created special interest in colonial relations, and have brought the Free-trade question into sudden prominence in a manner which challenges the commercial policy of Great Britain for the last half-century.

The problem of cementing more closely the interests and feelings of the colonies with the Mother Country is the immediate occasion. It is said that a new problem has arisen which calls for fresh economic treatment, and a proposal to effect the consolidation of the Empire, to render it a self-sufficing and a self-sustaining unity independent of all other countries, is advanced as constituting an aim worthy of statesmanship and an end to be achieved even if it involve some economic loss to Great Britain.

As a means for attaining this end, it is urged that a system of preferential trading be adopted between Great Britain and her colonies. It is proposed that the colonies should reduce their tariffs on British manufactures while retaining them on goods from other countries, in consideration of which special advantages are to be conferred by Great Britain upon goods imported from the colonies over those of other countries. Since, however, Great Britain is free-trading, this favour can only be offered through the imposition by Great Britain of duties upon foreign goods, those from the colonies alone being admitted free; in effect, Great Britain is to adopt protection against foreign trade in favour of colonial trade.

To render the proposal more acceptable at home it is supported by the promise of other advantages, one of which is that a fund for Old-Age Pensions will be provided by means of the taxes levied on foreign imports. Mr. Chamberlain writes: "As regards old-age pensions, I would not look at the matter unless

I felt able to promise that a large scheme for the provision of such pensions to all who have been thrifty and well-conducted would be assured by a revision of our system of import duties ". As a further argument in support of the scheme it is demanded that duties be levied on foreign goods to enable Great Britain to regain that power of bargaining for better terms in trading with foreign countries which it is asserted has been lost under her free-trade system. In the words of the Colonial Secretary: " There would be competition among foreign nations for our markets which would bring us nearer to real free-trade than we have ever been ".

Other results are predicted to follow from the proposed commercial system of discriminating protection: high wages and general prosperity, increased profit to the manufacturing and iron industries by the exclusion of competition, an impulse to agriculture, improved profits and wages to the farming classes, and a return of labourers to the land.

Fascinating as is the prospect there is one serious defect in this comprehensive beneficent project; no details are afforded of the working of the scheme, no logical proof is offered of the connection between the proposed measure and the consequences assumed to follow its adoption. Reflection detects inconsistencies and contradictions in these possibilities; scientific evidence based on experience, and reasoned grounds of belief, should be adduced in support of a policy which promises so much. The earlier history of this country affords illustration of experiments of a like nature disastrous in the extreme, and methods of reasoning point to consequences the very reverse of those promised from a return to the system of restricted trading in these islands.

It may be assumed that all true and loyal members of the Empire earnestly desire that the various sections of the Empire should be knit together in bonds of affection for mutual advantage and mutual defence, that ties should be strengthened and sentiments of brotherhood should grow, and that every measure that

can be devised which indubitably makes for the common
good of all sections of the Empire should be adopted.
But it would be fatal to all such hopes if the course
adopted led to economic loss, to conflict of interests,
to jealousies and animosities, to tariff-wars only little
less destructive to industry and well-being than actual
warfare. It should be noted that the existing warmth
of sentiment between the Mother Country and the
colonies has developed without preferential trading,
under the free-trade system of Great Britain and a
perfect freedom on the part of the colonies to adopt
their own fiscal systems, which for the most part
have been of a protective character. The proposition
that any form of zollverein (offensive and defensive
as regards other countries) will advance this feeling
and promote the industrial prosperity of all parts of
the Empire is purely hypothetical, and is unsupported
by anything of the nature of scientific proof.

It has been argued from the German zollverein
and from the common tariff for the whole of the
United States that protection to trade is a cause
of great prosperity, and it is suggested that if the
British Empire were similarly united under a common
fiscal system against all other countries it would increase the prosperity of the Empire, and at the same
time render it an independent economic and political
unit. This statement is a fallacy of false cause. Any
rational conclusion drawn from the examples of
Germany and the United States must be adverse to
protection. Germany has advanced in wealth exactly
as she has removed the obstacles to trade among the
various parts of her empire. Her prosperity followed
the extension of free-trade within her empire, and it
is fair to conclude that were she to extend that freedom to all external trade greater prosperity might be
expected to follow from the still greater removal of
obstacles to commerce. She is still far behind Great
Britain in the scale of wages and standard of living of
her people. Similarly, the United States has profited
by free-trade over her vast extent, and every new state
is included in the fiscal area. This internal free-trading

over so many states has proved beneficial, and is an argument for its extension; it is not the limitation that is placed upon its operation beyond the frontiers which has been profitable. The only valid conclusion from a study of the circumstances is that the true method of progress is in the removal of impediments to free commerce, and not in the building up of limited confederations each aiming at independence and isolation. If the latter were the case, Russia should be pre-eminently a wealthy and prosperous country instead of one in which the standard of living of the majority of its people is miserably low.

Peculiar difficulties would attend any attempt at a customs-union for the British Empire, with its geographical circumstances, detached parts, variety of people and conditions; no system of internal taxation could be common to people differing so much in the standard of life, habits, modes of production, history, and general material conditions as Great Britain and India, Canada, The West Indies, and Australia. The internal economy of each unit of the Empire has a character distinct from that of every other; a system of taxation adapted for one may be wholly unsuited for others.

The proposal of a customs-union is thus reduced to its most recent form, a demand for preferential trading within the Empire to the gradual discontinuance of trade with foreign countries; the ideal is a self-sufficing empire. Such an ideal implies at the outset a jealousy and fear of others, a minimum of external relations, a separation of interests, a Chinese wall to keep out foreigners—a state of things becoming daily less possible with the advance of science, the intermingling of peoples and the simplicity of travelling.

The economic difficulties are innumerable. Even our extensive empire cannot hope, within any period the present generation can contemplate, to produce in any adequate degree all the food consumed by Great Britain; the increased expense and loss to Great Britain in the interval of transition would be ruinous. Of food imports into Great Britain amounting to £175,000,000 only some £30,000,000, or about 16 per cent, come from British possessions; of raw materials for British industries amounting to £160,000,000 not quite one-third come from British possessions; for our supplies of cotton, rubber, hemp, hides, silk, iron, copper, lead, zinc, timber we are dependent almost entirely upon foreign countries, and the stock of useful minerals to meet our wants can never be obtained from our possessions. Similarly, our chief supplies of imported meat, butter, wheat, maize, oats and barley, fish, fruit and vegetables are foreign. Great Britain has no duties upon any of these commodities. To gain the dubious and remote advantage of a "splendid isolation" she is to encourage the import of these products from her distant possessions by a preferential tariff. Since none of these imported articles now pay any duty the only method of specially favouring the colonies is by putting a tax upon those which come from foreign countries. What would be the effect of artificially high prices on food and the raw materials of staple industries? Dear food and costly living, expensive manufactures, loss of employment to large numbers of workmen, reduction of exports; commerce, shipping and all its allied industries would decline, trade depression would set in, suffering and ruin to many industries must ensue.

But against this tendency it is held that a compensating demand would arise in the colonies. What is the ground for this assertion? Would colonists buy more from Great Britain when prices were raised? how could they afford to purchase more? Further, their own tariffs are imposed upon the manufactures of Great Britain mainly in order to encourage those very manufactures at home. At the present time, in Canada, the colony most favourable to inter-imperial trading, there is a demand for a higher protective duty for the iron and steel industries.

The colonies also, whenever it is to their economic advantage, import freely from the United States, Germany, and other countries the goods they require rather than obtain them from Great Britain. Whatever increase in exchange between the colonies and Great

Britain may take place must necessarily be slow in its development, and can in amount be only equivalent to a small fraction of the loss which would be inflicted on our industries by the imposition of import duties on foreign goods.

Again, it is to the white population that we must look for the chief increase in the demand for British goods; the white population of the British Empire outside Great Britain and Ireland only numbers some 11,000,000 or 12,000,000 — Canada has 5,670,000, Australia 3,577,000, New Zealand 767,000, British South Africa 1,000,000.

In course of time the natural development of the colonies (and of Canada in particular) will enable them to offer more produce, and they will take more manufactures in exchange, but this development must be gradual and cannot be forced. As the Prince of Wales pointed out in his tour, the chief want of the colonies is more white population, but the rate of increase of the white population has been very slow for many years; one of the causes of this slow increase is that, in spite of great natural resources, their unfortunate fiscal system of tariffs (and to this may be added the heavy loans to develop native industries) has hampered the colonies and made living relatively expensive. Further, the birth-rate is very low, immigration has fallen off, and the trend of population is to the towns. In New Zealand, with a magnificent climate and soil, the population scarcely advances at all; its total is only 820,000, of whom but 760,000 are of British extraction. The economic policy of New Zealand has not favoured increase of population. A debt of £53,000,000 or £65 per head encumbers her; legislative measures are passed which harass capital and do not really help labour, and heavy duties are placed on British imports. What hope is there of her rapidly-increasing power to purchase from Great Britain?

Against this set the growing population of Great Britain, 41,000,000, who are to be taxed in all the necessaries of life in order to give special (but not real) favours to the 11,000,000 of the colonies. While New

Zealand finds a market in Great Britain for her wool, meat, grain, butter, and tallow, &c., to the extent of ten and a half million pounds, she takes from Great Britain only five and a half million pounds out of a total external trade of £24,700,000. It cannot be hoped that the development of New Zealand's trade with Great Britain will be so rapid as to make any material compensation to Great Britain for loss of trade with foreign nations. The Premier of New Zealand has expressed himself forcibly in the demand for preferential treatment by Great Britain, and even threatened her with the loss of her present trade with New Zealand in case of non-compliance. But the fact remains that New Zealand wants a market for her produce; the best, if not the only, market for her food-products is in Great Britain; she wants to sell, and she will have to take payment in manufactures for such of her produce as is not interest on loans and payment for freights, for Great Britain does not produce "gold sovereigns" for export as Mr. Seddon seems to imagine. Though trade may be rendered more difficult by tariffs on British produce, yet settlement will not be frustrated, and the problem will be solved by economic needs and economic laws.

On examination it appears that the question of preferential trading is practically limited to Canada, Australia, and New Zealand; for these colonies have adopted protective tariffs, and those tariffs have been directed mainly against British manufactures with a view to stimulating manufactures in the colonies. Such industries have grown up under the shelter of the tariff and have created vested interests which now constitute one of the difficulties of any scheme of inter-colonial trading. The rest of the Empire, India, Straits Settlements, Ceylon, Hong Kong, the West Indies, West Africa, and other scattered parts (Malta, Gibraltar, &c.), have no tariffs of any importance, as their duties are for revenue; South Africa does not export food, nor is the tariff of South Africa to be considered protective. Practically they do not come into consideration; the proposed preferential treatment is therefore limited in its effects to Canada and Australasia.

A comparison of British trade with the various British possessions and foreign countries is instructive:—

1901 (STATISTICAL ABSTRACT).

	Imports From.	Per Cent.	Exports* To.	Per Cent.	Total Trade.	Population.
	£		£		£	
Canada and New- foundland	20,387,310	4	9,688,399	2¾	30,075,709	5,371,000
Australia	24,217,669	4½	23,513,662	6¾	47,731,331	3,777,000
New Zealand	10,594,587	2	6,068,230	1¾	16,662,817	819,000
	55,199,566	10½	39,270,291	11¼	94,469,857	9,967,000
Cape of Good Hope, Natal	5,032,308	1	18,939,147	5½	23,971,455	{ 1,000,000 (white)
British India	27,391,734	5¼	35,746,399	10¼	63,138,133	294,900,000
Other British Possessions	17,950,098	3¼	19,162,527	5½	37,112,625	43,500,000
	50,374,140	9½	73,848,073	21¼	124,222,213	
Foreign Countries	416,416,492	80	234,745,904	67½	651,162,396	
Total trade	521,990,198	100	347,864,268	100	869,854,466	

Thus it appears that 80 per cent of the British import trade and 67½ per cent of her export trade is with foreign countries. The British colonies and possessions, which require no protection and cannot be affected by a preferential scheme, send 9½ per cent of her imports and take 21¼ per cent of her exports. The colonies to which alone a preferential scheme would apply, send 10½ per cent of her imports and take 11¼ per cent of her exports. That is, a measure, details of which are not advanced to give any proof of its efficacy, is to be adopted for the benefit of that section of the Empire which provides one-tenth of the external trade of Great Britain to the detriment of that trade which concerns four-fifths of its imports and seven-tenths of its exports, with the aim of wiping out entirely that business and of making the Empire self-sufficing and isolated. Such

* The exports include £67,000,000 of foreign and colonial produce re-exported, as well as British produce.

an object is unattainable, and the attempt must be disastrous.

The cotton trade affords a useful example for consideration of the effects of a duty on the raw materials of an industry. The cotton manufacture is the chief industry of South Lancashire, and not only does it supply the nation with cotton goods, but it provides an export worth £72,000,000, or 25 per cent of the whole of British exports. Of this about £40,000,000 worth goes to foreign countries, a large amount to British non-protective possessions, and only £6,000,000 or £7,000,000 to the self-governing colonies. Canada severely protects this industry, her duty on most cotton goods being about 26 per cent even under the British preferential tariff. The whole of the raw material for this staple British industry is imported; 97 per cent comes from foreign countries (including 15 per cent from Egypt), and only 3 per cent from British possessions (mainly East and West Indies). An import duty on raw materials for preferential aid must include cotton. What amount of duty and what period of time would be required to transfer the supply of raw cotton from foreign countries to the colonies or other parts of the British Empire, and what would be the effect upon the British cotton industry in the interval? A cessation of supply during the American Civil War produced untold misery, and although strong efforts were made to encourage cotton-growing in various parts of the Empire, the result was very inadequate. A deliberate check on the main source of supply could only be followed by a very serious contraction of the industry.

It should be noted that 80 per cent of this supply comes from the United States, a friendly and English-speaking country. How would a duty on one of her chief exports, with the deliberate intent of displacing it, affect the amicable relations between the States and Great Britain? As a retaliatory and injurious proceeding the United States might reasonably consider that it could be met by an export duty on cotton, which, while it would raise the price of cotton in Great Britain to the same extent, would have the advantage of transferring the duty to the States, since they have practically a monopoly of the supply, which they would retain until cotton-growing had been extended in the British Empire.

Great Britain levies an export duty on coal (of which she has not got a monopoly), and the Government claims that it is paid by the foreigner. What would be more natural than that the Government of the United States should adopt the same policy? It would be popular with her cotton manufacturers. The most probable result would be that it would tend to foster the industry in the States and transfer a large part of this industry to the States. In any case it would be disastrous to the British cotton industry.

But the imposition of preferential duties by Great Britain on goods from foreign countries in favour of the colonies is also recommended to the working-classes of Great Britain by the promise of higher wages, and of a fund, to be raised by the yield of those duties, which will provide for an old-age pension scheme (calculated to cost from £20,000,000 to £25,000,000 per annum). These promises are unsupported by any proofs whatever, either from history or theory, that taxation of food and materials can raise wages, and it can readily be shown that it will have an exactly opposite effect.

At the outset the projects of encouraging colonial trade and at the same time raising a fund by a tariff present two incompatible positions, fundamentally opposed to one another. If the aim of preferential tariffs is successful, and the colonies alone take British exports and supply our imports, no revenue would be raised, as nothing would be imported from foreign lands, and therefore no fund would come into existence to be applied to old-age pensions or any other purpose. But if a fund is raised by such tariffs on foreign goods, then goods cannot have been excluded, and the colonies are not getting the trade. Logically both cannot be successfully attained; either the favoured colonial trade is successful or not.[1]

---

[1] It may be argued, as in the case of a partially protective duty, that the tax may be just so high as to give some trade to the colonies and permit

In one case the foreign goods are excluded and no duties are obtained; in the other the preferential scheme is a failure. The only assured results would be that food and materials for industries would have been made dearer. Great Britain would have reverted to the policy which yielded the misery and starvation of the period of taxed food prior to 1846. Such taxes would administer a severe check to all manufactures, to shipping and ship-building, to exports and to imports. Great Britain would be unable to maintain her large population of 41,000,000; skilled workmen would be compelled to leave her shores in armies and seek the means of sub-sistence elsewhere. An old-age pension fund at sixty-five to the few who managed to survive to enjoy it would be purchased at a cost to the nation of the ruin of her industries, and would have to be raised from the poor-rates.

The statement that high wages attend on protective tariffs is also not borne out by facts, and is contrary to all economic enquiry. The only example advanced is that of the United States. In protective Germany wages are lower generally and hours of work longer than in Great Britain. The same is true in France and other protective countries.[1] The economic con-dition of Russia is scarcely such as would induce British workmen to emulate its methods, and if higher money wages prevail in the colonies where natural resources favour production, the real wages (purchasing power) are not always superior to real wages in Great Britain.

As to wages in the United States, much evidence has been advanced in the last few years to explain any advantages which they possess over Great Britain. This

some goods to enter Great Britain. In this case it is a failure; neither aim is fully attained, and the ills attending a rise in price will follow.

[1] Average price of wheat per quarter, and duties on imported wheat in France and Germany, given in House of Commons (Votes and Proceedings) 2nd and 6th July, 1903:—

	France.	Germany.	United Kingdom.
Price	40s. 8½d.	35s. 6d.	27s. 6d.
Duty	12s. 2½d.	7s. 7½d.	None.

evidence proves that men in the United States work harder and for more hours per week; other causes also contribute to productiveness: they use the best tools and methods; they have no prejudices against labour-saving machinery, and men are encouraged by rewards to suggest inventions which will reduce cost. In short, from various causes, where wages are higher the labour is more efficient, more wealth is produced in the same time, and since wages and profits both ultimately come out of product there is a larger reward for both labour and capital.

But if wages are higher in the United States, cost of living is higher also. Other circumstances in the United States which make for prosperity and high wages are sufficient to disprove the fallacious statement often advanced that protection has been the cause of its rapid progress. These are the immense natural resources of the country, their extent and variety. The States are endowed with a rich virgin soil, capable of yielding, at little cost, corn, meat, fruit, cotton, tobacco, &c., and boundless supplies of minerals, coal, iron, copper, gold, oil. To this add the industry, inventiveness, restless energy and enterprise which characterize the people, who seem to combine in a manner exceptional in the history of the world an aptitude for incessant industry and commerce which makes for their material well-being, the enormous extent of the country, with its 80,000,000 of people enjoying free-trade over the whole of the Continent, also unlimited capital accumulated over a century of industrial progress and aided in its inception by large loans from England. Add to these, freedom from desolating war for forty years, and from any great drain upon their resources for naval and military defence as in Europe. Could a country in which these factors combine avoid becoming wealthy? To this inevitable march of progress protection has been a drag, but one relatively so small by comparison with the forces which make for prosperity that its effects are not easily detected by those unfamiliar with the intricacies of economic investigation. The same conditions remaining, the United States must necessarily advance in wealth. And this would take place even though they cut themselves adrift from European trade and intercourse with the Old World.

Taxation on food and materials cannot yield high wages; both history and reasoning disprove the statement.[1] Taxation increases cost. A rise in price diminishes demand, either for the article taxed or for other articles if a larger sum must be expended on obtaining the supply of the taxed commodity, as in the case of a necessary. If people pay more for their bread, butter, cheese, beef, they will have less to spend upon other articles (clothing, hardware, furniture, books, &c.). All these trades will experience a reduction in demand, employment will decline: the workers in these industries will find less demand for their labour, because others are poorer, while they themselves have to pay a higher price for all their food, &c. How can wages rise in such circumstances? Both wages and profits must fall and a period of great depression set in. A rise in general wages goes with increased demand or increased efficiency; there is no other possibility. To tax industrial materials and food as a means for raising wages is an expedient which as yet lacks any illustration of success. Let anyone study the history of this country from 1800 to 1849, during the period when taxes on food prevailed, and learn the results in the starvation-wages and the misery that was then general. No fact in history has received more decisive proof than that the taxation of food means low wages, little food, and

[1] Ricardo stated that a rise in the price of corn led to an increase of wages; this was true in the circumstances prevailing when he wrote (1817); the labourer then lived on the verge of starvation, he received a subsistence-wage, which was a corn-wage, varying with the price of bread as the poor-law allowance varied with the bread-scales: a man could not subsist and work on less than a certain amount of food which his money-wages must purchase. This was under a protective law which did not admit corn until it reached 80s. a quarter; labourers engaged on land in corn-growing could not afford to purchase meat or even sufficient of wheat flour. Happily circumstances are changed; subsistence-wage now is a term with a very different connotation, it implies the current standard of living adopted by a class, it is variable, and is constantly moving upwards; it may include meat daily, abundance of milk, butter, beer, tobacco, and such comforts as a man expects his labour to procure for him; it no longer refers merely to the price of corn.

want of employment.   Cheap food is of the nature of
a discovery or a great invention.   All improvements in
labour and skill aim at its attainment.   Methods parallel
to the taxation of food would be to reduce the fertility
of the soil, to flood the coal - mines and render them
unproductive, to disable our machinery and shipping
by prohibiting the use of steam-power, to cut off resources at their spring.   Could it be anticipated that
such measures would yield prosperity?   Lord Goschen's
phrase, "Gambling with the food of the people", is an
accurate description of such a proposal.

The advance in general comfort during the last fifty
years has gone *pari passu* with the fall in cost of production, and has been produced by it.   Free corn,
cheap and plentiful, was the first factor in reduced cost
of living, and it has been followed in many directions by
increased production, discovery, invention, skill, new
sources of supply (from abroad).   All have ministered to
cheapness and abundance, which mean high real-wages.
This is an economic fact which cannot be reversed.

Most of the arguments for protection rest upon the
fallacy of "making work", and can be traced to a
narrow, personal, and self-interested outlook.   Some
particular industry is seen to be expanded by the exclusion of competition, and its activity is regarded as
a gain to industry in general.   This comes of ignoring
the great waste and loss to the nation as a whole by
the direction of capital and labour to a less productive
employment.   It has at length been accepted that the
bounty-fed sugar industry of France is conducted at an
enormous loss to the nation at large; yet at the same
time it is possible to argue in this country "that an
import duty of 5s. per quarter on corn would increase
the wage fund by £9,000,000, employ a large number
of labourers by diverting grass-land to arable-land, and
would raise 20,000,000 quarters of wheat, thereby providing a home supply of food".   This is a statement
which has been widely distributed and widely accepted.

The effect of an addition of 5s. a quarter to the cost of
the bread of the poorer classes (a population larger than
the whole white population of Canada and Australasia),

the loss in buying power of other goods by the rest
of the community, and therefore of employment to
labour, the economic waste incurred in extracting corn
from poorer soil, the diminution in the supply of beef,
milk, and butter by the diversion of the land from cattle-
feeding to corn - growing, the additional expense of
customs' officers to collect duties and prevent smuggling,
the injury to British transport trade in the reduction
of commerce are all ignored in the assumption of an
increase of wages, arising out of the employment of a
few more labourers on arable land. But the aggregate
loss from all these joint effects would exceed in an immeasurable degree the small addition (if any) to gross
agricultural wages to be obtained by such a measure.

Similar effects must follow in the case of every industry fostered in any degree by a protective duty.
What must then be the cumulative effect of a retaliatory
policy placing import duties on a large number of commodities, in order to stimulate the production of those
articles in this country? It can be no other than a
wholesale decrease in the total production and in
wealth, and, far from increase of wages, a rise in prices
and a destruction of industry must ensue. Large sections of the population would suffer great loss with no
possible recompense; the small-salaried class, clerks
of every kind, railway-men, women-workers, unskilled
labourers, &c., would find their standard of living reduced: a rise in the cost of necessaries would fall with
the greatest severity upon the poorest labourers—the
class earning less than £1 a week.[1]

But the argument for creating a self-sufficing empire,
commercially independent and self - sustaining, is con-

[1] Mr. Chamberlain has recently stated that if bread be increased in price
the taxes on tea, sugar, and tobacco may be reduced, so that the cost of
living will not be increased. How is this to be accomplished? A convention has been adopted by which this country will lose some £6,000,000
a year on its sugar-supply: it has been shown that a duty on corn will
raise the price of bread and diminish industry, with no compensating advantage in this country; whence then are the funds to be derived for reducing
other taxes? and finally, how would a fall in the cost of tobacco—a luxury
consumed by a minority—compensate the majority, including women,
children, and non-smokers, for a rise in the cost of the first necessary of
life?

fused with still other issues with which it is in conflict. One of these is the project for securing better means of fighting foreign tariffs. Mr. Chamberlain writes: "At present we go into negotiations with foreign countries empty-handed. We have nothing to give, and we have to take what they are good enough to leave for us. If we were able to bargain on equal terms, I believe that the duties now imposed on our produce would be generally reduced. There would be a competition among foreign nations for our markets which would bring us nearer to real free-trade than we have ever been." But that will indeed be a remarkable policy which at the same time secures imperial independence and universal free-trade—the two are logical contradictories. The adhesion of the colonies is to be gained by exclusive preference for their trade, and by the same mechanism a better power of bargaining with other countries is to be gained which will extend our trade with them, a method of facing both ways at once which scarcely calls for serious examination. There is, however, a separate fallacy involved in the proposition for fighting foreign tariffs, it is the old complaint that the free-trade policy of this country has cost us the means of bargaining for lower tariffs with others. No doubt had we retained the tariff system we could have haggled over small reductions. Instead of this the country has enjoyed for half a century entire immunity from those taxes and the full advantage of the lowest prices for food and materials for its manufactures, the means of cheap living and abundant employment in its most productive industries. The mischievous assumption still obtains that trade is warfare instead of mutual benefit. If this be so why do nations trade at all? The answer is, that trade is an advantage, nations want imports, and to get them they must trade. But if we want commodities it is rational to get them as cheaply as possible no matter what restrictions other nations may place on their imports.

The fallacy of imposing a tax on our own purchases because the other party to the business transaction does so may be thus illustrated. If A can obtain a quarter of corn from B in exchange for a ton of coals, and if

B wastes the value of a cwt. out of every ton by requiring the coals to be carried over a useless barrier, it does not follow that A should throw half a bushel of every quarter of corn into the dust-bin lest he should profit too much by the exchange. He wants food, and the more he can get in exchange for his goods the better for him; to make it artificially dear to himself because that is B's method would be simple folly.

Great Britain is really in a better position than any other country for obtaining cheap imports, because she takes anything freely in exchange for her goods—she raises no barriers, and does not add to their cost artificially. On this account other countries compete to get her markets, and by their competition they lower the price so that she is the gainer by her open door; she has no wants unsupplied, for all nations are eager to serve her. Satisfaction of wants is the economic end of labour. To the old idea that the aim of trade is to find a market for exports it may be replied that exports are only the means for securing imports, and that if those imports could be obtained without any exports whatever in exchange, that is by free gift, we should be exceedingly fortunate; but there is no such probability, and the countries which are so eager to send us goods may be left to see that they are paid; they will require an equivalent, and to that end they must become British customers either directly or indirectly, and be paid by British products, British services, or claims upon Great Britain which are extinguished indirectly through a third country; there is no other way by which they can dispose of their products in our markets. The multitudes of farmers, merchants, and carriers in the United States and Argentina who live by providing Great Britain with corn do not live on bread alone, they have other wants, and they supply those various needs by selling that large part of their corn which has no market at home in the only market open to them, which is in this country. The same applies to the mutton of New Zealand and the beef of Argentina. To sell is to exchange, and British manufactures will directly or indirectly pay for them so long as we can offer a market. Not to sell the only commodity they can produce on their extensive corn-lands would mean ruin to them. They want clothes and commodities of many kinds, and they will be constrained to take them or cease selling. If Great Britain looks after her imports, she may afford to let the exports take care of themselves; the one fact is the complement of the other.

But we are told that "we require a fighting tariff", a weapon, "a big revolver", with which to put pressure upon foreign countries in bargaining and coerce them into a reduction of their tariffs. This is a policy of retaliation with the object of getting better terms from foreign nations: how is this to run with a preferential tariff which aims at exclusive trading within the Empire? How can both objects be achieved? If retaliation be the course adopted, the self-sufficing imperial measure disappears, and we go back to the old idea that trade is a species of warfare, with all its jealousies, animosities, and bitter struggles. The idea of retaliation is really based upon a misconception of the nature and aim of trade. The false analogy of fighting has done immeasurable harm, it is a stock fallacy with those who cannot see that the end of labour is living, and of commerce to get the means of subsistence more cheaply; that production is for consumption, and is not an end in itself; that buying means selling, importing means exporting. In any simple case of exchange each person seeks to get as much as possible, and regards the business as mutually desirable; trade as retaliation loses sight of this idea, and sets up a hostile attitude which is obstructive. The policy of retaliation is adverse to friendly relations; it has been tried and disproved. Sir Robert Peel's dictum has been abundantly verified, that "the best way to fight hostile tariffs is with free imports". Great Britain has prospered under the system of free imports, and it has tended to make for peace between this country and those countries which find in her markets the means of disposing of their produce; it has helped to make Great Britain the chief centre of commerce and exchange, to foster her great commercial navy and banking supremacy, and to put her in the forefront of wealthy and commercial peoples.

Any sober comparison of the circumstances and progress of this country and that of others the most advanced in the world, leads to the conclusion that the maintenance of 41,000,000 of people in these islands in the comparative comfort they enjoy would be impossible without that system; any departure therefrom must bring with it great injury and loss, and expel some of her population. The idea of retaliation is retrograde; it is antagonistic to the movements which make for better relations and intercourse throughout the world. Science is bringing nations nearer together, steam and electricity, common knowledge, better acquaintance, communication and travel are producing friendly relations and interests in every country, which make against war. Is commercial jealousy, retaliation, to be the instrument for disturbing the growth of amity and mutual understanding, for preventing fuller intercourse and the gradual approximation to universal free-trading? Great Britain has been the pioneer of progress on free-trade lines; shall she go back upon these traditions? It is surely illogical to assume that we shall convert other countries to free-trading by departing from it ourselves.

The whole history of tariffs is a series of struggles and hucksterings for small gains and advantages over others, call it rather partial remission of great losses. It has led to bickerings and strife, jealousy and intrigue, reprisals and open warfare; these are the products of the mischievous restraints upon trade and commerce, which, by creating special interests, favoured modes of production and monopolies, and by diverting production from natural courses, have caused immeasurable irritation and economic loss to the world; examples of these are to be found at the present day. To Great Britain retaliation is in a special degree difficult, as shown in an earlier chapter.[1] She exports merchandise and imports food and materials; any

[1] See page 123.

attempt at retaliation must imply a check on the import of food and materials, and thus cripple her industries and enhance the cost of living, while other countries could indefinitely reply by higher duties on the merchandise she exports.[1] Retaliation in the case of Great Britain would have to be its own reward, the mere satisfaction of reprisal, that is, of making other nations suffer a smaller trade by it. She could not possibly benefit herself, and would in all probability provoke further injury to herself. The scheme is either impossible or mischievous, and probably both. The great probability is that the attempt would lead to bad relations and losses all round. One result is certain, it would diminish the friendliness of the United States, which is one of the greatest securities for this country

[1] UNITED KINGDOM.

IMPORTS.		EXPORTS.
Raw materials,............£190,120,000	£33,376,644,	mostly coal.
Food,...................... 219,440,000	15,627,405,	mostly spirits, beer, jams, pickles, confectionery, &c.
Manufactured articles,. 111,000,006	231,494,000.	manufactures.

To retaliate on the imported manufactures would exclude the following materials of British industries:—goods imported in a primary stage of manufacture to be further manufactured here, *e.g.* wood-pulp from Canada and Scandinavia is already a kind of paper, but it is boiled up and remanufactured in Great Britain.

Cement, ...	£77,623
Cotton (manufactures), ...	4,778,226
Glass, ...	3,529,483
Glue, ...	474,369
Iron or steel, ...	5,104,502
Leather, ...	8,318,910
Linen yarn, ...	764,099
Machinery, ...	3,962,068
Mouldings, ...	274,296
Painters' colours and pigments, ...	1,288,295
Paper (unprinted), ...	2,965,691
Paper (printed), ...	421,912
Strawboards, ...	954,614
Straw-plaiting, ...	563,743
Silk manufactures, ...	13,029,261
Woollen yarn, ...	2,204,272
Woollen manufactures, ...	4,876,303
Manufactures of wood, ...	2,280,000
	£56,177,667

in case of a great European war, both as regards food-supply, as a protection for neutral rights, and as a make-weight for peace. Supporters of the preferential tariff have rather paradoxically advocated its adoption as a step towards a commercial treaty, which shall include the United States and all English-speaking peoples in the same union. What, in such a case, becomes of the self-sufficing, food-producing Empire, and the preference system which is especially aimed at the commerce of the United States with Great Britain?

Much has been made of German progress under protection; more correctly it should be German progress since the adoption of internal free-trade. Germany has advanced, especially in trades dependent on her progress in science, but for three years Germany has been suffering from great industrial depression, and a budget deficiency of £6,000,000 in time of peace indicates that Germany is far from that state of prosperity which is assumed. German progress is due to education and not to her external commercial policy; indeed her protective policy is a source of great difficulty to her, since she has to endeavour to favour the agricultural class by duties on corn, and the industrial class by duties on maufactured goods. These interests are in opposition; each of them, while seeking protection for its own source of income, desires free-trade for its expenditure, hence much angry controversy and political discord. This conflict of interests is less obvious in the United States because they are not importers of food, but the farmers are not less discontented with a system which taxes them in the manufacturing interest. The German struggle serves to prove the inability of a protective system to secure harmony between conflicting interests. Under free-trade, where no party is favoured, such a conflict cannot arise, for the cause is non-existent; it is created by the attempt to confer favours which must always be at the cost of some other class. Nor should it be forgotten that corruption inevitably attends a system in which trades are competing for political favours and privileged conditions.

Incidentally it may be noted that the same kind of
difficulty would attend any system of preference to the
colonies; their circumstances being widely different,
they would each require preferences in different degrees.
To frame a scheme which would be equally favourable
to all is impossible; the end would be disappointment,
dissatisfaction, discord. With the sacrifice of our own
fiscal system and the penalizing of our own people in
food for this end, there would arise a period of controversy and bargaining, of wrangling with the self-
governing colonies as to special treatment, which would
be a menace instead of a support to the stability of the
Empire.

The new fiscal proposal is defended by yet two other
lines of argument. It is said that times and circumstances have changed greatly within the last thirty
years, that two great industrial and commercial rivals
to Great Britain have arisen in the United States and
Germany, who will drive her out of the field of commerce unless her position is strengthened. Further,
it is stated that economic principles are not constant,
but need to be recast to fit altered conditions, and
that imperial federation is a wholly new problem
calling for a fresh adjustment of the economic doctrine. Neither statement is accurate, nor does it carry
the conclusion which is demanded; true, changes are
ever taking place, and among these is the fact that
fifty years of free-trade have seen great material advances in Great Britain in prosperity and well-being;
but the new phenomenon of the industrial growth of
Germany and the United States calls for no modification of the system which has favoured the prosperity
of Great Britain. The progress of other countries does
not militate against the well-being of Great Britain;
the doctrine that the material progress of one country is
detrimental to the welfare of others has been exploded
long ago.[1] Their increased production and wealth add

[1] On this point it is pleasant to quote Mr. Balfour's opinion, given at
the Iron and Steel Institute, 8th May, 1903: "The riches of one nation
conduce, believe me, not to the poverty, but to the wealth of another
nation; and if we could double or treble by the stroke of some fairy wand

to the wealth of the world; they become better customers to one another, and larger purchasers of the products of other countries; they add to the general comfort by their progress;[1] they help on general civilization by their skill, education, and intelligence; their populations are large, and the development of their resources enables them to support these populations in comfort. If they are rivals in neutral markets, these markets have also expanded in the interval and are by no means as yet satisfied; some are only on the threshold of developments which will make them great consumers of manufactures and centres of commercial enterprise at some future time. The vast East, Africa (North and South), and South America still afford an almost unlimited field for the consumption of the products of the industries which tend to supply the progressive wants of the more advanced countries. It would be both selfish and absurd for Great Britain to put in a claim for the monopoly of the world's markets for manufactures. She could not meet the growing demand. When she did possess something of a monopoly of certain industrial products the world of demand was very limited indeed; it did not extend much beyond France, a few of the most advanced European countries, and the undeveloped American colonies. That economic area has expanded vastly in the last fifty years, and presents a large vista for future business energy.

There is also an endless progression in human wants

the wealth of every other nation in the world but our own, depend upon it our nation would greatly profit by the process ".

[1] TABLE SHOWING THAT TRADE BETWEEN GREAT BRITAIN AND GERMANY HAS INCREASED SINCE GERMANY'S INDUSTRIAL DEVELOPMENT:—

	Imports from Germany.	Exports to Germany.
1879	21,604,890	29,623,776
1885	23,069,163	27,059,830
1890	26,073,331	30,516,281
1895	26,992,559	32,736,651
1900	31,181,667	38,142,790
1901	32,207,214	34,221,080
1902	34,000,000	34,100,000

and powers of consumption, a fact expressed economically as the law of variety; the only limit to demand is the power of purchasing, which is governed by the wealth of the buyer. The result is seen in the multitude of new kinds of commodities that come into existence

IMPORTS AND EXPORTS OF CERTAIN COUNTRIES,
EXCLUDING BULLION AND SPECIE.

The Imports are for Home consumption only—the Exports are all Domestic produce: ooo's omitted.

Calendar Years.	United Kingdom.	France.	Germany.	Russia.	United States, years ending 30th June.
1895—	£	£	£	£	£
Imports ...	356,986	148,796	206,035	53,851	149,547
Exports ...	226,128	134,952	165,895	68,908	165,290
Total ...	583,114	283,748	371,930	122,759	314,837
1896—					
Imports ...	385,575	151,944	215,360	58,981	158,400
Exports ...	246,146	136,036	176,255	68,993	179,833
Total ...	625,721	287,980	391,615	127,974	338,233
1897—					
Imports ...	391,075	158,240	234,035	56,000	155,363
Exports ...	234,220	143,920	181,750	72,612	215,002
Total ...	625,295	302,160	415,785	128,612	370,365
1898—					
Imports ...	409,890	178,902	254,032	59,324	128,343
Exports ...	233,360	140,436	187,828	74,828	252,144
Total ...	643,250	319,338	441,860	134,152	380,487
1899—					
Imports ...	419,994	180,732	259,850	62,745	145,239
Exports ...	264,492	166,105	199,571	63,507	250,819
Total ...	684,486	346,837	459,421	126,252	396,058
1900—					
Imports ...	460,534	176,341	277,900	60,430	177,024
Exports ...	291,451	163,121	220,700	72,680	285,516
Total ...	*751,985	339,462	498,600	133,110	462,540

* One-tenth of the trade is with the British possessions, the rest with foreign countries, yet it is said that Great Britain is being shut out from the markets of the world.

(electric light, cycles, and cameras will illustrate), articles of common consumption with multitudes who at an earlier period could not have purchased them. Their production calls into existence new industries, and finds employment for large multitudes. There is no limit to this kind of progress; Japan and China want cycles to-day; in time it will be the turn of the Sudan, Uganda, and the Congo, and they will be sending us raw produce (corn, rubber, &c.) in exchange. To suppose that Great Britain would remain the only manufacturing country in the world is ridiculous: it is a selfish and monopolistic idea, once paralleled by the idea that there could be only one wealthy man, the squire, in a village. Without diminishing the wealth of the squire, however, there are now many wealthy residents in villages. What is called the general standard of comfort has advanced with the larger consumption by the masses of all kinds of commodities; the very term poor has a different meaning to that which it had fifty years ago. The applications of electricity alone provide employment for some millions of well-paid artisans in the various progressive countries, and add to the comfort and happiness of all classes. Such progress could not be confined to one country, indeed it would never come into being were it not for the interchange of services, commodities, and ideas. It is due to the fact that other parts of the world can supply Great Britain with food and the products of the earth that she can devote so much labour to extend skilled and refined industries. This process of beneficial exchange and demand will go on, unless checked by measures such as those proposed.

Nor does the progress of other countries call for a reconsideration of the economic principles of free-trade; the doctrine of free-trade is a statement of efficiency, a principle which is as incontrovertible as the law of division of industry of which it is an example; it stands, when understood, a truth like those of physical science, on the solid basis of established fact. There is no room for doubt or suspended conviction on the point that a nation, like an individual, grows richer by producing

the commodities which it is best qualified to produce, and
by purchasing with these what it is less able to produce.
But it is retorted that cheapness is not everything, that
the question is not purely economic, that political considerations may override cheapness, and that the unity
of the Empire is one of those matters to which may be
applied Adam Smith's dictum that security is of more
importance than opulence; that, in short, it may be wise
to forego some economic advantages to obtain this
security by a united and strengthened empire. Certainly
if this unity can thus be secured, and only thus; but
that is the point at issue. As stated by its advocates it
begs the whole question; no proof is adduced that preferential trading makes for unity. The free-trader denies
it, and claims that his principles tend to that desired
end.   He rests his case upon history, experience, facts,
and arguments, not upon imagination or authority, or
respect for the exponents of a system.   The terms shib-
boleth, fetish, doctrinaire, Cobdenite, &c., used in this
connection do not stand for arguments, except by those
who employ them, and who are themselves the subjects
of such fallacies.   The fact is, that free-trading has
brought prosperity to Great Britain and made for peace
and harmony in the world; it tends to obtain from
nature the greatest results with the least labour; it is
an economic gain to the nation which practises it, and
indirectly to the nations that are in trade relations with
it: while the policy of protection wastes productive
energy, and tends to jealousy and discord.   Sir W.
Laurier stated the true principles of unity when he
said: "If the British Empire is to be maintained it can
only be upon the most absolute freedom, political and
commercial; to deviate from the principle of freedom
will be to weaken the ties and bonds which now hold it
together".   Great Britain has conferred that freedom
upon her self-governing colonies, and she practises it
herself not only in political and social matters, but also
in her fiscal system.   Further, the colonial problem is
not a new problem; it dates back a hundred and fifty
years to a system of restraint on trading which broke
up with disaster in 1776 when American independence

was declared. The policy of fiscal federation now urged, if it were attempted as a working system, would impose new restraints and fetters on all the parties to it, which would gall and chafe, and lead to perpetual demands for alteration; it would irritate foreign nations and check the prosperity of Great Britain by imposing taxation on the very necessaries of life and industry. From such a system can any permanent good be hoped?

If the colonies equally with Great Britain had adopted freedom in trading—freedom with all the world—they would have advanced more rapidly in wealth by natural development, and commerce with the mother country would have been on the most natural and easy footing. This now is difficult, because they are hampered by vested interests which have grown up under the protective system.

The proposal for commercial federation is an appeal to the business instincts, *i.e.* to self-interest, and not to human sentiment, it ignores the real bond of sympathy between Great Britain and the colonies, and professes to build on a foundation of economic interest. It assumes that it would be to the material advantage of both to make the union a fiscal one. Investigation shows this basis is impossible; it requires that the colonies should forego some business advantage, it demands that Great Britain shall make great sacrifices.

But when the appeal is to business instincts we must demonstrate advantages; instead of gains, however, both parties would have to incur immediate losses. Canada and Australia are to become food-producing colonies for Great Britain; but many of their active politicians are manufacturers, and they are not inclined to reduce their industries. Though the Canadian tariff has been reduced in some respects to Great Britain it is sufficiently high on Canadian manufactures to maintain their products against British goods, and it is really more favourable to the United States, her near neighbour, than to Great Britain: the Canadian iron industries are even now asking for higher tariffs against Great Britain.

The Canadian preferential treatment of Great Britain has not been so beneficial to Great Britain as is com-

monly imagined.   The British imports into Canada in
1883 were 51,680,000 dollars, out of a total of 121,861,000;
they declined from that date, and in 1902 were 49,023,000
dollars out of a total of 196,480,000.   The tariff reform
of 1897 caused a slight increase, but while it lowered
the duties on raw materials for Canadian industries it
maintained effective protection for its manufactures,
and even raised the duty against British cotton goods.
The effect is seen by a comparison of the proportion of
British imports into Canada with the whole of Canadian
imports over two quinquennial periods before and after
the alteration in tariff.

PERCENTAGE OF BRITISH IMPORTS INTO CANADA

Before the Preferential Tariff			After the Preferential Tariff		
Fiscal year		Per cent	Fiscal year		Per cent
1893		36.92	1898		25.36
1894		33.96	1899		24.72
1895		30.85	1900		25.66
1896		31.15	1901		24.10
1897		27.58	1902		24.95
Average,		32.09	Average,		24.96

On £8,921,000 worth of goods imported into Canada
from the United Kingdom (year ending June, 1901) the
duty was £1,634,000.   On £21,764,000 worth of goods
imported into the United Kingdom from Canada (year
ending Dec., 1900) the duty was £1020 (on spirits
only).

Australia is opposed to any measure which will tend to
check her manufacturing industries; her ideal is not to
be merely a producer of food and the materials for
British manufactures.   Even in so small and desirable a
matter as postal communication she has lately rejected
the proposal for a penny imperial rate, on the ground
that it would involve an immediate loss of revenue of
£295,586, a sacrifice which could probably soon be
recovered by increased business.   What expectation can
there be of a successful federation on the business
principle?

Again, to Great Britain the loss following on increased

cost of food and materials would be immense, good relations with other nations would be impaired, even the promised power of supplies from the colonies is very problematical and certainly remote. What probability is there that a people building on material advantages and suffering such consequences would long adhere to their contracts? Failure would be disastrous to colonial relations, the risk of rupture attending the attempt is alarming; instead of union, the scheme would mean disruption.

The problem of union is psychological as well as economic; it may appeal to different sides of human nature, to the selfish or the unselfish, to business or to sentiment, but not to both. But the impulses have an order and priority, and the pressing needs of subsistence take a front place; they are constant, always in evidence, always urgent; the feelings of sentiment are more spasmodic and intermittent. The colonies have proved that they can make great sacrifices to aid the Mother Country in an emergency; there is a time when blood shows thicker than water, affection comes out under trial; but even brothers can quarrel over money-matters, and it is proverbial that unsatisfactory business relations can make enemies of friends. This preferential scheme appeals to the wrong motive; it is to be based on business relations, and the business proposed is bad, since, as has been shown, it implies economic loss to all concerned. Is it a scheme on which to build an Empire? Freedom and sentiment form a better basis. Let the colonies be free to follow their own course in economic development. They have difficulties in the existence of a fiscal system which props up individual interests instead of merely providing revenue, but in time they may be able to amend it. Great Britain has no such difficulties; with an effort she rid herself of this protective burden more than fifty years ago, and she could not do worse than resume it.

There are other and stronger arguments for a closer union between Great Britain and her colonies: common origin, language and religion, sympathy of race and blood, free institutions, common liberty, mutual defence, a thousand ties of affection exist between them.   Shall we sacrifice all this sentiment for an illusory ideal built upon an appeal to selfish and conflicting interests, and to be attained by the mechanism of fiscal arrangements which can be demonstrated to yield economic loss?

DEFENCE OF THE EMPIRE

NAVY ESTIMATES OF GREAT BRITAIN (1902–3)

NAVAL EXPENDITURE OF THE EMPIRE			
	Population.	Naval Expenditure.	
		Aggregate.	Per Head.
		£	s. d.
United Kingdom ...	41,455,000	31,255,500	15 1
Australia	3,766,000	169,324	0 10¾
New Zealand	773,000	20,924	0 6½
Canada	5,313,000	Nil.	Nil.
Newfoundland	210,000	Nil.	Nil.
Cape Colony (White) ...	538,000	30,000	1 1¼
Natal (White)	54,000	12,000	4 5¾
India	—	414,000	—

MR. CHAMBERLAIN'S SPEECH, COLONIAL CONFERENCE, 1902.

At the present moment the estimates for the *naval and military expenditure* in the United Kingdom—not including the extraordinary war expenses—involve an expenditure per head of the population of the United Kingdom of 29s. 3d. per annum. . . . In Canada the same items involve an expenditure of only 2s. per head of the population, or about one-fifteenth of that incurred by the United Kingdom.   In New South Wales the expenditure is 3s. 5d.; in Victoria, 3s. 3d.; in New Zealand, 3s. 4d.; and in the Cape and Natal it is, I think, between 2s. and 3s.

BRITISH TRADE

British Imports and Exports—Total Trade.		Average Exports for periods of five years, ending:	
1855	£260,000,000	1850	£61,000,000
1860	378,000,000	1855	89,000,000
1870	547,000,000	1860	124,000,000
1880	697,000,000	1865	144,000,000
1890	749,000,000	1870	188,000,000
1900	877,000,000	1880	201,000,000
		1890	227,000,000
		1900	253,000,000

TOTAL TONNAGE (steam and sail) entered and cleared with cargoes or ballast at ports in the United Kingdom. Sir John Glover—(Statistical Society).

1850	...	...	...	32,634,000 tons.
1860	...	...	...	58,707,000 ,,
1870	...	...	...	73,198,000 ,,
1880	...	...	...	132,250,000 ,,
1890	...	...	...	164,340,000 ,,
1900	...	...	...	208,777,000 ,,

TOTAL WEIGHTS of Imports and Exports.—Statistics of Mr. John Williamson for Liverpool Chamber of Shipping:

1880	...	...	...	53,000,000 tons.
1890	...	...	...	76,500,000 ,,
1900	...	...	...	102,500,000 ,,

Total tonnage of ships owned:

	1870	1901
British under Free Trade... ...	4,229,000	8,422,000
American under Protection ...	1,449,000	880,000

Index